WHY BELIEVE IN JESUS?

TIM LaHAYE

HARVEST HOUSE PUBLISHERS

EUGENE, OREGON

Cover by Terry Dugan Design, Minneapolis, Minnesota

Cover photo © Diana Healey/The Image Bank/Getty Images

WHY BELIEVE IN JESUS?
Revised edition of *Jesus: Who Is He?*
Copyright © 2004 by Tim LaHaye
Published by Harvest House Publishers
Eugene, Oregon 97402
www.harvesthousepublishers.com

Library of Congress Cataloging-in-Publication Data
LaHaye, Tim F.
    Why believe in Jesus? / Tim LaHaye.
        p. cm.
    Originally published: Sisters, Or.: Multnomah Books, 1996. Includes bibliographical references.
    ISBN 0-7369-1354-8 (pbk.) — ISBN 0-7369-1364-5 (hardcover) 1. Jesus Christ—Person and offices. I. Title.
    BT203.L34 2004
    232—dc22   2003020407

Printed in the United States of America

    04 05 06 07 08 09 10 11 / DP-MS / 10 9 8 7 6 5 4 3 2 1

To all those who believe that the historic Jesus of Nazareth
was the Son of God in human flesh,
who really died on the cross and rose again three days later—
‣ and for all those who wish they could find logical,
convincing reasons to believe.

Contents

Almost a Skeptic

I almost became a skeptic in Sunday school. Maybe that is why I can understand and be patient with those who retain unanswered questions and honest philosophical doubts about God, the Bible, and Jesus Christ.

My Sunday-school teacher was a good man. I am sure he meant well, but he had little education and almost no time for adequately preparing his lesson. He was a sweeper on the night shift at the Ford plant in Dearborn, Michigan, just out of Detroit. Our class of boys met in the choir loft of a little white church on Williamson Avenue.

Unfortunately for us, our teacher had only scant knowledge of the Bible and knew little about how to teach. Almost every Sunday he would stand in front of us, frantically twisting his quarterly, and say the same thing: "I didn't have time to study my lesson this week, boys, but let's see what God has for us." I must confess that whatever God had for us, our teacher failed to give us. Yet somehow this man was our teacher for both the seventh and the eighth grades!

To make matters worse, my biology teacher in junior high was an ardent evolutionist and an evangelist of atheism. He repeatedly told us there was no God, no life after death, and that miracles were impossible. Mr. Babel (believe it or not, his real name) had earned his master's degree in science from the University of Michigan. He always came to class prepared and could be very convincing.

I don't consider myself an intellectual or profound thinker, but I am blessed (or as some of my friends would say, "cursed") with a very busy and inquisitive mind. I find it difficult to accept anything without logical reasons to back it up. No matter what is said, if I haven't reasoned it out already, I can usually think of some question to probe its validity.

One day, I pushed my well-meaning Sunday-school teacher beyond his limits by my endless chain of questions. "Why did Jesus do that?" "Can you prove this?" "How do we know that is true?"

Finally, in what must have been complete exasperation, he bellowed, "Tim LaHaye, if you don't stop asking all these questions, I'm going to kick you out of this class!" Then he added something that I had to reject completely: "Why don't you just believe?"

Quite honestly, I found that intolerable. *Just believe?* Was that all the logic Christianity could muster? Was faith like a viral infection that some people "caught" and others didn't? Even though I had accepted Jesus as my Lord and Savior in the fourth grade, I was having a hard time believing it was all true. I wanted to know all about Jesus, from His claims about Himself to the testimonies of others. Even as an eighth grader I knew enough about Christianity to identify Jesus Christ as its central figure. If His assertions could not be supported, if the things the Bible claimed for Him could not be verified, then He was not who He said He was. And like a house of cards, Christianity would come crashing down.

A few weeks later, our faithful pastor said something I never forgot. "To those of you who have doubts about Christianity, and particularly about Christ," he said, "don't be afraid to admit them to God and search for answers in the Bible. God doesn't expect us to believe blindly. To the contrary, He expects us to use our minds." Then he quoted from the Hebrew prophet Isaiah, "'Come now, and let us *reason* together,' says the LORD."[1] For the first time I realized that I was permitted, even encouraged, to have an inquiring mind. I saw that God Himself challenged us to use reason in determining what we believe.

That moment inaugurated a lifetime quest for truth that has resulted in the discovery of many logical and historical reasons for our faith. Eventually I found more-than-adequate reasons for believing that Jesus Christ, the central figure of Christianity, is who He said He was: "the Son of Man" who came "to seek and to save that which was lost."[2]

Today I can honestly say that my doubts and questions have been more than answered. The answers I found should challenge any honest skeptic to examine the demanding evidence for the real identity of Jesus of Nazareth. I believe there is far more evidence for *believing* the claims of Christ than for rejecting them, more *answered* questions than unanswered ones. In fact, I am convinced that when we follow our questions and thoroughly examine the evidence, we will conclude that Jesus of Nazareth was one of a kind. We will also find that it is excruciatingly difficult to offer credible reasons for His powerful impact on human history…short of recognizing that He was, indeed, deity in human flesh.

This book should prove helpful to all sincere doubters whether Christians who entertain unanswered questions, unbelievers, or honest skeptics. I have seen many Christians increase their love for and dedication to Jesus Christ as they became more convinced of who He really is. As their nagging doubts and lingering questions were laid to rest, their faith grew strong. I have also seen the attitudes of unbelievers and skeptics change as they realized, in the words of the apostle Peter, "We did not follow cunningly devised fables."[3] When they saw we are a logical people whose belief in and acceptance of the person and deity of the historical Jesus Christ is intellectually sound and logically reasonable, they, too, came to faith.

The Most Important Question of All

As he was interviewing my fiction partner Jerry Jenkins and me about the popularity of the Left Behind® series, talk show host

Larry King posed what has become one of the most common questions we are asked today. "Do you believe Jesus Christ is the only way to heaven?" Morley Safer of *60 Minutes* fame put forward the same question to me a year later. As I explained to them, that is the wrong question. The real question is, Who is Jesus Christ? If He was simply a unique and influential man, even the most unique man who ever lived, yet still a man, He could not die for the sins of the world. For even the best man in the world is but a man. But if He was the Son of God in human flesh, as the Bible presents Him, then He very well could be the only way to heaven. For only God, being superior to man, could pay for the sins of all mankind in one climactic moment.

Which brings us back to the most important question in the universe: Who is Jesus? I believe, when examined carefully, the evidence is clearly in favor of the fact that Jesus could not have been just a superb human being. There must be some reason why this man who started from the humblest of beginnings became the most influential person in all of history. He was the only person to fulfill 109 prophecies written between 500 and 1500 years before His birth. He was the only person to heal all manner of diseases and perform incredible miracles. To say that these and other supernatural evidences were mere coincidence or are false—or whatever excuse people use to disbelieve—flies in the face of the fact that no human has ever influenced the world for good like Jesus of Nazareth.

Take, for example, the three most influential Greek philosophers from the ancient world: Plato, Socrates, and Aristotle. They taught in the center of Greek civilization for a combined total of 150 years and had a great impact on their society. Yet Jesus of Nazareth, with little formal education and without assistance from anyone, influenced the world more than all three of these famous Greek philosophers put together...and He did it in a mere three-and-a-half years.

Which is why I ask, Who is this Jesus Christ? You will never be asked a more important question because your eternal destiny hinges on your response. If you can accept that He is "the only begotten Son of God" who died for the sins of the whole world and rose again as evidence that God the Father accepted His sacrifice, you can be saved by believing on Him and receiving Him as your Lord and Savior. If you can't accept that, then you are on your own for eternity. Sound reasoning, fulfilled prophecy, and unparalleled influence on this world all provide formidable evidence for faith. There is no evidence, however, for unbelief.

The Need for This Book

Dewey Bertolini is a friend of mine who has been a high school and college youth speaker and pastor for more than 30 years. Dewey has spoken to well over several hundred groups of modern teens. He contends that young people today are growing up with little or no knowledge of Jesus Christ. Mention of Him in anything but profanity has been all but forbidden in either public education or on television; consequently, unless parents regularly take their sons and daughters to church, many don't have a clue as to who the Son of God really is.

To illustrate this sad fact, Dewey described how he was given an opportunity to teach a class of high-school seniors just one month away from graduation. He brought up the name of Jesus Christ and was stunned by the sheer ignorance of the class. Curious about this spiritual illiteracy, he divided the class into discussion groups and gave the students 20 minutes to formulate a definition of Jesus. Finally the groups combined their findings and brought the following conclusion, which represented the thinking of the entire class: "Jesus Christ is some religious dude who lived about 200 years ago." Dewey added, "They thought He was a contemporary of George Washington."

Dewey then told of walking through the halls of one of the largest high schools in his city when he saw a student accidentally slam a locker door on the hand of his friend. The injured student began swearing in the name of Jesus Christ. Instead of ignoring the outburst, Dewey approached the young man, expressed his sympathy, then asked, "Do you mind if I ask why you used my friend's name that way?"

"Whose name?" wondered the puzzled student.

"Jesus Christ," replied Dewey.

"Who's he?" the boy asked.

Believe it or not, that young man knew nothing about that "name which is above every name"[4] other than that it was used, along with God's name, as a term of profanity when things do not go well.

I know that these ill-informed young people may not represent the consensus of American youth, but who can deny they represent the growing ignorance of and disrespect for the most important person who ever lived? It is my prayer that this book will not only describe who He is, but prove it in terms all can understand.

Why Believe in Jesus? is the culmination of a lifetime of research. It doesn't contain all the answers I have found, but it does include the best. I suspect you will find these answers convincing. It is my hope you will share them with others who, like the former Tim LaHaye, are plagued with sincere questions and doubts.

Honest skeptics do not doubt because there are no answers to their questions about Jesus' identity; they doubt because they lack exposure to those answers. The apostle Peter challenged Christians everywhere to "always be ready to give a defense to everyone who asks you a reason for the hope that is in you."[5]

This book will not only encourage Christians and provide them with ready answers to the sincere doubters they meet, but I expect it may also answer those who have been victimized by the Mr. Babels of this world. Take it from a former Sunday-school "doubting Thomas": the journey down the highway of knowledge is more than worth the trip.

Part I:
Who Is This?

Chapter One

The Most Extraordinary Person Who Ever Lived

In His day He was known as Jesus of Nazareth. For most of His adult life He worked as a carpenter. Yet He was so extraordinary in the way He lived and the influence He exerted on humanity that the word *extraordinary* doesn't begin to describe Him.

No one else—no king, dictator, scientist, educator, or military leader—has made a greater contribution to world history than Jesus has. At least twelve billion people have come and gone on this planet, but today, almost 2000 years after His death, no one has come close to replicating His unique place in history.

This world has not lacked for great men and women. History is replete with such names as Solomon, David, Hammurabi, Cyrus, Alexander the Great, Caesar, Genghis Khan, Joan of Arc, Napoléon Bonaparte, George Washington, Isaac Newton, Florence Nightingale...the list goes on and on. But no one comes close to equaling Jesus Christ in His influence on mankind.

Even H. G. Wells, the English novelist and historian whose five volumes on world history grace the shelves of almost all college and university libraries, ended up giving more space to Jesus Christ than to anyone else. And Wells was no friend of faith! In fact, his biographers portray him as a skeptic or possibly an atheist.

Yet as a true historian, he could not ignore the greatest personality who ever lived.

Unique in His Life and Teachings

Beyond all doubt, Jesus Christ is the most discussed, debated, and scrutinized person who ever lived. Even after 20 centuries, He has more defenders and opponents than any other single figure. While there are literally thousands of academicians with the highest of degrees who willingly confess Him as Lord, there are also thousands of others who would, if they could, destroy His credibility. From the very beginning He had both followers and detractors, and we are told that this pattern will continue until the very end.

In the next chapter we shall briefly discuss the much publicized "Jesus Seminar," a group of 70-plus liberal scholars who meet twice each year in an effort to redesign the life and character of Jesus. In recasting Him as a mere "sage or cynic," they try to strip Him of His uniqueness. Yet despite their ready access to the popular media, including *Newsweek, Time,* and *U.S. News & World Report,* they have not succeeded in gaining many converts. In fact, their biggest success has come in prompting many scholars, writers, and theologians—brilliant men who have examined the evidence for Jesus' uniqueness—to put into print solid, credible reasons for continuing to believe that Jesus Christ was in fact who the Gospels portray Him to be, the most extraordinary and influential person who ever lived.

The Jesus Seminar scholars and others like them are at a loss to explain how a mere sage or cynic could have influenced the world to the fantastic degree that Jesus has. The Big Question boils down to this: Who was Jesus of Nazareth? If He was merely a remarkable carpenter born in an obscure country, even the sharpest of skeptical minds has trouble explaining why, of all the brilliant people who ever lived, Jesus remains in a category by Himself.

Sir Isaac Newton is considered by many experts to be the most brilliant scientist who ever lived. Yet this man never tried to compare himself with Jesus Christ; instead, as we shall see, he was an ardent believer in and follower of the Nazarene. Blaise Pascal is considered one of the world's greatest philosophers, yet like

Newton, he never attempted to usurp the place of Jesus Christ. Pascal ardently believed in the Savior, all the way to a painful deathbed. The same could be said of William Gladstone, Louis Pasteur, and multiplied thousands of brilliant scholars, scientists, jurists, and authors, as well as millions of ordinary people. They studied His life and teachings, examined both sides of the evidence, and yet came to believe more than ever that Jesus is the Son of God—unique among all who have ever lived.

Unique in His Impact

To put Jesus' influence into perspective, consider several major areas of His uniqueness.

Jesus of Nazareth is unparalleled as a *moral influence.* His life and teachings remain unsurpassed in their ability to guide cultures, tribes, and peoples out of moral confusion.

Jesus of Nazareth is unparalleled as an *artistic influence.* He has inspired more of the world's great art and music than any other person. Some of the greatest oratorios and hymns of history were written about Him or to Him. He is the object of more books, music, and literature than any other individual. The Library of Congress, considered the most complete repository of books in the world, catalogs more works about Jesus than any other person.

Jesus of Nazareth is unparalleled as a *humanitarian influence.* More hospitals, orphanages, rest homes, and rescue missions have been dedicated to Him than to all other religious leaders combined. More people-helping efforts have been founded, financed, and perpetuated by His followers than all others.

Jesus is unparalleled in His ability to *inspire devotion.* No other individual in the last 2000 years has prompted greater commitment among his followers. Although Jesus never raised an army during His three-and-a-half years of ministry, multiplied millions of His followers have scattered to the uttermost parts of the earth to carry His message—not for money, lands, or earthly reward, but out of pure devotion to Him.

Jesus of Nazareth is unparalleled as a *scholastic influence.* Though He never founded a college, His teachings and followers have contributed to more literacy and educational institutions—of all levels, from kindergarten to graduate school—than all others combined. In America alone, a land of educational institutions, 128 colleges were established in the first 100 years of the nation's history—all founded by a church, denomination, or religious group. Harvard, Princeton, and Yale, which for 200 years served as the headwaters of American education, were created to prepare ministers, missionaries, and Christian leaders. In addition, scores of Christian colleges have been established in His honor.

Before the gospel ever came to America, it was the followers of Jesus Christ who brought education to the children of ordinary citizens. Prior to the time of Martin Luther in Germany and John Calvin in France and Switzerland, only the rich or royalty or the geniuses of the world were considered fit for education. But these great Reformers saw education as the means of teaching the Bible to whole generations who, for the first time, could read the Scriptures in their mother tongues. The Pilgrims and Puritans furthered that pattern in the New World. It was no accident that this quest for educating children in the sixteenth to eighteenth centuries laid the foundation for the explosive growth of the Industrial Revolution in the nineteenth century.

By contrast, the secular cultures of the world have done little to bring literacy to the thousands of tribes and indigenous peoples who once lacked a written language. Yet the followers of Jesus have translated the Bible into countless tongues and have taught millions to read. They intend to bring literacy and the Bible to all tribes of the world by the early part of the twenty-first century. Their reason? Dedication to Jesus Christ.

Jesus of Nazareth is unparalleled in His *impact on women.* No one has done so much to raise the status of womanhood and motherhood as has Jesus Christ. He came into a world where women were considered only one step above animals. Many were traded for cattle and few enjoyed personal rights before the law or the marriage altar. Where the message of Christ has permeated, women have been ennobled and respected as human beings made in the image of God. The followers of Christ led the women's suffrage movements throughout Europe, England, and America. And His disciples today make up the bulk of those who stand in defense of the unborn. Secular women in the West may not understand the debt they owe to Jesus Christ and His teachings, but they have the Nazarene and His followers to thank for the exalted status they enjoy today.

Jesus of Nazareth is unparalleled in His influence on *freedom and justice.* No one has more deeply promoted personal freedom and justice before the law than Jesus' followers, armed with His standard of law. English and American law, once considered the model throughout the world, was made possible primarily through John Locke, William Gladstone, William Wilberforce, William Blackstone (of England) and James Witherspoon, John Adams, James Madison, and John Marshall (of America). All were committed followers of Christ who knew and applied His principles and teachings to the preservation of individual rights and freedom under the law. All of these influential men freely admitted they owed their greatness to Him.

The climax of this commitment to individual freedom came in the United States Declaration of Independence, in which the words "all men are created equal" became the cornerstone of the freest nation in world history. America was founded to preserve religious freedom: "life, liberty, and the pursuit of happiness" for everyone. As you can see, the evidence is staggering. No matter what sphere of wholesome human activity you consider, Jesus Christ's influence on Western civilization looms larger than anyone else's. History shows that wherever the story of His life and message has been taken, lives have been transformed, resulting in tremendous gains in education, law, society, and culture.

Unique in His Personal Life

It was no accident that the man who most influenced human history for good also lived the most extraordinary life in history. Consider His birth. Every Christmas, billions of Christians and non-Christians celebrate His birth and mention the most unusual feature of it: His mother was a virgin.

Jesus' holy life also sets Him apart from anyone else, for as we will show later in this book, even His enemies could not find any fault in Him. In all human history, only one man who claimed to be perfect has ever been taken seriously by both His friends and His enemies. Jesus never had to apologize or ask for forgiveness. He is unique in that He never sinned.

The magnificent teachings of this humble carpenter from Galilee also lift Jesus into a category by Himself. Most Western historians and philosophers, and many from other traditions, acknowledge Him as the greatest teacher who ever lived. Consider His standard of "love your enemies"[1] or "pray for those who spitefully use you"[2] or "give, and it will be given to you."[3] Almost all historians agree that this world would be a far better place if everyone followed the teachings of the Nazarene.

The miracles of Jesus set Him apart as well. As we shall prove, they truly happened, they are still believable, and His ability to relieve every malady and cure every infirmity shows He had the power of God within Him like no one else.

Finally, to cap off His incomparable life, He gave Himself sacrificially for the sins of the world, then performed the greatest of all His miracles: He rose from the dead. That event, commemorated each year as one of the two most sacred dates on the Christian calendar, sets Him apart as the most extraordinary person who ever lived.

The Unique Titles Used of Jesus

No person other than Jesus has been addressed by the following titles, because no other person qualifies for them. Some of these titles were given to Him by angels, others by disciples or followers or even by Hebrew prophets. No one title fully describes Him. To understand who He really was and who He is in His second coming, all must be considered together. One fact is certain: No one else comes close to deserving even one of these titles.

The Almighty
The Mighty God
The Word
My Lord and my God
The great God
Our Savior Jesus Christ
Wonderful
Counselor
The Father of eternity
The Prince of Peace
Alpha and Omega
First and last
God blessed forever
The Christ
The Son of God
Jehovah
The beginning and the end
The Lord
Savior
The Holy One
Lord of all
Emmanuel
The way, the truth, the life
King of kings
Lord of lords

In the history of the world, no one has ever risen from a carpenter's shop to assume such lofty titles. His life can be explained only by the fact that He was indeed "the Son of God" in a unique sense.

His Unique Effect on People

The power of Jesus' unique and unparalleled life has produced a near-universal response in those who accept His claims to deity. People who come to know Him want to live righteously. I have spent my whole life persuading people to accept Him by faith. Every time someone receives Him, the response is always the same: an intense desire to cease from harmful or sinful behavior and to live a righteous life. While some fell back into the evil habits of their past, in no case can I recall anyone who accepted the salvation of Jesus Christ becoming worse than before.

The very weekend I wrote these words, God provided a perfect example of this. I gave the commencement address for the twenty-fifth graduating class of Christian Heritage College in San Diego, California (the college founded by Dr. Henry Morris, Dr. Arthur Peters, and myself). One graduate gave an incredible testimony.

This man, all six feet and five inches and 280 pounds of him, recounted a long history of being in and out of prison. The last time in, he was thrown into the "tank," a facility housing 11 men. The first thing he did was throw a man off the most desirable bunk in the place and say, "This is now my bunk. Want to make something of it?" With that, he crawled into the bunk to get some sleep. Instead, he found a lump in his mattress that turned out to be the first Bible he had ever seen. He began reading it and didn't stop until he finished the Gospel of John—at which time he invited Christ to forgive his sins and become his Lord and Savior. Seven years later he was not only a transformed man who had no further troubles with the law, but he was graduating from a Christian college and intended to go on to seminary to study for the ministry.

The influence of the Nazarene had struck again, changing yet another fallen man's nature and life direction.

I can say without reservation that no one ever has had such a positive influence on more people than Jesus of Nazareth!

The Reason for His Uniqueness

The single fact that Jesus of Nazareth has influenced this world more than anyone who ever lived should be sufficient to establish His unique place in human history. But when you factor in the many other unique features of His life, we are struck with an incredibly difficult dilemma. How do you explain this on a purely human level, particularly when He made His entire life contribution in only three-and-a-half years? When one man stands on such a lofty pedestal, far above all others in human history, surely there must be some reason. What was it?

It was not His parentage, for His mother was a simple Jewish maiden and His father a humble village carpenter.

It was not His material possessions, for He had no money, not even a place "to lay His head."[4] He was tried before legal officials in a borrowed robe and buried in a borrowed tomb.

It was not His education, for there is no record that He attended school. Yet at age 12, He confounded the doctors of theology by teaching in the temple at Jerusalem.

It was not His world travels, for with the exception of a brief trip to Egypt when He was an infant, He never journeyed more than one hundred miles from where He was reared.

It was not because He lived and ministered in an influential country, for He spent His entire life in the obscure little land of Israel. He was reared in a city that prompted the question, "Can anything good come out of Nazareth?"[5]

It was not because He had influential friends, for only fishermen, tax collectors, and other ordinary men and women followed Him.

It was not because all the people loved Him, for the religious leaders and political elite repeatedly tried to stone Him and finally crucified Him.

It was not because He lived a long and successful life, for He was only 33 when He sacrificed His life for others.

It was not because He had a long and extensive ministry, for He ministered only three-and-a-half years. By human standards He died an ignominious failure on a rough-hewn cross.

It was not because He established so many organizations to perpetuate His memory, for He founded only one, His church, and that was not begun until after His death.

So what accounts for the unique status of Jesus Christ? I have read the suggestions of those who reject His claim to be God in human flesh and have found them wanting. They are far more difficult to accept than the simple Gospel accounts. How did this man influence more lives and affect human history more deeply than all others? In all history, no one else even comes close. And yet He did all this in only three-and-a-half-years! All honest doubters must answer the question, "How did He manage it?"

As Jesus Christ walks through the pages of human history, He is lifted into a category all by himself. Unbelievers cannot ignore Him, so great have been His incredible contributions to humanity; neither can they explain His existence without acknowledging His deity. Albert Schweitzer, a victim of a wave of skepticism at the beginning of the twentieth century, had to concede that the historical Jesus is, to our time, a stranger and enigma. As Dr. Carl F. H. Henry, one of the last of the past generation's truly conservative Bible scholars, wrote,

> Many scholars who reject that Jesus is true God and true man, and who instead hold to a one-nature view of Jesus, nonetheless distinguish him from the entirety of the human race. Tributes paid to Jesus even by scholars who disavow the historic christological creeds not only revere the Nazarene above his

contemporaries, but elevate him as well above all human beings ancient and modern. These assessments of Jesus Christ exhaust ordinary anthropological categories in explaining him.[6]

Then he concludes, "Those who do not begin with the fundamental Christian assumption that 'the Word was made flesh,' but attempt to show how a complete man as they suppose Christ to have been was united (somehow) to God, cannot but end in confused and self-contradictory views."[7]

In reality, all portraits of Jesus that conflict with the one presented in the four Gospels are "unhistorical." Jesus is who He said He was: God in human flesh.

There just is no merely human explanation why a simple though brilliant man—a man who should have been forgotten long ago by the entire world—would still be the most loved and respected person who ever lived, 2000 years after His death. Human explanations alone cannot account for the astonishing grip He still holds over this planet. No, only one fact explains the uniqueness of Jesus Christ: Jesus truly was the divine Son of God who came in human flesh, just as He claimed.

You see, assigning humanity alone to Jesus is not good enough. To accomplish what He did in both His life and teachings requires both God and man, working together in one person. That person is Jesus of Nazareth.

It is the purpose of this book to demonstrate that conviction both logically and reasonably. To begin our investigation, let's consider the skepticism of some of those who reject Jesus' unique status as the God-Man. We will see that while no good evidence supports their skepticism, mountains of evidence uphold Jesus' claim to be the unique Son of God, the Lord of Glory in human flesh.

Chapter Two

What About the Skeptics?

For more than 1600 years the deity of Jesus Christ was seldom questioned. Most people readily accepted the eyewitness accounts of His life contained in the Gospels, which made it clear that Jesus must be God in human flesh. Even the people of His day exclaimed, "No one can do these signs unless God is with him."[1]

The same could be said for His teachings, for He spoke as one with authority. Not even the greatest Old Testament prophet ever dared to say, "You have heard that it was said to those of old, 'You shall not murder'....But I say to you..."[2] thus putting Himself on an equal plane with the voice of God. Jesus' universally acknowledged impact on world civilization impelled men to accept Him as God, for no one had ever impacted the nations as He did or accomplished what He did in so short a time.

Of course, even while Jesus walked this earth not everyone accepted His claim to be the Son of God. Not all who heard Him speak, viewed His miracles, and were exposed to the evidence He provided believed in Him. Many of the Jews of His day rejected Him because He failed to match their preconceived idea of the Messiah.

Yet from the very beginning, those who accepted Him as their Messiah also accepted His claims to deity. The vast bulk of the church followed that pattern for centuries afterwards. History records few voices that were raised to offer reasons for questioning the deity of Jesus Christ. That is, until about 400 years ago.

Belief in God Is Challenged

Beginning in the seventeenth century with the philosopher René Descartes, many men were smitten with the idea that they could not believe anything they couldn't see. And because they could not see God, they refused to believe in His existence.

This, of course, was a radical departure from the norm. For millennia, most of mankind accepted that creation demands a Creator, that a world of infinite design demands a Designer. Yet Descartes and those who followed in his skeptical footsteps rejected the whole notion of God.

It was natural, then, for seventeenth-century French skeptics and eighteenth-century German rationalists to question whether Jesus was God. Already they had rejected belief in God and propounded a philosophy of life independent of Him; it was a logical step, then, to apply their skepticism to Jesus.

One basic principle of logic is that if you begin with a wrong premise, inevitably you will reach a faulty conclusion. In regard to the deity of Christ, once a person has rejected God, he must dismiss belief in the supernatural. This prejudice will force him to wear philosophical blinders, preventing a fair evaluation of any claim related to the deity of Jesus. A skeptic simply cannot admit the possibility that Jesus is God. Were he to do so, he would deny the very core of his belief, "There is no God." Therefore he arbitrarily rules out Christ's claims to divinity; since God does not exist, Jesus could not have been divine. In this way, long before beginning an evaluation of the life of Christ, he has concluded that Jesus was nothing more than a mere man.

Amazingly, most of those who reject God and the deity of Jesus are like the atheist Tom Paine, who wrote his very influential book *The Age of Reason* without ever having read the Bible! Most who have concluded that Jesus is less than the Son of God (a claim He made repeatedly) have failed to examine His life personally. In most cases they have reviewed only what others have written, and most of those writings are 1600 years or more removed from the events in question!

Some skeptics, though admitting the incredible impact of Jesus' life on the world, insist that He never claimed to be God or to possess the attributes of God. They would have us believe that Jesus was a good man, but not divine.

That is exactly the situation with the notorious "Jesus Seminar" that has received so much media attention over the past couple decades.

The Jesus Seminar: Who Are They and What Do They Do?

In 1985, Robert Funk invited a number of liberal scholars to meet in Berkeley, California, to reconsider the identity of Jesus and the authenticity of the Gospel records. The Jesus Seminar, as it became known, has continued to meet twice a year to sit in judgment on the accuracy of the New Testament Scriptures. Swelling to over 200 from its original membership of 30, the number of attendees has dwindled in recent years to less than 75. Of these, nearly half either teach at or have received degrees from three of the most liberal theological institutions in America (Harvard, Claremont, and Vanderbilt).

The "objectivity" of the group can be seen in its conclusions. According to the Jesus Seminar, the vast majority of the New Testament in general, and the Gospel of John in particular, is a mistake (despite the fact that biblical scholars have found more manuscripts to authenticate John than any of the other Gospels).

But that is the way it was intended by this group. The conclusions were predetermined from the beginning. Keep in mind that no "scholarship" was involved and no new evidence was examined. So how did these people arrive at their results? The panel simply voted on whether or not *they believed* a passage of Scripture was true! In fact, the group began with the dictum that the supernatural cannot occur, thus denying some cardinal doctrines of the Christian faith, including the virgin birth, the deity of Christ, His atonement for sins, His resurrection from the dead, and His ascension into heaven. Is it any wonder that the Seminar labeled as "inauthentic" any scriptures that support these doctrines?

The primary goal of the Jesus Seminar has always been to garner as much publicity for its "findings" as possible. Without extensive and favorable news coverage in such publications as *Time, Newsweek, U.S. News & World Report,* and the *Los Angeles Times* and *New York Times,* the opinions of the Seminar would have been quickly forgotten. In addition, it was the Jesus Seminar that served as the foundation for ABC's two-hour prime-time television special *The Search for Jesus,* hosted by Peter Jennings and watched by over 16 million viewers. This same media, however, has failed to report that the "scholarship" and methodology of the Seminar has come under intense fire from legitimate scholars in the United States and Europe, both Christian *and* secular.

The first book published by the Seminar, *The Five Gospels: The Search for the Authentic Jesus,* revealed the group's true bias. This 1993 work attempted to elevate the gospel of Thomas above the level of the four biblical Gospels. The blatantly antibiblical gospel of Thomas, which was not discovered until 1945, paints Jesus as a "sage" and a "cynic" rather than as the Son of God. Why the Seminar's fascination with Thomas? One can only assume it's because the members feel more comfortable with Thomas' gnosticism and occultism than they do with the Bible's orthodoxy.

While the Jesus Seminar continues to meet, it has not accomplished much more than to raise troubling questions about its own objectivity, methodology, and scholastic merit. Certainly, it has not in the least shown why anyone should abandon confidence in the Gospel records and instead put trust in its own flights of fancy. [7]

The skeptics I know are generally better at raising objections than they are in answering the simple question, "How do you explain Christianity without the supernatural?" You see this tendency in the shallow, sometimes silly theories they devise, which often create more difficulties than they solve. And it's instructive that they don't seem to develop any truly new theories or find any new proofs against Jesus' claims. Several of the books I read during my research for this book are over 50 to 100 years old, and I find that the questions we are answering for skeptics today are essentially the same ones they raised back then.

In short, modern skeptics have nothing new to offer. They simply refurbish and revise the ideas concocted by French skeptics and German rationalists of two and three centuries ago. Even the Jesus Seminar participants have not devised anything new (the overblown media attention notwithstanding). So far, the best they can offer are some updated versions of the 300-year-old inventions of Voltaire, Rousseau, Hegel, and others. Were their theories even partially correct, you might think the science of archaeology would by this time have provided them with more than enough solid evidence to destroy the credibility of Jesus' deity and resurrection (or at least allow them to discredit the Gospel records of His life). Yet the truth is that archaeological digs continue to *confirm* the 2000-year-old record.

How Skeptics Are Made

It is astounding that many of those who are skeptical of either the deity of Jesus or His bodily resurrection from the dead have never read the Gospels, the records which claim to be eyewitness accounts of the life of Christ. Voltaire, the notorious infidel of the eighteenth century, rejected the deity of Jesus, the resurrection, and the Bible. How did he become so skeptical? Because he was so brilliant? Hardly. His parents were faithful French Catholics who realized their son was unusually intelligent, so they hired a former priest to be his private teacher in an attempt to provide him with a quality education.

Sadly, they didn't check into why the tutor was a *former* priest. The man had been expelled from the Catholic church for his skepticism; in turn, he pumped massive doses of skepticism into the mind of his brilliant young charge. Objectivity had nothing to do with Voltaire's skepticism. Indoctrination by a skeptic made Voltaire a skeptic!

In fact, it has been my experience that most skeptics have been influenced by some book or teacher who passed on his own skepticism. Once a skeptic has his mind made up, personal pride will usually prevent him from changing his position, no matter how many facts to the contrary might confront him.

That is particularly true of many academics. These men and women love to pass on their skepticism to young, impressionable minds—even though they do not have the facts in their favor. Perhaps that is why the largest number of skeptics are found on university campuses, where a few agnostic professors can undermine the faith of many in the next generation.

Under the cloak of "academic freedom," atheistic skeptics in our colleges and universities (and sometimes in our middle schools and high schools) question everything in the Christian faith from creation to the resurrection. Yet they refuse to consider Christian arguments.

Now, anyone who is exposed to only one side of an argument is prone to adopt that viewpoint (particularly youths). Today's universities are cranking out skeptics not because Christians lack adequate evidences for the deity of Christ and His bodily resurrection, but due to the fact students lack exposure to that evidence. I am convinced that the evidence for the deity and resurrection of Jesus Christ is so overwhelming that any objective person who examines both sides of the arguments will conclude that the Christian faith is based on solid facts of history.

The Case of the Unscientific Atheist

When I was a pastor, not many atheists attended my church. So you can understand my surprise when a sharp young engineer shook hands with me one Sunday after the service and announced, "I am an unscientific atheist. I have just earned my master's degree from Stanford University and wish to attend your church. I am working for one year at General Dynamics here in San Diego to earn enough money to attend Brandeis University next fall in pursuit of my Ph.D. degree." He then explained, "An unscientific atheist is one who has examined only one side of the evidence before reaching a conclusion. In all my training, I have been instructed never to reach a conclusion until after examining both sides of the evidence. I have just realized that all my training has been from a skeptical or atheistic perspective. So during this nine months when I do not have heavy academic pursuits, I have chosen to attend your church to allow me to examine the Christian viewpoint."

Then he requested something few people ever have asked of me: "Would you be willing to spend one hour each week with me to help direct my research?" Of course I said, "Yes." But first I extracted one promise from him: that he would read at least one chapter from the Bible each day as I assigned them.

Stan agreed and we met every Wednesday night before the midweek service. He was one disciplined academic. He read the Bible daily, as he promised, and all the books and assignments I gave him. We started with the virgin birth and the deity of Christ, but I soon found he was so thorough it would take him much more time than we had available. So I challenged him to jump to the resurrection alone, for as I told him, "If the resurrection is valid, so is the deity of Christ, including the virgin birth." We worked furiously during the remainder of our nine months, and at my suggestion he started making a list of reasons in favor of the resurrection and another list of reasons against it. Josh McDowell had not yet written his classic apologetic books, so we had to do a lot of research on our own.

You can imagine my disappointment in early September when Stan announced, "This will be our last meeting; I leave for Brandeis in the morning." I tried to get him to reach a decision on the basis of his research, which already showed twice as much evidence for the resurrection as against it—but he "wasn't ready," and I knew better than to push him. He did promise to spend some time in the library each week in an effort to "reach some kind of conclusion during the Thanksgiving break."

Very honestly, I thought we had lost him. After all, in those days almost the entire Brandeis faculty was Jewish and 98 percent of the students were Jewish or atheistic.

I didn't hear from Stan until Christmas vacation, when he called for an appointment. To my great surprise, he had called to tell me, "Next Sunday I plan to come forward at the close of the service and become a Christian." Naturally, I was elated! Then he told me what had happened.

Stan had kept his promise and spent considerable time in the libraries at and near Brandeis, and continued to amass evidence for and against the resurrection. His conclusion? "There was five times as much evidence for the resurrection of Jesus as there was against. Once I reached that conclusion, it was easy to kneel by my bed (in the frat house at Brandeis) and invite Jesus, the living Christ, into my life. The most wonderful peace came over me, as if at last the search was over!"

Then a most unusual thing happened. He went downstairs, where five fellow graduate students were (believe it or not) discussing how incredible it was that Christians could accept anything so outrageous as the resurrection of Jesus. Stan, a gentle-spirited introvert by nature, could take it only so long. Suddenly he found himself entering into the discussion and sharing some of the evidences he had discovered, much to the amazement of the others. For like most unbelievers, they had erroneously concluded there were no arguments in favor of the resurrection because they had never heard any.

When I asked Stan why he didn't consider himself a Christian—he had invited Christ into his life already—he explained that the Lord expected him to give a public testimony of his faith. He was right about that, but had a mistaken idea about what a public testimony was. He had seen people go forward at the invitation given after our sermons each week, and that's what he had in mind.

I explained that he had already given his first public testimony; it came on that day after Thanksgiving in the frat house when he spoke up in defense of his newfound Savior's resurrection from the tomb. And it was given before five Jewish witnesses! That proved he was saved. Stan evidently was thinking of the scripture that promises, "If you confess with your mouth the Lord Jesus and believe in your heart that God has raised Him from the dead, you will be saved. For with the heart one believes unto righteousness, and with the mouth confession is made unto salvation."[8]

True to his word, Stan came forward that next Sunday morning to confess before the church what he had already confessed before men—that the Christ who rose bodily from the dead after the crucifixion was indeed his personal Lord and Savior.

It must have been a genuine experience, for that former unscientific atheist has been a consistent Christian for over 30 years now. The last I heard of him, he was a professor in a Christian college— further evidence that skepticism usually can't stand exposure to the overwhelming evidence for the resurrection of Jesus. If, that is, the skeptic is willing to be objective and to examine both sides of the evidence.

Some Skepticism Isn't Intellectually Honest

Christians have nothing to fear from the arguments of skeptics. When all the evidence is weighed, it becomes clear that belief in the risen Christ makes better sense than belief in any alternate system.

Yet Christians should also realize that the skeptics' weapon of choice never has been rational argument based on the best available evidence; skeptics realized long ago that ridicule and sarcasm serve their purposes far better. Believers need to know that many skeptics cling to their unbelief not on the basis of overwhelming evidence, but simply because they choose to disbelieve. They are not intellectually honest. For example, Josh McDowell tells of being invited as a guest lecturer to a philosophy class by a professor.

The professor who invited me was also the department head. After I presented literary and historical evidence for the deity of Christ, the professor began to badger me with questions and accusations on the resurrection. After about ten minutes, a student interrupted and asked the professor a very perceptive question.

"Sir, what do you think happened that first Easter?"

The professor looked at me, then back at the student. "I don't know what happened," he said. "But it wasn't a resurrection!"

"Is your answer the result of examining the evidence?" the student responded.

The reply was, "No! It is because of my philosophical outlook."

At another major university, several students took my first book, *Evidence That Demands a Verdict*, to the chairman of the history department for evaluation. After several months, one of the students visited the chairman and asked for his opinion of it.

"It contains some of the most conclusive arguments historically for Christianity I've ever read," the professor responded.

The student got all excited. Then the department head added, "But I won't come to the same conclusion as Mr. McDowell."

"Why?" the student asked, puzzled.

"Because of my philosophical outlook," the answer came back.

There was no lack of evidence. The conclusion was reached in spite of it.[9]

A Matter of the Will

A poet has wisely said, "A mind convinced against its will is of the same mind still." Some people just refuse to believe, even when presented with overwhelming facts. Others may have run out of answers, but still refuse to bend their knee to Jesus. In that case, their rejection of Christ and His resurrection is no longer a matter of reason and logic; it is one of rebellion against God.

Such a case occurred several years ago in the church I pastored in San Diego, California. A highly intelligent aerospace engineer came to church regularly with his lovely wife and daughter, but admitted he was not a believer. He openly stated he was an atheist, or at best, a skeptic. I'm not sure which he was. Don was different from most unbelieving husbands in that he enjoyed the company of some of the men in our church. He even came waterskiing with our church men early on Saturdays.

One Sunday morning, after about five years of attendance, Don was deeply moved and after the service said, "Pastor, I have two serious questions I would like to ask you sometime, and if you can answer them, I am ready to become a Christian." I was elated and asked when he would like to talk. He announced the next day would be fine, for he was on vacation all that week.

At two o'clock I arrived at his home and he asked his two critical questions about Christianity. Would you believe that I had studied about both of them within ten days of the visit? For two-and-a-half hours we talked. At the end I asked if he had any more questions. "No," he replied; I had answered them all to his satisfaction.

"Don," I asked, "are you ready to get down on your knees with me and invite Christ into your heart?" To my amazement he said, "Now, let's not get too hasty about this. I don't want to rush into anything." I went away sad, reminded that salvation is more a matter of the will than it is of the mind.

Fortunately, Don kept coming to church with his wife. Later they moved away, and two years after relocating his family, he finally made the decision he should have in his home that Monday afternoon almost ten years before.

Remain Open to Truth

One of Shakespeare's classic lines reads, "To thine own self be true." As you read this book, I challenge you to remain open to truth, evidence, and logic. Be careful not to be swayed by those who refuse to believe—especially when they refuse to examine the evidence. The primary source of evidence for the life of Jesus of Nazareth is the four Gospels, three of which were written by eyewitnesses. As you will see in the next chapter, these records of His life are the most reliable documents of any that came out of the ancient world.

Chapter Three

The Credibility of the Gospel Accounts

Since all the essential facts we know about Jesus come from the Gospels, in a very real sense, all of Christianity is based on the credibility of those four Gospel accounts.

It is therefore easy to see why modern skeptics—men who lived at least 1700 years after the events—insist that long periods of time elapsed between the life of Jesus and the writing of the Gospels. This allows them to claim that the Gospels were written by men who lacked firsthand information about the events in question. They contend that the Gospels tell us little about the "historical Jesus" and much about what the church invented many decades after His death. In other words, they discount the Gospels as reliable accounts of the life of Jesus. While they admit the Gospels give us interesting insights into what the early church taught about its Messiah, they do not believe either the synoptics or John give us much (if any) accurate information about the life and death of the Jesus who actually ministered in first-century Palestine.

If these critics are right, then we can never hope to know much of value about the life of Jesus, and the historic Christian faith crumbles into dust. Yet if they are wrong and we can indeed trust that the Gospels have accurately recorded actual events in the life of Jesus—which I hope to clearly show in this chapter— then we have a solid foundation on which to build our hopes, our faith, and our very lives.

The Importance of the Gospels

It is impossible to overestimate the importance of the Gospel accounts of Jesus' life. Henry H. Halley says,

> The four Gospels are, by all odds, the most important part of the Bible: more important than all the rest of the Bible put together. More important than all the rest of the books in the world put together: for we could better afford to be without the knowledge of everything else than to be without the knowledge of Christ. Bible books that precede are anticipatory, and those that follow are explanatory, of the Hero of the four Gospels.[1]

It is true that Josephus, Tacitus, and other writers of that period refer to the "Jesus of history," but they do not provide any information about Him that is not already mentioned in the Gospels. Consequently, it is of paramount importance that we establish the credibility of the Gospels. Let us begin by briefly considering the Gospel of John, and then we'll look at the three *synoptic* Gospels— so-called because, when set side by side, they reveal a similar treatment of the life and death of Jesus of Nazareth.

The Gospel of John

John's Gospel is customarily set apart from the others because he did not intend to write an account of Jesus' life in chronological form. His desire near the end of the first century was to present the supernaturalness of Jesus in such a way that his readers would be led to faith. He makes that clear in his classic comment near the end of his book: "These are written that you may believe that Jesus is the Christ, the Son of God, and that believing you may have life in His name."[2]

No other Gospel has been more vigorously attacked by skeptics, agnostics, and unbelievers—not because any first-century evidence questions its authority, but largely because it presents the deity of Jesus in unmistakable terms.

John had long outlived the other apostles and had noticed a tendency for some people to think of Jesus' deity in terms similar to that found in the Greek mythologies (for example, as gods who took human or animal form). John wanted to make it clear that Jesus had come in the flesh, that He was every bit human (albeit sinless) *and* every bit God. That is why he emphasized the miracles of Jesus—to show that while the Savior was truly man so that He could die for the sins of mankind, He was also God and could therefore perform miracles like no one else before or since. John presented Jesus as the "Logos" or "the Word," meaning He is the exact expression of God. If you truly desire to know God and understand how He would react in any given situation, study the life of Jesus, for He reveals Him.

Laypeople probably find John's Gospel the easiest of the four Gospels to understand. It was written by a longtime pastor (of the church at Ephesus), an intimate associate of Peter and of the other church leaders. And, of course, John was an eyewitness to all the events he describes. It is interesting that several of the places John mentions—such as Jacob's Well at Sychar, the Pool of Siloam, the pavement *(Gabbatha)* where Jesus was tried before Pilate, and others—have been discovered by archaeologists, putting to silence many of the objections of the skeptics.

John had probably read the synoptic Gospels when they were first written, some 30 years before he wrote the Gospel of John. He wanted his record to be unique; that may be why he presents several miracles and many of Jesus' teachings that are not mentioned in the other Gospels. That is probably why he also presented Jesus as the Creator of all things "in the beginning" (1:1-3). In addition he presents Jesus as Judge, equal with God, the Resurrector and the Rewarder, the Redeemer and the Revealer. John very respectfully and factually presents Jesus as all of these.

One uncomfortable fact confronting skeptics is that more ancient manuscripts attest to the reliability (and late first-century date) of John's Gospel than exist for any other literary work of antiquity. It should be remembered that ancient manuscripts are rare, primarily because they were not written on paper as we know it today, but largely on papyrus, a material extremely vulnerable to weather, moisture, molding, and decay (vellum was not invented until around the fourth century). Yet many pieces of papyri have been discovered from that period which validate the Bible (and especially John) more than any other ancient document.

In 1885 in central Egypt, where the air is dry, many ancient documents were discovered under centuries of protective sands. For the next ten years many fragments of Scripture were unearthed. In 1920, a papyrus fragment of the Gospel of John was discovered, measuring 3½ inches by 2½ inches, with John 18:31-33 on one side and 18:37-39 on the other.

Scholars date this fragment to the first part of the second century. It is the oldest known Bible manuscript, and is evidence that the Gospel of John was in existence, and was in circulation in Egypt, in the years immediately following the death of John.[3]

This important fragment is under glass in the Chester Beatty Collection of the Rylands Library in Manchester, England.[4] It is considered one of the most significant manuscript discoveries in history (although it is no longer the oldest known Bible text; see below) and it helps validate the early authorship and accuracy of the Gospel of John.

In addition to the celebrated John Rylands manuscript fragment, other evidence exists for the early date of John's Gospel:

> The use of John as an authoritative Gospel alongside the other three is attested by the Egerton Papyrus 2, also dated before 150. It was also used by Tatian in his Diatessaron. John was certainly also known and used in heretical Gnostic circles—e.g., by Ptolemaeus, a disciple of Valentinus, by the Gospel of

Peter (c. 150), and (fairly certainly) by the author of the Valentinian Gospel of Truth.[5]

Yet further evidence for the authenticity of this important Gospel is found in its instant acceptance by all the early church leaders. For example, Ignatius, in his *Seven Letters,* written about A.D. 110, quotes from all four Gospels. Papias, who lived from A.D. 70–155, was a disciple of John and quoted his writings as Scripture, along with the other Gospels in his book *An Explanation of the Lord's Discourses.* Similar quotations can be found in the writings of Irenaeus (A.D. 130–200), a pupil of Polycarp (himself a student of John's), as well as Justin Martyr and other early church fathers. Keep in mind, only a fraction of their writings have been preserved; but the ones still extant confirm the existence of and early acceptance of the Gospel of John (and other New Testament books).

With good reason, the most read and loved book in the world is the Bible. And among the most read and loved books in the New Testament is the Gospel of John.

Its message, in accordance with its own stated purpose, has been used throughout the centuries to win multitudes to saving faith in the Lord Jesus Christ, and this is perhaps the crowning proof of its authenticity and divine inspiration.[6]

The Three Synoptic Writers

All three writers of the synoptic Gospels were either eyewitnesses of the events of Jesus' life or had access to those who were. In evaluating the synoptics, the student should bear in mind that the theme and intended audience often took precedence in the mind of the writer over the chronology of events.

Matthew's Gospel is thought to have been written primarily to the Jews because he continually emphasized the fulfillment by Jesus of Old Testament prophecies, proving He was indeed the Messiah.

From the earliest days of Christianity, Matthew was considered the writer of the Gospel which bears his name. Matthew is mentioned in both lists of disciples,[7] confirming that he was an eyewitness to the events. He admits to being a "publican" or tax collector who had left everything to follow Jesus.

And just how old is the Gospel according to Matthew?

Skeptics would have us believe that it dates from at least a generation or two after the events it purports to record. Yet this is impossible. Under glass for almost 100 years in the library of Magdalen College in Oxford, England, is what is now regarded as the oldest extant papyrus fragment of the New Testament. Not only does it confirm the accuracy of the text of Matthew it preserves, it proves that the Gospel was in circulation well within the lifespan of the eyewitnesses to the events it describes—just as the church has believed for two millennia.

On Christmas Eve, 1994, the director of the Institute for Basic Epistemological Research—a German scholar, Dr. Carsten Peter Thiede—released to the press his scientific evidence that dated this fragment of Matthew's Gospel not only prior to A.D. 70, but perhaps as early as A.D. 30. He and British scholar Matthew D'Ancona, in their 1996 book *Eyewitness to Jesus,* state, "It now appears that the finished Gospel according to St. Matthew was also circulating in codex form at that time [A.D. 30 to 60]. It could conceivably have been read and handled by an eyewitness to the Crucifixion."[8]

In a personal magazine interview in late 1996, Dr. Thiede made this important assertion based on his scientific discovery:

> What the papyrus fragments can prove is that the first records, the first complete Gospels, were copied and spread and multiplied during the first decades of the apostolic era in close vicinity to what actually happened among eyewitnesses. *So you could not invent the historical Jesus.* You might still dispute certain details if you like, but you could not dispute the basic fact of his existence and what he did.[9]

This scholar believes the Gospel of Matthew and probably the other two synoptics were written and distributed A.D. 30–60, when many other eyewitnesses were still living and able to judge their accuracy.

This early date for the first Gospel means that Matthew stood the test of scrutiny by the only people qualified to judge it—not "scholars" 1900 years removed from the events, men who are bent on disproving the Bible and the claims of Christ—but by the very eyewitnesses to the events themselves. No wonder the early church accepted the Gospel accounts immediately and gave them status as "other Scriptures," placing them alongside the Old Testament in their worship services!

Mark, traditionally considered the author of the second Gospel, was probably the first to compile a life of Christ for the ever-expanding early church. Mark was not an apostle, but he knew both Peter and Paul well and traveled with them frequently. It is thought that Mark was especially attached to Peter, and in fact he was with the apostle in "Babylon" when Peter wrote his first epistle (see 1 Peter 5:13). Mark had heard both Peter and Paul preach many times and thoroughly knew the events of Jesus' life. Because the disciples met in his mother's home in Jerusalem, it is assumed that in his youth Mark had heard the Savior speak frequently.

Recent scholars think Mark's Gospel may have been written as early as A.D. 55. Gregory A. Boyd, in his excellent answer to the Jesus Seminar skeptics, points out several factors in the book that indicate an early date for Mark. For example,

> In 15:21 Mark refers, without explanation, to "A certain man from Cyrene, Simon, the father of Alexander and Rufus" who was forced to help Jesus carry his cross. The statement is utterly inexplicable except on the assumption that Mark's audience was well-acquainted with Alexander and Rufus. Matthew

and Luke, interestingly enough, make no reference to them.[10]

This not only establishes the event in real history, but locates the time of composition within the memory of the readers, which comfortably would be ten to twenty years, or at most, a generation. Otherwise, such obscure names would likely be forgotten.

Boyd continues:

> Mark mentions Pilate without feeling the need to tell his readers who he was (Matthew and Luke note that he was "governor"), and, conversely, Mark refers to "the high priest" without feeling the need to name him (whereas Matthew and Luke correctly name him as Caiphas, Mark 14:53-54; 15:1). The most natural explanation of this is that Mark's audience did not need to be told what position Pilate held or who held the distinctive position of "high priest" when Jesus was crucified. Since Pilate ceased to be governor in A.D. 36, and Caiphas ceased to be high priest in A.D. 37, the farther away from these dates we move in dating Mark's Gospel, the less intelligible these Markan assumptions become.[11]

Boyd's conclusion is appropriate; the evidence suggests an early date, written by one very familiar with the facts and the people involved.

I might add that recent archaeological finds have confirmed that Pilate was indeed governor in Jerusalem at that very time, which confirms the reliability of the Gospel accounts. Imagine, if you can, some archaeological discovery in the last 100 years that placed Pilate 20 years before or after the crucifixion. Howls would instantly arise from the skeptics in the scholarly community about the lack of reliability of the Scriptures. Yet only deafening silence from these same quarters greets the recent discoveries that confirm the dates, people, and historical accuracy of the records.

In fact, the science of archaeology has not been kind to skeptics during the past 150 years. Instead of confirming their skepticism by proving the Bible was "filled with falsehoods," as some have proclaimed in the past, thousands of archaeological discoveries have instead confirmed the scriptural text. In fact, to date there have been more than 25,000 archaeological digs that have unearthed evidence supporting the claims of the Old Testament portion of the Bible alone. Highly respected archaeologist Nelson Glueck has said,

> It may be stated categorically that no archaeological discovery has ever contradicted a Biblical reference.

One archaeological find of special note made worldwide headlines in the fall of 2002. An ossuary, or burial box, was unearthed containing the inscription "James, son of Joseph, brother of Jesus." CNN stated that "the 2000-year-old box provided the oldest known archaeological record of Jesus of Nazareth." The artifact had been dated to right around A.D. 65, the precise time of James' death. However, what is most interesting is the fact that normally only the names of the father and the deceased person would have appeared on an ossuary. Indeed, the inclusion of the deceased's brother's name on such an artifact would not have occurred *unless* the brother happened to be an important, well-known figure. And no one was more well-known than Jesus Christ in that area of the world at that particular time.

Following the announcement of the find to the media, a number of individuals with an anti-Christian agenda surfaced, claiming the artifact must be a forgery. Now I ask: Would a person who is simply a good man or wise teacher still be stirring up such heated controversy 2000 years later?

Excellent evidence exists that Mark not only wrote the Gospel, but had help from an actual eyewitness. Early tradition suggests that the apostle Peter was the moving force behind Mark's Gospel.

Some even go so far as to say it is the Gospel according to Peter (through Mark). What is important is that the Gospel was written by someone with firsthand acquaintance with the events and it was accepted by the church very early after its writing.

Papias, A.D. 70–155, a pupil of the apostle John, wrote, in his *Explanation of the Lord's Discourses,* that he had made it his business to inquire of the Elders and followers of the Elders, and "The Elder said this also: Mark, having become the Interpreter of Peter, wrote down accurately all that he remembered—not, however, in order—of the Words and Deeds of Christ. For neither did he hear the Lord, nor was he a follower of His, but later on, as I said, he attached himself to Peter, who would adapt his instruction to the need of the occasion, but not teach as though he were composing a connected account of the Lord's Oracles; so that Mark made no mistake in thus writing down some things as he remembered them. For one object was in his thought—to omit nothing that he had heard, and to make no false statements."[12]

Luke, "the beloved physician"[13] and author of the third Gospel, was well educated and gifted as a historical writer. Even those skeptics who malign the Gospel records admit the quality of literary style in Luke. He was a Greek medical doctor who traveled extensively with the apostle Paul in spreading the gospel. It is thought that his book was written about A.D. 70. It is further thought that he had read the Gospel of Mark prior to writing, for he quotes 320 verses of Mark in the 1129 verses of his Gospel.

As a Greek, Luke tended to write to the Greek mind, which gives his Gospel a more universal appeal than Matthew. He emphasizes the humanity of Jesus more than the other writers, which may be why the *Jesus* film (produced and distributed by Campus Crusade for Christ)—which is simply the Gospel of Luke read to dramatic action on screen—does not need much editing when translated into other languages. The film has been produced in more than 75 languages, and reports indicate it has been instrumental in leading millions of people to make decisions for Christ.

Luke was not an eyewitness to the events he relates in his Gospel, but he turns that deficit to an advantage by interviewing those who were there, producing a highly accurate and believable record. No one person could have been privy to all the details found in Luke's Gospel, but by interviewing the eyewitnesses, the good doctor produced a compelling account of Jesus' life, ministry, and death. Because Luke refers to so many specific geographical locations in his writings, he made himself vulnerable to careful examination. He listed 53 geographical locations, and in every instance, archaeology has proven him accurate. His accuracy is so startling that several archaeologists, such as W. F. Albright, have seen their faith restored or have turned from infidelity to faith. An example of the latter is Sir William M. Ramsay, one of the greatest classical archaeologists and geographers ever to have lived.

Trained in the German historical school, Ramsay originally was no friend of the faith. He thought the Bible made itself vulnerable to criticism because it referred to so many places, events, and people. Like many others, his attempt to discredit the New Testament turned him to faith. He had assumed that Acts was not written by Luke, the companion of the apostle Paul. In an attempt to prove this hypothesis he took a trip through Asia Minor, and ended up being so impressed by the accuracy of the book when it referred to local places and things that he reversed himself, saying, "Luke's history is unsurpassed in respect of its trustworthiness."[14] He later wrote in a book supporting Christianity, "This author, Luke, should be placed along with the very greatest of historians."[15]

For another testimony to the accuracy of Luke's writings, Dr. Wilbur Smith—an outstanding scholar of the last generation and one of my own beloved professors—quoted from an unfriendly source, Dr. James T. Shotwell. In his book *The History of History*, Shotwell instructively wrote, "Luke, as the Acts of the Apostles shows, was an educated man who compiled his history out of various sources, was accurate in geography and painstaking, and his work stands easily alongside the best pagan histories of his time."[16]

You can be sure that Luke applied the same kind of crafts-manship to the Gospel that bears his name!

All of the four Gospels are important. To gain a complete picture of Jesus' unique life you must study all four. Each one emphasizes a different aspect of His character. Matthew, writing to the Jews, presents Him as King. Mark presents Him as a servant, while Luke presents Him as the perfect man. Last, John presents Him as God in human flesh. All four are accurate pictures of Jesus of Nazareth and help us to understand the Lord in all His uniqueness.

The Pre-Gospel Writings

Several modern Bible scholars suggest that Mark, considered the first of the Gospel writers, had access to other documents concerning Jesus' life, which he used to write his own Gospel. If at first you consider that heretical, please remember it was Luke who said:

> Inasmuch as *many have taken in hand to set in order a narrative of those things* which have been fulfilled among us, just as those who from the beginning were eyewitnesses and ministers of the word delivered them to us, it seemed good to me also, having had perfect understanding of all things from the very first, to write to you an orderly account (Luke 1:1-3).

Unless only two writers (Mark and Matthew) count as "many," Luke had in mind other accounts of the life, times, and death of Jesus that God did not see fit to include in the canon of Scripture. These "other documents" have been lost in the passing of time. Perhaps some listeners wrote down Jesus' sermons and teachings and provided an unknown author with them, thus putting their notes within hours or days of His speeches. Others may have been eyewitnesses to His miracles and other events of His life. Mark may well have had some of these unpreserved writings at his disposal. No one knows for sure. It is well within the realm of possibility that all three authors of the synoptic Gospels had many bits and pieces or even whole documents from which they could draw.

At least one such document seems to have been quite complete, and some experts believe it was incorporated into our Gospels. As Dr. Smith points out, "We know that before anything was written, the church possessed records of Jesus, but how they originated or what was their earliest character, we shall never know."[17] Scholars have dubbed those pre-Gospel writings as "Q," taken from a German word meaning "source" document. There is reason to believe that their existence accounts for the similarity of the verses in all three synoptic accounts.

The following valuable summary offers some helpful suggestions:

> "Q" was a guide to Christian life and conduct, specially written to meet the needs of the Antiochene church at the time of crisis. It was a Gospel Manual for a Gentile Church. Quite clearly it did not contain all the teaching of Jesus, but only as much as was necessary to meet the special problems and circumstances of a special Church at a special stage in its history. It could only have been written before the Apostolic Council (A.D. 50). A date before the first Mission of Barnabas and Saul, i.e. nearer A.D. 47 is probable. Professor Streeter goes so far as to say that "Q" was probably written twenty years before Mark, and as Professor Robertson comments, "Q" was written during the lifetime of Jesus and for this reason does not include the Passion Week. What the contents of "Q" were, we probably will never know, as no one has ever seen such a document, nor did any of the ancient fathers tell us that they had seen it.[18]

Though the existence of such a valuable resource as "Q" is not required, it is certainly feasible. We know Luke based his Gospel

51

on extensive research; nothing limits his efforts to oral histories. It would seem natural that many people would record their witness of a healing or of one of Jesus' sermons. In all probability, each of the Gospel writers had access to many pieces of such material. It is distinctly possible that Matthew took notes of his experiences and later used some of them for resource material in writing his Gospel. If this is true, it shortens the time even more between the actual events in the life of Christ and the time they were recorded in the Gospels.

Synoptics All Written Before A.D. 70

The longest period between the events of Jesus' life and the writing of the Gospels as we know them today could only be about 35 years. This became clear shortly after seventeenth-century skeptics suggested the Gospels were not committed to writing until after the first century and possibly even later. The objective of these skeptics was not difficult to ascertain; they wanted to put the writing of Jesus' life long after the death of all the disciples. By doing so they could brand the whole story a fraud, since the Gospels are attributed to men who were alive at the time the events transpired. A Gospel that does not contain the testimony of a single eyewitness is not much of an authentic record. Yet like most of the skeptical attacks on the authenticity of Scripture, this argument does not hold water.

All three synoptic writers include the Lord's prophetic discourse taught on the Mount of Olives just hours before He was crucified. In all of them He is quoted as predicting the destruction of the temple in Jerusalem, a prophecy that was fulfilled in A.D. 70, yet none of them mention that the catastrophe had occurred by the time they wrote. It taxes credibility that Matthew and Mark, both Jewish nationals, would have failed to record such a culture-destroying event as the capture of their city and the destruction of their temple, if in fact it had occurred by the time they wrote their Gospels. Most likely, then, these Gospels were written before that date; and since it is highly improbable that all three were written in the same year, at least one of them could have been written two to ten years prior to that awesome event described so carefully by the Jewish historian Josephus. So we are still within 30 to 37 years of the events in question—well within the scope of reliability.

An Endorsement from a French Skeptic

If the Gospels did not accurately record the events that took place in the life of Jesus, where did the writers get their picture of Him? How likely is it that the authors of the Gospels simply "made up" the career and character of Jesus? Consider the opinion of the famous French skeptic Jean-Jacques Rousseau:

> Shall we say that the Gospel story is a work of the imagination? Friend, that is not how one invents; the facts about Socrates which no one doubts, are not so well attested as those about Jesus Christ. At best you are only putting the difficulty away from you, without getting rid of it. It would be more incredible that four men should have agreed to manufacture this book than that there was a single man who supplied the subject matter for it. No Jews could have hit upon its tone of morality; the Gospel has notes of reality which are so great, so striking, so absolutely inimitable, that their inventor would be a more astonishing person than their Hero.[19]

Anyone familiar with Rousseau knows he was no friend of faith. He was a thoroughgoing rationalist who probably did more than any other man to bring on the French Revolution and introduce humanism into the Americas. Yet Rousseau believed the Bible possessed at least as much credibility as any other ancient book. His argument still carries great weight.

History Favors Biblical Reliability

Why do some scholars not subject other ancient works to the same unreasonable standards they apply to the Gospels? There is many times more evidence for the reliability of the Bible than of any other book of the ancient world.

Consider just a few examples from antiquity. Aristotle, an often-quoted Greek philosopher, lived between 384 and 322 B.C. The earliest copy of his works still in existence was produced some 1400 years after he wrote the originals. Plato lived from 427 to 347 B.C., and the oldest copies we have of his works date from at least 1100 years after the originals were produced. Yet almost no one denies the authenticity of either of these authors' writings.

Now, compare that to the situation with the synoptic Gospels. Complete copies of the Gospels, which date back to within 200 to 300 years of their writing, are in museums in several places of the world, and some fragments of the Gospels can be dated much earlier than that. Yet the same "scholars" who accept Aristotle and Plato often seem to choke on Jesus. Does that sound like bias to you?

Beyond that, the entire New Testament can be reproduced from books written by early Christians within 150 years of the events! Yet the same skeptics who have difficulty accepting the Bible rarely hesitate to accept their philosopher friends from Greece. Why? Certainly not because they have more evidence; far more likely is that these scholars have severe philosophical disagreements with the Bible. So the issue is not evidence, but philosophy!

This goes a long way toward explaining why some scholars are so eager to accept something like the gnostic gospel of Thomas (which the vast majority of scholars, evangelical or not, date much later than the canonical Gospels and, in fact, believe is dependent on them). Ordinarily an ancient document is accepted for what it claims to be unless the historian can prove otherwise. That puts the burden of proof on those who would discredit the document. So far, the opponents of the historical reliability of the Gospel accounts have failed to supply such evidence. It is time for the skeptics either to prove that the Gospels date from a much later period than has been traditionally held, or to accept them as authentic.

The truth is, no ancient book has anywhere near the number of whole copies or parts of manuscripts that we possess of the New Testament. Josh McDowell writes,

> When I finished my research into biblical reliability and released *Evidence That Demands a Verdict* in 1973, I was able to document 14,000 manuscripts of the New Testament alone. In 1980 I reissued and updated *Evidence* because of the vast amount of new research material available. Now, I am able to document 24,633 manuscripts of the New Testament alone. The significance of the number of manuscripts documenting the New Testament is even greater when one realizes that in all of history the number two book in manuscript authority is *The Iliad,* by Homer. It has 643 surviving manuscripts. The great number of manuscripts authenticating the New Testament motivated Sir Frederick Kenyon, one of the leading authorities on the reliability of ancient manuscripts, to write: "The interval, then, between the dates of original composition and the earliest extant evidence becomes so small as to be in fact negligible, and the last foundation for any doubt that the Scriptures have come down to us substantially as they were written now has been removed. Both the authenticity and the general integrity of the books of the New Testament may be regarded as finally established."[20]

In any event, the burden of proof lies on the skeptics. They have yet to provide any hard evidence that the Gospel records of Jesus' life are unreliable. Take away their philosophical antagonism to anything supernatural, and their arguments vanish like mist in a blazing sun. History, geography, and logic all cry out that God has indeed left a reliable record of the life of His Son, Jesus of Nazareth. And that record is found in the Gospels.

Years ago my youthful doubts were magnified by the skeptics who ridiculed faith in the Bible because many of its details could not be verified by extrabiblical sources. For example, the Bible mentioned 44 kings by name, yet no "secular" history corroborated their existence. Dr. Harry Rimmer, a crusader for biblical accuracy in an age of scientific discovery, pointed out that in the last 100 years of archaeological digging, the names of 40 of those kings had been discovered. He often pointed out in his lectures that it doesn't take much faith to trust the accuracy of the Bible for the missing four kings! At one time the Bible was ridiculed for mentioning the great "Hittite nation," particularly because the available nonbiblical sources never mentioned the Hittites. Today, thanks to the spade work of the archaeologist, everyone accepts the historicity of the Hittites, a people the Bible described 2500 years ago.

As Professor Eduard Meyer, a rationalist, honestly testified, "There is no ground at all for refusing to accept these oldest traditions as historically trustworthy in all essentials, in their chronological ordering of history."[21]

In the years since those words were penned, so much evidence from the first century and so many fragments of manuscripts have been found that even some of the most skeptical scientists and scholars have had to revise their late dating of the Gospels in the end, much closer to the time tradition has always claimed for them. In fact, Thiede and D'Ancona predict that science and scholarship will have to "redate" their long-held estimates. They conclude,

> There is now good reason to suppose that the Gospel according to St. Matthew, with its detailed accounts of the Sermon on the Mount and the Great Commission, was written not long after the Crucifixion and certainly before the destruction of the Temple in A.D. 70; that the Gospel according to St. Mark was

distributed early enough to reach Qumran (also destroyed before A.D. 70); that the Gospel according to St. Luke belonged to the very first generation of Christian codices.[22]

During the past 200 years, science has often been hostile to faith. It now appears that, just to be academically honest, science has begun to support what Christians always have believed: that the Gospels were written by eyewitnesses to the events they describe and are therefore reliable accounts of history.

My godly mentor was right after all:

> Out of these Gospel records, more power for good has proceeded than out of any other documents of the same size ever written by the hand of men. Upon the testimony of these records, the Christian church has stood solidly for nineteen centuries. Thousands of great scholars in every age have gladly testified that after years of the most careful study, they were compelled uncompromisingly to accept the words of the Gospel records as historically trustworthy. By the preaching of these early disciples, the whole world was transformed, and transformed for the better. By the continued preaching of the truth of these Gospels millions of lives have been transformed in every age.[23]

No book in the ancient world has been more consistently attacked than the amazing book, the Bible, yet it stands unscathed by higher or lower criticism, distortions, and outright prejudice. It is still the world's bestselling book, and, more importantly, the most loved one. It was the first book produced on the printing press because it was "the first book." That was over 500 years ago, and it is still "the first book" today.

No other book has been copied, quoted, or used as much to inspire more individuals to greatness or to nobility of character.

It is easily the world's most inspirational and motivational book. It contains much of the wisdom of God and it is the best manual on human behavior ever written. Those who created philosophies divergent from the Bible have been proven wrong over time, while those who charted their course according to the principles contained in the Bible enjoy "peace with God" unobtainable anywhere else. In times of need or guidance, more people go to the Bible for help than to any other source.

Jesus Guaranteed the Accuracy of His Record

The Christian need not worry about the reliability of the Gospel records or the accuracy of our Lord's messages to His followers. He took great care that they would be infallible. It makes sense that if He was to go to such enormous lengths to save mankind, He would assure the accuracy of the narration of those events. That Christianity has existed for two millennia, all the while depending on the Gospels to tell His story, did not take Him by surprise. Not even the German rationalist and French skeptic movements took Him by surprise. He had taken more than adequate precautions.

It was John who recorded His promise: "The Helper, the Holy Spirit, whom the Father will send in My name, He will teach you all things, *and bring to your remembrance all things that I said to you.*"[24] The Holy Spirit, whom Jesus also called "the Spirit of Truth," was assigned the task of assuring the accuracy of the Gospel records and their inclusion into the canon of the New Testament. We have already seen that other Christian writings most likely existed, but none have survived to this day. Why? Evidently they did not measure up to the standard of excellence that the Holy Spirit required when assembling the New Testament.

We can indeed read the Gospels and other New Testament books with the confidence that we are reading true reports of what Jesus of Nazareth actually did and said. For that reason we can base our eternal salvation and destiny on them. If we want to know who Jesus of Nazareth really was, we needn't wait for the most recent declarations of skeptical scholars such as those who are part of the Jesus Seminar. The best strategy is to read closely what the Gospels and the rest of the New Testament have to say about Him. Only there will we be on solid ground.

Chapter Four

Various Opinions of Jesus of Nazareth

Almost everyone who has heard of Jesus has an opinion about Him. That is to be expected, for He is not only the most famous person in world history, but also the most controversial. Most of the popular views about Him can be reduced to two: Either He was God in human flesh, or He was merely a good man. Both cannot be right. It is impossible to view Him as a good man if He is not the Son of God, for that is precisely who He claimed to be (as we will see in chapter 5). If He was not God but claimed to be, then He was not good; rather, He was either deranged or utterly evil.

Because of Jesus' upright character and charitable deeds, hardly anyone considers Him in a negative light. Even those who bristled at his name—Hegel, Voltaire, Stalin, Mao Tse-tung, and Marx, to name a few—were unable to ignore Him. Some were even respectful of Him. Yet they knew His teaching and their own could not coexist, so they spared no effort in a futile attempt to stamp out His influence.

It boils down to this: If Jesus was and is God in human flesh, then He should be worshiped. If He is not, He should be forgotten and labeled an impostor or lunatic.

Over the past 2000 years, billions of people have indeed worshiped Jesus. Billions of others have never heard of Him or have not gained access to full evidence of who He is. Many in this latter group have formulated their opinions about Him based on the claims of others, but that is dangerous, for a prejudicial view can lead to an erroneous conclusion.

In the eternal plan of God for man, according to the Bible, the most crucial decision facing every individual relates to the identity of Jesus of Nazareth. "Who is Jesus?" is the most important question any person can ever answer.

What People Say About Jesus

The Opinions of Unbelievers

Of all the views regarding Jesus of Nazareth, none are so foolish as the one that asserts He never really lived. Such a claim defies all history and reason, for the Nazarene's footprints are irrevocably stamped all over the Middle East, the Roman era, and Western civilization. Most Jews in Israel have rejected Him as their Messiah, but they cannot and do not deny His existence in history. Many of them today concede that He is the greatest Hebrew since the close of the Old Testament.

In 1995 I led two busloads of Christians on a tour of Israel. Our guide, a major in the army reserve, also held a master's degree in history from the Hebrew University. He was very respectful of Jesus the man—but stated he did not accept Jesus as the Messiah, even though he acknowledged "many similarities" between Jesus and the Jewish perception of the promised Messiah. When I asked him if most Jews believe He truly lived, he responded, "Yes, of course!" To my query, "Who do they think He was?" he replied, "The most famous Jew in all history." Much of the economy of Israel today is based on Christian tourists coming to the Holy Land to pay homage to Him. Every tour bus reminds residents that the Nazarene lived in their land and was one of them, however much they may deny His claim to be their Messiah.

Even those who do not accept Jesus' claim to be God admit that He left an indelible impact on humanity. For example, J. Oswald Sanders, a respected English minister and writer, collected statements from both unbelievers and believers about the person of Jesus, and we'll look first at the unbelievers.

It would seem unbelievers and even infidels have tried to outdo each other in applauding the character of Christ, and in a court of law, favorable evidence from a witness for the opposite side carries great weight. There follow, therefore, some tributes from unbelievers and even enemies of Christianity.

Ernest Renan, the French infidel, wrote: "Repose now in Thy glory, noble Founder. Thy work is finished! Thy divinity is established. Between Thee and God there will no longer be any distinction. Whatever may be the surprises of the future, Jesus will never be surpassed."

Rt. Hon. W. Lecky, of Dublin, the historian of rationalism, says: "Christ has exerted so deep an influence that it may be truly said that the simple record of three short years of active life has done more to regenerate and soften mankind than all the disquisitions of philosophers, and all the exhortations of moralists."

Lord Byron, profligate poet as he was, affirmed: "If ever man was God, or God was man, Jesus Christ was both."

Spinoza, apostate Jew: "Jesus Christ was the Temple; in Him God had most fully revealed Himself."

J. J. Rousseau, immoral atheist: "If the life and death of Socrates were those of a sage, the life and death of Jesus were those of a God."

James Martineau, famous Unitarian: "Jesus Christ must be called the Regenerator of the human race."

Robert Ingersoll, the atheist lecturer: "For the man Christ I have the highest admiration and respect. Had I lived in His day I would have been His friend."

Pecaut, another noted French infidel: "Christ's moral character rose beyond comparison above that of any other great man of antiquity. No one was ever so gentle, so humble, so kind as He. In His spirit He lived in the house of His Heavenly Father. His moral life is wholly penetrated with God."[1]

One wonders how these men could come so far and yet not surrender to the claims of the Son of God, for admiration alone will not save.

The Testimony of Napoléon Bonaparte

Little is mentioned by modern historians about the spiritual life of the would-be dictator of Europe after he was exiled to St. Helena, an island in the South Atlantic Ocean. It is said that to while away the hours of almost seven years of imprisonment, Napoléon did an in-depth study of the life and person of Jesus Christ. His conclusion will interest you.

From first to last, Jesus is the same; always the same—majestic and simple, infinitely severe and infinitely gentle. Throughout a life passed under the public eye, He never gives occasion to find fault. The prudence of His conduct compels our admiration by its union of force and gentleness. Alike in speech and action, He is enlightened, consistent, and calm. Sublimity is said to be an attribute of divinity: what name, then, shall we give Him in whose character were united every element of the sublime?

I know men; and I tell you that Jesus is not a man. Everything in Him amazes me. His spirit outreaches mine, and His will confounds me. Comparison is impossible between Him and any other being in the world. He is truly a being by Himself. His ideas and His sentiments; the truth that He announces; His manner of convincing; are all beyond humanity and the natural order of things.

His birth, and the story of His life; the profoundness of His doctrine, which overturns all difficulties, and is their most complete solution; His Gospel; the singularity of His mysterious being; His appearance; His empire; His progress through all centuries and kingdoms; all this is to me a prodigy, an unfathomable mystery.

I see nothing here of man. Near as I may approach, closely as I may examine, all remains above my comprehension—great with a greatness that crushes me. It is in vain that I reflect—all remains unaccountable! *I defy you to cite another life like that of Christ.*[2]

The Evidence of Profanity

In the introduction to this book I told the story of a high-school student who had never heard the name of Jesus Christ used in anything but profanity. He is not rare; his tribe is legion, thanks to the void of teachings about the historical Jesus in public education and to the widespread use of His name in curses. Unfortunately, this practice permeates the media and the entertainment business. The use of Jesus' name in profanity is so second nature to many they seem not to be aware of what they're doing.

Take television, for example. It seems to me that while media people are embarrassed whenever Jesus' name is used respectfully, they hardly seem to notice when it is used as profanity. I have noticed that sportscasters interviewing the hero of a given event are rattled if he or she happens to spontaneously give "all the credit to my Lord and Savior Jesus Christ," as star athletes have been known to do. When that happens the announcers quickly change the subject, as if afraid their network or station might be used to suggest that Jesus is someone special. Those same individuals, however, seem unconcerned when Jesus' name is used to blaspheme.

But why *His* name? Why—if, as some skeptics suggest, Jesus is merely a "religious teacher" or "a philosopher" or a "great person from history"—are not the names of other famous teachers or philosophers or great historical heroes used in a similar fashion? Have you ever heard anyone smash his finger with a hammer and curse in the name of Buddha or Socrates or Muhammad? Probably not. Why is the name of Jesus singled out? And it is, with one exception: God Himself. Why are these two names used in blasphemy, and no others?

It is very simple. There are no greater names to use when a person wants to "damn" something or verbally condemn someone to hell. Heedless of the Ten Commandments' warning that "the LORD will not hold him guiltless who takes His name in vain,"[3] people continue to speak the name of Jesus as if it were nothing more than a colorful way of saying, "Ow!" In a twist of irony, the skeptic or atheist who uses the name of Jesus in profanity is not only invoking the wrath of almighty God on himself, he is actually acknowledging His supremacy above all other beings.

The Opinion of Other Religions

How do the various religions of the world view Jesus Christ? It seems there are as many opinions about who He is as there are religions. Generally speaking, however, most non-Christian religions attempt to simply place Jesus into the good man/religious prophet/wise teacher category, which, as explained at the beginning of the chapter, cannot logically be done.

One such religion is Islam, one of the fastest-growing religions in the world. Currently, nearly one-fifth of the planet's population is Islamic. The events of September 11, 2001, focused the world's attention on this predominantly Middle Eastern religion, for all 19 of the hijackers who flew the airplanes into the World Trade Center towers and the Pentagon were practicing Muslims.

According to the Qur'an, the holy book of the Muslims, the Islamic Jesus, referred to as *Isa*, is simply a prophet and messenger of Allah. Muslims are careful not to let Jesus upstage Muhammad, whom they consider to be their true leader. Muslims view Jesus as purely human and not the Son of God and thus have no concept of salvation through Him. Although they do not believe Jesus is the Messiah, they have no problem using the word *Christ* when referring to Him because they have redefined the term to mean "one who is anointed to proclaim Allah's truth."

While Muslims affirm that Mary was a virgin at the time of Jesus' birth, the Islamic account of the Lord's birth differs substantially from the biblical record. According to the Qur'an, Jesus was not conceived as a result of the Holy Spirit working in Mary (Muslims do not believe in the Holy Spirit), but was instead created by Allah from dust, similar to the method in which Adam was created.

Islam teaches that Jesus never claimed to be God, and that the Jews were in error when they brought the charge of blasphemy against Him. Islam also teaches that Jesus was never crucified and rejects the entire crucifixion story. The cross is viewed as a "death of disgrace" unworthy of a prophet of Allah. In fact, according to Muslim scholars, the concept of the vicarious atonement of sins by Christ is unnecessary within Islam. Muslims believe that each person must atone for his or her own sins by outweighing his or her evil deeds with good ones. One surefire method for a Muslim to guarantee himself a place in Paradise is to die in *jihad*, or holy war, which is viewed as the ultimate good deed. This was the primary motivation of those who attacked the World Trade Center and the Pentagon and continues to be the primary motivation behind the ever-increasing number of Islamic suicide bombers today.

Muslims view Christians as apostates who have abandoned the truth of Allah, and unless they return to the path of Islam, they will find themselves assigned to the fifth level of hell, known as *Laza*. According to Muslim teacher Shaikh Ahmed Zaki Yamani,

> Issues like the Trinity, the divinity of Christ, and the crucifixion, so central to Christian beliefs, have no place in Islamic faith, having been categorically refuted by the Qur'an.

The identity of Jesus Christ cannot be ignored by the other religions of the world, for the evidence that confirms He lived exactly when and where the Bible says He did is overwhelming. The question is, Who is He? Man or God? The dilemma for all religions is like that of Islam: to relegate Jesus to simply being a good man or mere prophet or wise teacher is ridiculous, for He Himself claimed to be God. However, to admit that Jesus is God makes Him greater than the founder of their particular religion. Therefore, their conclusions regarding the personhood of Jesus are at best suspect, and at worst false.

The Opinion of Believers

It is easy to find testimonies of believers in the deity of Jesus, for their numbers are massive. In the upcoming chapters we will consider the testimonies of those who were eyewitnesses of the life of Jesus. For now, we'll look at a few sample testimonies of believers from postbiblical times who confessed Jesus as Lord. Note that belief in Jesus' deity did not expand with the passing of the centuries, as usually happens with characters in folklore. From the first century on, believers have acknowledged the divinity of Christ. Consider the following testimonies:

> *Polycarp* (A.D. 69–155): Bishop of Smyrna, Polycarp was a disciple of the apostle John. Polycarp wrote, "Now may the God and Father of our Lord Jesus Christ, and the High Priest Himself, the [Son of] God Jesus Christ, build you up in faith…"[4]

Ignatius (died A.D. 110): Head of the Church at Antioch, Ignatius was a contemporary of Polycarp, Clement, and Barnabas, and was martyred in the Colosseum. In his epistle to the Ephesians, he wrote of Christ as "Our God, Jesus Christ."[5] In another letter Ignatius admonished Polycarp to "await Him that is above every season, the Eternal, the Invisible, who became visible for our sake, who suffered for our sake."[6] To the above he added in correspondence to the Smyrneans that "if they believe not in the blood of Christ, (who is God), judgment awaiteth them also."[7]

Additional quotes from the writings of Ignatius:

"Jesus Christ our God..." (Ephesians 1, greeting)

"...by the blood of God..." (Ephesians 1:1)

"...who is God in man..." (Ephesians 2:7)

"For our God, Jesus the Christ..." (Ephesians 2:18)

"Jesus Christ, our God" (twice) (Romans, greeting)[8]

Irenaeus (c. A.D. 125–200): A disciple of Polycarp, Irenaeus explained in *Against Heresies* (4:10) how Christ was often seen by Moses and that it was Christ who spoke from the burning bush. Irenaeus continued elaborating on Christ's relationship to God the Father: "For with Him were always present the Word and Wisdom, the Son and the Spirit, by whom and in whom, freely and spontaneously, He made all things, to whom also He speaks, saying, 'Let us make man after our image and likeness.'"[9]

Justin Martyr (A.D. 110–166): An apologist who defended the faith in a very scholarly manner, Justin Martyr acknowledged, "Our Christ conversed with Moses under the appearance of fire from a bush." It was not the Father of the universe who thus spoke to Moses, but "Jesus the Christ," "the Angel and Apostle," "who is also God," yea "the God of Abraham, Isaac, and Jacob," "the I AM that I AM."[10]

Credal testimony to the deity of Christ abounds, commencing with the first declaration given by Peter, which our Lord attributed to divine revelation: "You are the Christ, the Son of the living God."[11] The Apostles' Creed, whose date is uncertain but whose tenets can all be found in theological formulas current around A.D. 100, states: "I believe in God the Father Almighty, Maker of heaven and earth, and in Jesus Christ, his only Son, our Lord." The Nicene Creed (A.D. 325), formulated to correct some errors which had sprung up in the Church, is even more explicit: "I believe in one Lord Jesus Christ, the only begotten Son of God being of one substance with the Father."

Other creeds and confessions are equally unambiguous as to the deity of Jesus of Nazareth. One contains the distilled wisdom of all the creeds before it. The Westminster Confession, now more than three centuries old, affirms, "The Son of God, the second person in the Trinity, being very and eternal God, of one substance, and equal with the Father, did, when the fullness of time was come, take upon Him man's nature."[12]

Beyond the creeds, many famous writers, thinkers, and leaders of history witnessed to their belief in Jesus' deity. Consider the following:

> William Shakespeare (playwright): "Jesus Christ, my Savior."

> John Milton (poet): "Begotten Son, Divine Similitude."

> Blaise Pascal (mathematician): "Knowledge without Jesus Christ is useless and barren."

> Daniel Webster (American statesman): "I believe Jesus Christ to be the Son of God."

> W. E. Gladstone (British prime minister): "All that I live for is based on the divinity of Christ."

> C. S. Lewis (writer): "God has landed on this enemy-occupied world in human form. The perfect

surrender and humiliation was undergone by Christ...perfect because He was God."[13]

As the foregoing testimonies make clear, the deity of Christ has been clearly believed and propagated in unchanging form by those who knew and served Him throughout the ages. Many great men and women worldwide have been humble believers in Jesus the Christ, the Son of God.

One of the finest tributes to the Nazarene that ever was put to print remains among the most loved pieces of literature:

One Solitary Life

He was born in an obscure village, the child of a peasant woman. He grew up in another obscure village, where He worked in a carpenter shop until He was thirty.

Then for three years He was an itinerant preacher. He never had a family or owned a home. He never set foot inside a big city. He never traveled two hundred miles from the place He was born. He never wrote a book or held an office. He did none of the things that usually accompany greatness.

While He was still a young man, the tide of popular opinion turned against Him. His friends deserted Him. He was turned over to His enemies and went through the mockery of a trial. He was nailed to a cross between two thieves. While He was dying, His executioners gambled for the only piece of property He had—His coat. When He was dead, He was taken down and laid in a borrowed grave.

Nineteen centuries have come and gone, and today He is the central figure for much of the human race. All the armies that ever marched, and all the navies that ever sailed, and all the parliaments that ever sat, and all the kings that ever reigned, put together, have

not affected the life of man upon this earth as power-
fully as this "One Solitary Life."[14]

—Adapted from James A. Francis

Who Is This Man?

In Jesus' day, unlike our own, men customarily accepted the
existence of God. Consequently, His many claims to deity were
either received or rejected on their own merit. As we shall see, not
all who heard Him speak, viewed His miracles, and were exposed
to the evidence He provided believed in Him. Many of the Jews
of His day rejected Him because He did not fit their idea of what
the Messiah should be.

Nowadays some skeptics, though admitting the incredible
impact of Jesus' life on the world, insist that He never claimed to
be God or to possess the attributes of God. They would have us
believe that Jesus was a good man, but not divine. It makes one
wonder if they ever read the four Gospels, for as we shall see, He
made His claim to deity abundantly clear.

Chapter Five

Who Jesus Said He Was

The human beginnings of Jesus can be traced to a humble carpentry shop in the obscure village of Nazareth. Yet despite His lowly stature, at no time was He confused about His person or purpose. Almost immediately upon commencing His public ministry, He began to teach and demonstrate that He was more than human, that in fact He was God come in the flesh. When His enemies recognized the significance of His claims, they took up stones to kill Him.[1]

Eventually thousands of His friends and followers believed in Him. They confessed that "no man ever spoke like this Man!"[2] They had never heard anyone claim that one "greater than Jonah" is here, or one "greater than Solomon" is here, or "the chief cornerstone" is here, or the ultimate: "I AM" is here![3] Yet Jesus made every one of those claims, and more. He knew exactly who He was: the divine Son of God, the second person of the Trinity.

Bold Claims That Call for a Response

My longtime friend and colleague Dr. Henry Morris II, one of the three greatest scholars I have ever been privileged to know, had this to say about Jesus' claims to deity:

> These claims must be studied carefully and regarded with utmost seriousness. They were actually made by Christ Himself and, by all rules

of reason and logic, should be accepted as absolute truth. They amount *in toto* to an absolute and dogmatic claim that He, Jesus Christ, is Himself the eternal God! If this be so, and it *is* so, then a person can ignore or reject this fact only at the cost of tragic and eternal loss to his own soul.

The claims are many and varied, but all add up both individually and collectively to affirmation of Jesus' own unique deity as the eternal Son of God. A sampling of these claims is given below, without comment (for none is needed), taken from the King James Version of the Bible:

"I am the way, the truth, and the life. No one comes to the Father except through Me" (John 14:6).

"The Son of man has power on earth to forgive sins" (Matthew 9:6).

"Therefore whoever confesses Me before men, him I will also confess before My Father who is in heaven" (Matthew 10:32).

"All things have been delivered to Me by My Father, and no one knows the Son except the Father. Nor does anyone know the Father, except the Son, and the one to whom the Son wills to reveal Him" (Matthew 11:27).

"I am the resurrection and the life. He who believes in Me, though he may die, he shall live. And whoever lives and believes in Me shall never die" (John 11:25-26).

"The Son of man is also Lord of the Sabbath" (Mark 2:28).

"Whoever loses his life for My sake will save it" (Luke 9:24).

"I am the light of the world. He who follows me shall not walk in darkness, but have the light of life" (John 8:12).

"When the Son of man comes, will He really find faith on the earth?" (Luke 18:8).

"The Son of Man [came]...to give his life a ransom for many" (Mark 10:45).

"Whoever drinks of the water that I shall give him will never thirst" (John 4:14).

"The Father...has committed all judgment to the Son" (John 5:22).

"Come to Me, all you who labor and are heavy laden, and I will give you rest" (Matthew 11:28).

"The dead will hear the voice of the Son of God: and those who hear will live" (John 5:25).

"Heaven and earth will pass away: but My words will by no means pass away" (Luke 21:33).

"Before Abraham was, I AM" (John 8:58).

"On this rock I will build my church: and the gates of Hades shall not prevail against it" (Matthew 16:18).

"I am the door of the sheep. All that ever came before Me are thieves and robbers" (John 10:7-8).

"I and My Father are one" (John 10:30).

"I am the bread of life. He who comes to me shall never hunger" (John 6:35).

Statements like these can be found in great numbers in the Bible. Remember that He who was sinless would never deceive us, and He who was the wisest Teacher could not be mistaken. The claims are true and the promises sure. In the face of such incontrovertible evidence, we can only say with the once-doubting Thomas, "My Lord and my God!" (John 20:28).[4]

An Unambiguous Piece of Evidence

Those who claim Jesus was confused about His identity must never have read the Gospel records. There is no doubt Jesus knew

He was the Messiah; an incident recorded in John chapter 4 proves this.

One day Jesus met a Samaritan woman at the famous landmark known as Jacob's Well. Jesus, who had never met the woman before, showed His divine nature by telling her (much to her amazement) that she had gone through five husbands and was currently living with a man out of wedlock. Instantly she recognized that Jesus was "a prophet" (verse 19).

After Jesus ministered to her soul, she made a statement that indicates that knowledge of a coming Messiah was widespread, even in Samaria. This fallen Samaritan woman said, "'I know that Messiah is coming' (who is called Christ). 'When He comes, He will tell us all things'" (John 4:25). Notice how Jesus responded: "I who speak to you am He" (verse 26).

The importance of this conversation cannot be overemphasized, for it proves that even laypeople in that day knew about the coming Messiah. Jesus' statement is also a clear and forthright admission by Himself that He was the Messiah for whom the people were looking. This text makes it clear Jesus was not confused about who He was.

Six Specific Claims to Deity

The fifth chapter of John contains some of the clearest of Jesus' claims to deity to be found anywhere in the New Testament. That they are not the only ones in the Gospels is obvious from the list compiled by Dr. Morris, which we looked at a moment ago. But the six found here are the most to be found in a single chapter. John, an eyewitness to the events of Jesus' life, on a single day, heard Jesus proclaim these six characteristics of His deity. Taken together, they prove He believed He was more than a man, and that in fact He was God in human flesh.

Now, these six assertions of deity were delivered to a hostile audience of Jewish leaders who objected when, on the Sabbath, Jesus healed an invalid. Jesus was in Jerusalem for the feast of the

Passover, which all Israelite men were required to observe annually. While there, He visited the Pool of Bethesda, where "a great multitude of sick people, blind, lame, paralyzed, [were] waiting for the moving of the water" (John 5:3). John, an eyewitness, relates the story:

> Now a certain man was there who had an infirmity thirty-eight years. When Jesus saw him lying there, and knew that he already had been in that condition a long time, He said to him, "Do you want to be made well?" The sick man answered Him, "Sir, I have no man to put me into the pool when the water is stirred up; but while I am coming, another steps down before me."
>
> Jesus said to him, "Rise, take up your bed and walk." And immediately the man was made well, took up his bed, and walked. And that day was the Sabbath.
>
> The Jews therefore said to him who was cured, "It is the Sabbath; it is not lawful for you to carry your bed." He answered them, "He who made me well said to me, 'Take up your bed and walk.'" Then they asked him, "Who is the Man who said to you, 'Take up your bed and walk'?" But the one who was healed did not know who it was, for Jesus had withdrawn, a multitude being in that place.
>
> Afterward Jesus found him in the temple, and said to him, "See, you have been made well. Sin no more, lest a worse thing come upon you." The man departed and told the Jews that it was Jesus who had made him well. For this reason the Jews persecuted Jesus, and sought to kill Him, because He had done these things on the Sabbath (John 5:5-16).

The teaching that follows this event was precipitated by the Jews' ardent commitment to Sabbath-keeping, in response to the fifth commandment. They disregarded the fact that God had already provided some exceptions to that commandment for emergencies and acts of benevolence.[5] They were so upset by this miracle being performed on the Sabbath day that some sought to kill Jesus, even though that would have been a violation of the seventh commandment. To them, He had committed the unpardonable sin: He had made Himself "equal with God." Jesus justified His actions by making six classic assertions of His deity.

Again, while these hallmarks of His deity do not begin to cover all the claims of deity Jesus made during His life, they do show quite clearly that within weeks of leaving His humble carpenter's shack in Nazareth, Jesus unwaveringly proclaimed who He was: God in human flesh. And He never recanted any of those claims.

1. *Jesus claimed to be God in the flesh*

When Jesus was confronted about healing the man at the Pool of Bethesda on the Sabbath, He responded, "My Father has been working until now, and I have been working" (John 5:17). John then tells us, "Therefore the Jews sought all the more to kill Him, because He not only broke the Sabbath, but also said that God was His Father, making Himself equal with God" (John 5:18).

In defense of His working on the Sabbath, Jesus resorted to the model of God the Father, who had labored on the Sabbath day even after the six days of creation. True, He "rested" in that He did no creative acts on the seventh day, but He sustained His creation on that first Sabbath and has done so every Sabbath since. When Jesus pointed out that He was "working" (or doing good) on the Sabbath day, He was claiming to perform deeds akin to those of "My Father." The Jews instantly recognized He was saying that He was the Son of God and therefore equal with God. That is why they attempted "the more to kill Him." Jesus' message could not have been clearer. He considered Himself "equal with God."

In verse 19 He expands His assertion, maintaining that He was so united to the Father that "the Son" did things in the same manner as the Father. Jesus did not hesitate to personalize His relationship to God in a way other Jews could not. Abraham, Isaac, and Jacob, their esteemed fathers, had never said, "God is my Father," yet Jesus did not hesitate to do so. Why? Because He was the Son of God come in the flesh! He never flinched from using that title.

And never did He call Himself "a Son of God," but always "*the* Son of God." To the Jews it was brazen blasphemy; to Him it was a statement of fact.

2. *Jesus claimed power to raise the dead*

Later in chapter 5, Jesus said, "As the Father raises the dead and gives life to them, even so the Son gives life to whom He will.... Do not marvel at this; for the hour is coming in which all who are in the graves will hear His voice and come forth—those who have done good, to the resurrection of life, and those who have done evil, to the resurrection of condemnation" (verses 21,28-29).

The Jews of Jesus' day (except one sect, the Sadducees) believed in life after death through resurrection. That is why Martha could say to Jesus of her dead brother, Lazarus, "I know that he will rise again in the resurrection at the last day."[6] Like most Jews, she had been taught this doctrine from childhood. However, Jews believed that only God could raise the dead. In this passage, Jesus claims that He will be the one to raise the dead.

Let me ask you something: Have you ever been tempted to raise the dead? Of course not. We humans never assume such authority and power. Many times as a minister of the gospel I have wished that I had the power to resurrect that young father to his wife and three girls, to return that baby to her parents, to reanimate that young man cut off in the zenith of his life. But frankly, though I could yearn for such power, I have never even been tempted to try such deeds. Why not? Only God can raise the dead! And that is Jesus' point.

There are, of course, four illustrations in the Scriptures when two prophets (Elijah and Elisha) raised the dead, and when two apostles (Paul and Peter) did the same. But in each instance these men made it clear it was God who was using them to accomplish the miracle. Jesus raised the dead in His own power and is the only one who raised a man who had been dead four days (which is significant because Jewish tradition said that by the fourth day, there was no question a person was dead). What also should not be overlooked is that Jesus not only raised three people, but claimed He would raise both the righteous and the unrighteous on Judgment Day. His audience was thoroughly familiar with Daniel's prediction that there were two resurrections coming—"some to everlasting life, some to shame and everlasting contempt."[7] In John 5:29, Jesus is obviously claiming to be the one who performs those resurrections. Such a claim could only be made by God or a mentally deranged person. And since Jesus' life, teachings, and ministry show no signs that He was mentally deranged, but as we shall see, manifest His many divine characteristics, we are left to conclude that He was the unique Son of God in human flesh.

The fact that Jesus demonstrated His power to raise the dead three times during His ministry and then Himself rose the third day from His own grave, laying the foundation of the religion that bears His name, confronts all mankind with the essential question: "Who has life in Himself and the power to raise the dead?" Answer: "God alone!"

3. *Jesus claimed to be the future judge of all men*

Jesus said, "The Father judges no one, but has committed all judgment to the Son" (John 5:22).

Human beings intuitively know that someday they will be judged by God for the way they have lived. Many of those who sow wild oats adopt atheism out of fear of God's justice. It is their attempt to reject both Christ and God, and thus, Judgment Day. They figure if they can somehow reject the existence of God, then they can cast doubt upon their ultimate meeting with God. But at the moment of death, all such fantasies evaporate. At that point, some—like the French skeptic Voltaire or the modern French humanist Sartre—enter into a Christless eternity, screaming in fear and dread.

For our purposes here, it is important to note that Jesus Christ publicly stated in essence what no sane person would ever think: "I am the sovereign God who will sit in judgment on all men." This claim is impossible for anyone to make—unless, of course, He really is God. Jesus of Nazareth made exactly this claim. Therefore He considered Himself divine and openly taught that one day, all human beings will appear before Him for judgment.

Jesus clearly taught that a final judgment is coming, and we know from the Scriptures that the verdicts will last for eternity. If you have never accepted Christ as your Savior, realize that when you stand for judgment at the "great white throne,"[8] you will face the very member of the Trinity who died for your sins on the cross as a willing substitute. At that moment, you will have to admit you rejected Him. Anyone who believes that God will overlook his sinful ways and his rejection of Christ is basing his beliefs on something other than the Bible, for Scripture makes it clear that Jesus is the *only* way of salvation.[9] And those who reject Him will answer to Him for their rejection.

> Of how much worse punishment, do you suppose, will he be thought worthy who has trampled the Son of God underfoot, counted the blood of the covenant by which he was sanctified a common thing, and insulted the Spirit of grace? For we know Him who said, "Vengeance is Mine, I will repay," says the Lord. And again, "The LORD will judge His people." It is a fearful thing to fall into the hands of the living God (Hebrews 10:29-31).

4. *Jesus claimed equal honor with God*

Jesus proclaimed, "All should honor the Son just as they honor the Father. He who does not honor the Son does not honor the Father who sent Him" (John 5:23). When Jesus said that, He was making another claim that denies He possessed a merely human nature. Proof that the Jews considered His statement gross blasphemy is seen in their subsequent attempt to kill Him. Honor and worship of God was a centuries-old part of the Jewish faith. They so revered God they would not even say His name aloud. Yet here was Jesus, plainly affirming that His equality with God earned Him the same honor given to God.

Almost 50 years after Jesus' statement, the apostle John wrote that one of the requirements for salvation is that we honor the Son as we honor the Father.[10] A man does no disservice to God the Father when he honors equally the Father and His Son. In fact, we receive the blessing of God whenever we honor the Son with the Father.

5. *Jesus claimed the authority to dispense eternal life*

Continuing onward in John 5, Jesus said, "Most assuredly, I say to you, he who hears My word and believes in Him who sent Me has everlasting life, and shall not come into judgment, but has passed from death into life" (verse 24).

One universal desire stamped indelibly on the human heart is the wish to live forever. The religions of the world proclaim life after death in "the happy hunting grounds," "Nirvana," or whatever they choose to call "heaven."

Only thoroughly indoctrinated secularists can say, "When you're dead, you're dead" with any sense of confidence. And even some of them have recanted after they walked alone into the valley of death.

All religions of the world are inadequate when addressing *how* people can be assured of gaining access to eternal bliss. Invariably they prescribe a system of good works or self-effort. Not so Christianity. Jesus pointedly said He had the authority to impart eternal salvation and would grant it to anyone who hears His "word and believes in Him who sent Me."[11]

The key here is to believe that Jesus was sent by God and can give life to those who believe in Him (that is, put their faith in Him). He claimed to be the proper object of faith and the dispenser of salvation. This, of course, is nonsense if Jesus were only a man.

But if He is God, as He claimed, then of course He has the capacity to bestow eternal life. That's what God does!

6. *Jesus claimed to be the source of life*

Jesus went on to say, "For as the Father has life in Himself, so He has granted the Son to have life in Himself, and has given Him authority to execute judgment also, because He is the Son of Man" (John 5:26-27).

Jesus boldly claimed He shared the divine nature of God in that He was the source of life. The Jews had an expression for that divine trait, which was used by God Himself when He spoke to Moses at the burning bush. When the people asked Moses, "Who sent you?" he was instructed to say, "I AM has sent me."[12] That was and is the ultimate name for and expression of God. It means that God is "the uncaused cause of all things."

For Jesus to claim that He possessed "life in Himself," even as did the Father, was tantamount to equating Himself with "I AM," the uncaused cause of all things. It is no surprise, then, to find Him in John 8:58 using that very title to identify Himself. He announced to the Jews, "Before Abraham was, I AM."

Throughout His ministry Jesus elaborated on that title, saying at one time or another, "I AM the light of the world...I AM the way...I AM the truth...I AM the Messiah...I AM the door of the sheep...I AM the good shepherd...I AM the Son of God."[13] No stronger claim to deity could be made by anyone. The Jews understood that perfectly—which is why they took up stones to kill Jesus. "You, being a Man, make Yourself God," they raged (John 10:33).

After reading this list of six claims, we cannot evade the conclusion that Jesus was never content to think of Himself as a mere human being. He knew that He was the Son of God and that all power and authority resided in Him. That is why, in the Great Commission given after His resurrection, He admonished His disciples, "All authority has been given to Me."[14]

The claims we examined prove clearly that Jesus thought of Himself as God in human flesh. He declared these statements in public so others could reach that same conclusion. Those who accepted His words became ardent followers; others rejected them and went their own way. That's the way people are about salvation; God has given us the freedom to choose to believe in God or to reject Him.

Part II:
The Testimony of the Eyewitnesses

Chapter Six

The Testimony of
John the Baptist

*There is another who bears witness of Me, and I know
that the witness which He witnesses of Me is true. You
have sent to John, and he has borne witness to the truth.
Yet I do not receive testimony from man, but I say these
things that you may be saved. He was the burning and
shining lamp, and you were willing for a time to rejoice
in his light* (John 5:32-35).

The quality of a witness in court is often as important as the
testimony itself. If an attorney can impugn the witness's character, he will destroy the effectiveness of what the witness says.
In a nationally televised jury trial of a National Football League
icon, a detective's testimony was discounted by the jury
members when they discovered he had lied under oath.

Jesus Christ could not have chosen a better first witness to validate His claims of personal deity than John the Baptist. On one
occasion He Himself said of John, "Among those born of women
there has not risen one greater than John the Baptist."[1] Since all
Jews revered the prophets as the most holy of men, this would
make John the most impeccable eyewitness to Jesus' identity.

Quoting the Hebrew prophet Malachi, Jesus said that John was
"more than a prophet"[2]; he was a special messenger of God who
would "prepare the way before Me."[3] Bible teacher Arthur W. Pink
said of John, "He was the subject of Old Testament prophecy (Isaiah
40); his birth was due to the direct and miraculous intervention

of God (Luke 1:7, 13); he was filled with the Holy Spirit even from his mother's womb (Luke 1:15); he was a man sent from God (John 1:6); he was sent to prepare the way of the Lord (Matthew 3:3)."[4]

John Was Supernaturally Conceived

Although John the Baptist was not born of a virgin, as was Jesus, he was specially conceived. Like Isaac long before him, John was born to aged parents by the miraculous intervention of God. It may be more than coincidental that the one Gospel writer who includes the details of John's miraculous conception was himself a medical doctor. John's father, Zacharias (a priest), and his mother, Elizabeth, were godly people, for Dr. Luke tells us,

> They were both righteous before God, walking in all the commandments and ordinances of the Lord blameless. But they had no child, because Elizabeth was barren, and they were both well advanced in years. So it was, that while he was serving as priest before God in the order of his division, according to the custom of the priesthood, his lot fell to burn incense when he went into the temple of the Lord (Luke 1:6-9).

As Zacharias was ministering before the Lord, the angel Gabriel came to him and prophesied that he and Elizabeth would have a son, who should be named John. The possibility of giving birth to a child at their age was so remote that Zacharias questioned the angel's promise. Because of his lack of faith, he lost his voice for the nine months of Elizabeth's pregnancy; it did not return until the day the child was named shortly after birth.

Six months into her pregnancy, Mary, the niece of Elizabeth, also received a visitation from the angel Gabriel. She was told that she, a virgin, would give birth to the Messiah. When Mary visited her aunt and uncle and related her vision, "the babe [John the Baptist] leaped in her [Elizabeth's] womb; and Elizabeth was filled with the Holy Spirit."[5] After John was born the Bible tells us, "And the hand of the Lord was with him. Now his father Zacharias was filled with the Holy Spirit, and prophesied, saying [of John]...'And you, child, will be called the prophet of the Highest; for you will go before the face of the Lord to prepare His ways, to give knowledge of salvation to His people by the remission of their sins...to give light to those who sit in darkness and the shadow of death, to guide our feet into the way of peace.' So the child grew and became strong in spirit, and was in the deserts till the day of his manifestation to Israel."[6]

Quite clearly John the Baptist was a specially conceived and anointed individual. Although he served only a short time before losing his head by the order of King Herod, this spokesman for God and symbol of spiritual revival in Israel did not disappoint us when it came to bearing witness to the identity of Jesus.

John Understood Who He Was

No one who takes the time to read John's testimony can come away believing that the prophet had trouble with his identity. Because the people anticipated the coming of the Messiah in his day, many pointed to John as that "promised one." In fact, when the "Jews sent priests and Levites from Jerusalem to ask him, 'Who are you?' he confessed...'I am not the Christ [Messiah]'" (John 1:19-20). Neither was he Elijah, for he told them. "I am the voice of one crying in the wilderness: 'Make straight the way of the Lord,' as the prophet Isaiah said" (verse 23). By quoting the prophet Isaiah, John made clear that his role was to herald the coming of Messiah, not to be the Messiah himself. He was obviously comfortable with his role, for he did not try to upstage Christ. John forthrightly said of Him, "He must increase, but I must decrease."[7] John was of both noble birth and impeccable character.

Humility always has been a priority with God. Even today it is a true sign of greatness. John exhibited that humility when, at the zenith of his short career, when people were flocking to him by the thousands to hear him preach righteousness and to be baptized by him, he deferred to the coming Messiah, saying, "There stands One among you whom you do not know. It is He who, coming after me [Jesus was six months younger than John], is preferred before me, whose sandal strap I am not worthy to loose."[8]

What could be clearer? John humbly identified himself as the forerunner of the Christ and willingly fulfilled his calling in hastening the coming of the Messiah, who was preferred before him.

John Was Sent from God to Be a Light

The apostle John, writing more than 50 years after these events, said, "There was a man sent from God, whose name was John. This man came for a witness, to bear witness of the Light, that all through him might believe. He was not that Light, but was sent to bear witness of that Light. That was the true Light which gives light to every man coming into the world."[9]

From God's perspective, John the Baptist had a most significant purpose for living—to be a witness to "the Light of the world," Jesus the Messiah. John's most important role was not as a prophet, even though he was the first to come to Israel in 500 years. It was not even as "the voice of one crying in the wilderness" or as the fulfillment of prophecy (though these were true as well). His greatest characteristic was identified by the apostle John: He "was a man sent from God"!

John's Sevenfold Testimony About Jesus

Having established John the Baptist's impeccable character and seeing that he was the most credible witness of his day to identify Jesus as the Messiah of Israel, we must now turn to his testimony. One thing is certain: His declarations cannot be dismissed or expunged from the record.

1. *The preexistence of Jesus*

"John bore witness of Him and cried out, saying, 'This was He of whom I said, "He who comes after me is preferred before me, for He was before me."'"[10]

It is important to note that Jesus Christ did not begin to exist when "that holy thing,"[11] the fertilized egg of the incarnation, was planted in the womb of the virgin Mary. He had already existed before the foundation of the world. Jesus was "the Word" that was "in the beginning with God." In fact, that "Word was God."[12] John the Baptist affirmed that although his own birth antedated Jesus' by six months, "He [Jesus] was before me." In other words, John confessed that Jesus existed prior to his own conception.

2. *The lordship of Jesus*

John told the crowds that followed him that his purpose was to "make straight the way of the LORD" (John 1:23), in fulfillment of Isaiah's prophecy. In saying this he was testifying that Jesus was the God (or Lord) of the Old Testament, confirming what Jesus would later say of Himself: "I and the Father are one" (John 10:30). This explains why Jesus never rebuked anyone who worshiped Him, even though He knew that only God should be worshiped. Jesus did not consider it blasphemy to permit such adoration, which can only be explained in the light of who He was: The Lord, or God in human flesh.

3. *The absolutely holy life of Jesus*

"Then Jesus came from Galilee to John at the Jordan to be baptized by him. And John tried to prevent Him, saying, 'I need to be baptized by You, and are You coming to me?'"[13]

In order to comprehend the significance of this event, one must picture the scene at the Jordan River. John, the first prophet to minister to Israel in almost 500 years, was preaching against the sins of the people and the religious leaders. A spirit of revival had broken out, people everywhere were repenting, and John was baptizing people from all walks of life. Tax collectors, prostitutes, a few priests and rabbis, and thousands of common people came to be baptized by John in the River Jordan. John baptized all who came to him in true repentance.

Then one day an astonishing thing happened. A certain man came to the shore of the river seeking baptism, and John looked at him and declared, "I can't baptize You; I need You to baptize me!"

Now, get the picture clearly. John knew Jesus well. As cousins, their homes were close enough and their mothers neighborly enough so that they probably knew each other as children. John was giving a subconscious but spontaneous witness that Jesus did not need baptism. Never before or afterward did John offer to exempt anyone else from his baptism—only Jesus. Do not miss the point. John wanted everyone to understand that his cousin, whom he knew well, had lived a sinless life and thus did not need to seek repentance. Such a powerful testimony should stand up in any court in the world, even the court of public opinion.

4. *Jesus identified as "the Lamb of God"*

"The next day John saw Jesus coming toward him, and said, 'Behold! The Lamb of God who takes away the sin of the world!' "[14]

John the Baptist was schooled in the writings of the Old Testament prophets. He knew well the requirements of the special sacrifice for sin—a pure white lamb "without blemish and without spot."[15] It must be perfect. John was saying that Jesus was sinless and therefore qualified to be "the Lamb of God," the sacrifice of God for the sins of the whole world. Jesus, who had just begun His public ministry at this point, had not yet uttered a single word to indicate that He would die on a cross as a sacrifice for sin. That sacrifice was mentioned by the prophets, but neither the disciples nor the religious leaders of the day expected the Messiah to come and die for the sins of the people. In fact, the Jews later rejected Jesus not because He failed to fulfill all the requirements of the prophets, but because He had come to die as a sacrifice for sin. Despite the clear prophecies of Isaiah and other Hebrew prophets, they wanted their Messiah to assume the role of a ruling king, to throw off the shackles of the Romans and set up His kingdom.

The crowds might have been willing to accept Jesus as their sovereign, but not as a suffering Messiah. John knew instantly that Jesus was "the Lamb of God" who would suffer—even before Jesus said that was the case.

This is the only time in the Gospels where Jesus is called the Lamb of God. The apostle Philip used the term when explaining the gospel to the Ethiopian eunuch in Acts 8, but he was quoting Isaiah 53:7-8, where the prophet had written, "He was led as a lamb to the slaughter, and as a sheep before its shearers is silent, so He opened not His mouth. He was taken from prison and from judgment, and who will declare His generation? For He was cut off from the land of the living."

Elsewhere in the New Testament, the apostle Paul calls Jesus "our Passover lamb" (1 Corinthians 5:7 NIV) and Peter calls Him "a lamb without blemish and without spot" (1 Peter 1:19). But the real champion of this term is the book of Revelation, which uses "lamb" to describe Jesus no fewer than 31 times!

We recognize today that Jesus was indeed the Lamb of God who died on the cross, not for His own sins, but for the sins of the whole world. This recognition, however, came after the fact.

How did John know to call Jesus by this title? By divine inspiration only! More than the testimony of John the Baptist, it is also the witness of God.

5. *Jesus identified as the Messiah*

When the people asked John the Baptist if he were "the Christ" (or Messiah; John 1:25), he answered, "No," and told them that he baptized with water only. Yet God had instructed him how to identify the Messiah:

> John bore witness, saying, "I saw the Spirit descending from heaven like a dove, and He remained upon Him. I did not know Him, but He who sent me to baptize with water said to me, 'Upon whom you see the Spirit descending, and remaining on Him, this is He who baptizes with the Holy Spirit.' And I have

seen and testified that this is the Son of God" (John 1:32-34).

John acknowledged his cousin's spiritual superiority when he stated, "I am not worthy to baptize you; you should baptize me." He was not, however, aware in advance that Jesus was the Messiah. Evidently he was certain that the Messiah was living in his day, for he knew he was to serve as His herald, but he did not know who the Messiah would be. Consequently, the Holy Spirit had explained to John how to identify the Messiah. "Upon whom you see the Spirit descending, and remaining on Him, this is He who baptizes with the Holy Spirit" (verse 33). So after Jesus prevailed on John to baptize Him, thus enabling Him to identify with the revival movement of the Spirit in that day and "fulfill all righteousness," it happened! And John "bore witness, saying, 'I saw the Spirit descending from heaven like a dove, and He remained upon Him….This is He who baptizes with the Holy Spirit.'" Thus John identified Jesus by sight as the Messiah of God, the Lamb of God, and the Son of God.

To illustrate the importance of this incredible event, consider a contrasting illustration. Suppose the Holy Spirit had descended and rested on the shoulder of Peter or one of the other apostles. John the Baptist could have been justified in protesting, "Oh no, not him! He is just an undisciplined fisherman! What does he know?" Or he could have said, "I have more qualified disciples than that one!" But he didn't. Instead, when the Spirit fulfilled that prearranged sign—when the Spirit in bodily form like a dove came upon Jesus "and remained on Him"—John immediately responded that He was the Son of God and would baptize with the Holy Spirit.

6. *Jesus declared to have the divine right to baptize with the Holy Spirit*

"Upon whom you see the Spirit descending, and remaining on Him, this is He who baptizes with the Holy Spirit" (John 1:33).

John knew that his baptism was a symbol of repentance and faith, a commitment of one's life to God—not the baptism of salvation. Our baptism today signals that we were "born of the Spirit" when we were "born again."

The baptism of the Messiah was very different. He would baptize with the Holy Spirit, which He has done through His disciples millions of times during the past two thousand years.

Thus John testified that Jesus has the right to dispense salvation through the ministry or baptism of the Holy Spirit, which is available to anyone who believes that Jesus died sacrificially for their sins on the cross (as the Lamb of God), was buried, and rose again on the third day.

7. Jesus was "the Son of God"

"I have seen and testified that this is the Son of God" (John 1:34).

Assessing all he knew about his cousin, Jesus of Nazareth—the stories of His birth to a virgin; His sinless life as a child, teenager, and adult; prophecies of Messiah that Jesus fulfilled; but most of all, that the Holy Spirit "descended on Him like a dove, and remained on Him"—John paid Jesus the highest tribute anyone could express: "This is the Son of God." He did not omit the definite article as though Jesus was *a* son of God, but made it clear that Jesus was *"the* Son of God." In so doing he ascribed to Him the unique identity of Sonship to the Supreme Being. This term, used 40 times in the Gospels, is unique to Jesus.

John's Testimony: Jesus Is God in Human Flesh

Were John to appear in a court of law today and be asked to identify Jesus, he doubtless would proclaim, "He is the preexistent Lord who lived a sinless life, the Lamb of God who was anointed by the Holy Spirit and baptizes with the Holy Spirit. I saw and bear record that this is the Son of God."

John the Baptist, who knew Jesus longer than any of the Lord's disciples, could not have made it any clearer. Jesus of Nazareth was *the* Son of God while on this earth, God in human flesh.

Still, John is only one witness. What did other eyewitnesses say about Jesus? What did those who were closest to Him say? It's time to call them to the stand.

Chapter Seven

The Testimony of
the Apostle Peter

[Jesus] said to them, "But who do you say that I am?"
Peter answered and said to Him, "You are the Christ"
(Mark 8:29).

No defense attorney ever had a more credible witness to his client's life, character, activities, and identity, than Christians today have to the life of Jesus of Nazareth in the person of the apostle Peter. He is clearly the most prominent character in the Gospels (except for Christ Himself). As far as the records are concerned, he spoke more than all the other 11 disciples put together, he was part of the "inner circle" (along with James and John), and he was with Jesus at all the major events of His life, including His death and postresurrection appearances.

When it comes to qualifications as a witness, Peter said it best himself: "We did not follow cunningly devised fables when we made known to you the power and coming of our Lord Jesus Christ, but were eyewitnesses of His majesty. For He received from God the Father honor and glory when such a voice came to Him from the Excellent Glory: 'This is My beloved Son, in whom I am well pleased.'"[1]

Peter's testimony would stand up in any court of our day. He was a man of integrity; he was the leader and spokesman of the early church and one of the most influential of all the disciples. He was respected by the early church right up until his death, about 35 years after the death of his Lord. The influence of the apostle Paul was as yet all but nonexistent in those early years; it was left to Peter to be the leader and human driving force for the primitive church. Consequently, his testimony about Jesus of Nazareth is of paramount importance.

Fortunately, we are not left in doubt about what Peter believed. His convictions about Jesus are contained in the sermons he preached in Acts, in the two epistles he wrote, and almost unquestionably in the Gospel of Mark (which, as we have seen, could well be called "the Gospel of Peter as told to Mark").

Peter's Testimony in Mark

As we have noted, many scholars believe Mark was the first of the four Gospels to be written. And while Mark does not deal with the virgin birth and childhood of Jesus, but instead jumps right into His life and ministry, beginning with His baptism, he does attest to the supernatural nature of Jesus in every respect.

Consider the following highlights from Mark's Gospel:

On the identity of Jesus: "[Jesus] said to them, 'But who do you say that I am?' And Peter answered and said to Him, 'You are the Christ'" (8:29).

On the death and resurrection of Jesus: "[Jesus] began to teach them that the Son of Man must suffer many things, and be rejected by the elders and chief priests and scribes, and be killed, and after three days rise again. He spoke this word openly. Then Peter took Him aside and began to rebuke Him. But when He had turned around and looked at His disciples, He rebuked Peter, saying, 'Get behind Me, Satan! For you are not mindful of the things of God, but the things of men'" (8:31-33). This is an interesting testimony indeed, for it not only records one of Jesus' predictions of His passion, but also that Peter did *not* expect such a thing to happen!

On the transfiguration of Jesus: "Then Peter answered and said to Jesus, 'Rabbi, it is good for us to be here; and let us make three tabernacles: one for You, one for Moses, and one for Elijah'—

because he did not know what to say, for they were greatly afraid" (9:5-6).

This testimony is interesting not only because of Peter's witness of the transfiguration, but also because of his obvious surprise at its occurrence.

On Jesus' promise of eternal reward: "Then Peter began to say to Him, 'See, we have left all and followed You.' So Jesus answered and said, 'Assuredly, I say to you, there is no one who has left house or brothers or sisters or father or mother or wife or children or lands, for My sake and the gospel's, who shall not receive a hundredfold now in this time—houses and brothers and sisters and mothers and children and lands, with persecutions—and in the age to come, eternal life'" (10:28-30).

On the accuracy and power of Jesus' prophetic word: "Now the next day, when they had come out from Bethany, He was hungry. And seeing from afar a fig tree having leaves, He went to see if perhaps He would find something on it. And when He came to it, He found nothing but leaves, for it was not the season for figs. In response Jesus said to it, 'Let no one eat fruit from you ever again.' And His disciples heard it....Now in the morning, as they passed by, they saw the fig tree dried up from the roots. And Peter, remembering, said to Him, 'Rabbi, look! The fig tree which You cursed has withered away'" (11:12-14,20-21).

On Jesus' ability to forecast the future: "Now as He sat on the Mount of Olives opposite the temple, Peter...asked Him privately, 'Tell us, when will these things be? And what will be the sign when all these things will be fulfilled?'" (13:3-4).

On Jesus' ability to predict personal behavior: "Peter said to Him, 'Even if all are made to stumble, yet I will not be.' And Jesus said to him, 'Assuredly, I say to you that today, even this night, before the rooster crows twice, you will deny Me three times.' But he spoke more vehemently, 'If I have to die with You, I will not deny You!'....A second time the rooster crowed. Then Peter called to mind the word that Jesus had said to him, 'Before the rooster crows twice, you will deny Me three times.' And when he thought about it, he wept" (14:29-31,72).

Again, an interesting testimony because it highlights the Lord's supernatural abilities at the expense of Peter's personal record.

Peter's Testimony in Acts

The Bible teaches that the Holy Spirit fell upon the people in the Upper Room on the day of Pentecost, fulfilling the prophecy of Joel 2:28-30. The sermons Peter and others gave that day were well known to the members of the early church and were written down within 30 years of the events they describe, which is still during the lifetime of many of the eyewitnesses to these events.

If Luke had erred in his report, you can be sure many eyewitnesses would have objected. Yet in all of church history, no objections have been found. Luke was extremely careful to record accurately what these eyewitnesses told him.

In the first sermon preached by Peter on the day of Pentecost (Acts 2:14-40), note the references to the following events in the life of Jesus of Nazareth:

"A Man attested [proven] by God to you by miracles, wonders, and signs" (verse 22)

"You have...crucified and put to death" (verse 23)

"Whom God raised up, having loosed the pains of death..." (verse 24)

"God had sworn...He would raise up the Christ to sit on his throne" (verse 30)

"He...spoke concerning the resurrection of the Christ" (verse 31)

"This Jesus God has raised up, of which we are all witnesses..." (verse 32)

"Therefore being exalted to the right hand of God..." (verse 33)

"God has made this Jesus, whom you crucified, both Lord and Christ" (verse 36)

"Repent, and let every one of you be baptized in the name of Jesus Christ for the remission of sins" (verse 38)

Throughout the book of Acts Peter gives strong testimony to the identity, mission, and actions of Jesus Christ. Note especially the following texts, which make clear the apostle's convictions about who this Jesus was:

"In the name of Jesus Christ of Nazareth, rise up and walk" (3:6)

"So, he [the formerly lame man], leaping up, stood... walking, leaping, and praising God" (3:8)

"The God of our fathers, glorified His Servant Jesus [by the resurrection]..." (3:13)

"You denied the Holy One and the Just [Jesus]" (3:14)

"[You]...killed the Prince of life" (3:15)

"...whom God raised from the dead, of which we are witnesses" (3:15)

"His name, through faith in His name, has made this man strong" (3:16)

"God foretold by the mouth of all His prophets, that the Christ would suffer" (3:18)

"That He may send Jesus Christ...whom heaven must receive [or hold] until the times of restoration" (3:20-21)

"For Moses truly said to the fathers, 'The LORD your God will raise up for you a Prophet, like me from your brethren. Him you shall hear in all things'" (3:22)

"To you first, God, having raised up His Servant Jesus, sent Him to bless you" (3:26)

"To all the people of Israel, that by the name of Jesus Christ of Nazareth, whom you crucified, whom God raised from the dead..." (4:10)

"This is the 'stone which was rejected by you builders, which has become the chief cornerstone'" (4:11)

"Nor is there salvation in any other..." (4:12)

"There is no other name under heaven given among men by which we must be saved" (4:12)

"With great power the apostles [including Peter] gave witness to the resurrection of the Lord Jesus" (4:33)

"The God of our Fathers raised up Jesus whom you murdered by hanging on a tree" (5:30)

"Him God has exalted to His right hand to be Prince and Savior..." (5:31)

"...to give repentance to Israel and forgiveness of sins" (5:31)

"We are His witnesses to these things" (5:32)

"Daily in the temple, and in every house, they did not cease teaching and preaching Jesus as the Christ" (5:42)

"Jesus Christ—He is Lord of all" (10:36)

"God anointed Jesus of Nazareth with the Holy Spirit and with power, who went about doing good and healing all who were oppressed by the devil, for God was with Him" (10:38)

"...whom they killed by hanging on a tree. Him God raised up on the third day, and showed Him openly" (10:39-40)

"Witnesses chosen before by God, even to us who ate and drank with him after He arose from the dead" (10:41)

"To Him all the prophets witness that, through His name, whoever believes in Him will receive remission of sins" (10:43)

Remember that all the preceding references to Jesus came from Peter spontaneously. He did not plan out ahead of time what he was going to say; what he spoke conveyed his faith in the core doctrines of the Christian faith, including Jesus' sinless life, powerful ministry of healing, fulfillment of prophecy, His bodily resurrection, and His ability to forgive sins and give eternal life.

Anyone with eyes to see should be convinced that Peter, speaking publicly for the followers of Jesus at the moment in history when the church came into being, believed Jesus to be the divine Son of God come in human flesh. He also acknowledged that Jesus was crucified and had been raised bodily by God as a testimony of His divine approval.

Peter's Testimony in His Epistles

A man's writings are usually an even more deliberate reflection of what he believes than any of his spontaneously delivered public speeches. With that in mind, let us examine the two books that bear Peter's name to see what he believed about Jesus, 30 or more years after the resurrection. In 1 Peter, Jesus is presented as...

> A member of the Godhead (note that all three members are mentioned in one verse): "elect according to the foreknowledge of *God the Father*, in sanctification of the *Spirit*, for obedience and sprinkling of the blood of *Jesus Christ*" (1:2).

> "...a living hope through the resurrection of Jesus Christ from the dead, to an inheritance incorruptible and undefiled and that does not fade away, reserved in heaven for you" (1:3-4)

> At the "revelation of Jesus Christ" (1:7, a reference to the second coming), He will reward the faithful

> The prophets "searched carefully" about "this salvation"; the Spirit of Christ was in them "indicating...the sufferings of Christ and the glories that would follow" (1:10-11)

"You were...redeemed...with the precious blood of Christ, as of a lamb without blemish and without spot" (1:18-19)

"God, who raised Him from the dead and gave Him glory..." (1:21)

"Coming to Him [Jesus] as to a living stone....[He] has become the chief cornerstone" (2:4,7)

"Christ also suffered for us, leaving us an example" (2:21)

"Who committed no sin, nor was guile found in His mouth" (2:22)

"...who, when He was reviled, did not revile in return; when He suffered, He did not threaten, but committed Himself to Him [God]" (2:23)

"...who Himself bore our sins on His own body on the tree...by whose stripes you were healed" (2:24)

"...the Shepherd and Overseer of your souls" (2:25)

"For Christ also suffered once for sins, the just for the unjust, that He might bring us to God, being put to death in the flesh but made alive by the Spirit" (3:18)

"...a good conscience toward God, through the resurrection of Jesus Christ, who has gone into heaven and is at the right hand of God, angels and authorities and powers having been made subject to Him" (3:21-22)

"Since Christ suffered for us in the flesh...live according to God in the spirit" (4:1,6)

"I who am a...witness of the sufferings of Christ, and also a partaker of the glory that will be revealed..." (5:1)

"May the God of all grace, who called us to His eternal glory by Christ Jesus..." (5:10)

Second Peter was written near the very end of Peter's life, when the apostle knew his time on earth was growing short. Many years before, the Lord had predicted Peter would be martyred (see

John 21:18-19), and the apostle realized that the time had arrived. If ever there were an opportunity to recant his beliefs and save his skin, it was now. But we see that his convictions remained as firm as ever about the identity of Jesus of Nazareth:

> "Grace and peace be multiplied to you in the knowledge of God and of Jesus our Lord" (1:2)

> "Entrance will be supplied to you abundantly into the everlasting kingdom of our Lord and Savior Jesus Christ" (1:11)

> "Shortly I must put off my tent, just as our Lord Jesus Christ showed me" (1:14)

> "We made known to you the power and coming of our Lord Jesus Christ….[We] were eyewitnesses of His majesty" (1:16, a reference to the transfiguration)

> "For He received from God the Father honor and glory when such a voice came to Him from the Excellent Glory: 'This is my beloved Son, in whom I am well pleased'" (1:17)

> "The Lord is not slack concerning His promise….The day of the Lord will come as a thief in the night" (3:9-10)

> "…our Lord and Savior Jesus Christ. To Him be the glory both now and forever. Amen" (3:18)

It is obvious Peter's theological understanding had matured during the 30 or more years he had grown in his faith, for he reveals some truths in his second epistle that are not found elsewhere. Yet one element remains unchanged: Christ is given primary position and is described as living a sinless life, performing miracles and signs to glorify God, and letting the people know who He really was.

Peter's Testimony Never Changed

Peter is adamant in his writings that he was an eyewitness to the resurrected Christ after He suffered for our sins. There is no hint of waffling in his testimony, even though he confesses that he knew his death as a martyr was imminent.

Peter lived and died with the testimony on his lips (and from his pen) that Jesus was the supernatural Son of God who died for our sins and rose again the third day—just as the prophets said He would! From Pentecost on, Peter never wavered in his convictions.

Fortunately for us, he was not alone.

Chapter Eight

The Testimony of the Apostle John

Truly Jesus did many other signs in the presence of His disciples, which are not written in this book; but these are written that you may believe that Jesus is the Christ, the Son of God, and that believing you may have life in His name (John 20:30-31).

It is generally accepted that John was the disciple closest to Jesus personally. He refers to himself as "the disciple whom Jesus loved"[1] with good reason. Apparently he was a young man during the ministry of the Lord, and reliable tradition says he outlived all the other disciples. As such he was the last living apostolic eyewitness of the resurrected Christ. He was a close associate of Peter in the early days of the church, usually deferring to his elder's leadership.

John's most distinguishing ministry came as the chief elder at the church of Ephesus, as well as through the enormous contribution he made to Christianity through the five books he wrote. All five books were accepted by the church as soon as they were completed. It is assumed that John lived and ministered in and around Jerusalem for many years, but had gone to Ephesus by the time Titus destroyed the Holy City in A.D. 70.

The Gospel of John is almost universally recognized as having been written later than the three synoptic Gospels, perhaps as late as A.D. 90. Also, John made no attempt to write a chronological history of Jesus' life and ministry, as did the other writers. Most likely he had a much different purpose in mind when he wrote.

It is thought by some that a heresy was creeping into the early church that suggested Jesus had come as a spirit being. No one tried to suggest that Jesus had not lived; they were still too close to the events of His life to deny Him as a figure of history. So instead, the satanically inspired false teachers invented some type of "spirit being" idea. That is why both the Gospel of John and 1 John make it clear that Jesus had indeed "come in the flesh."

John insisted that what he wrote was based on his personal contact with Jesus. He wrote of that "which we have seen with our eyes, which we have looked upon, and our hands have handled, concerning the Word of life" (1 John 1:1). There could be no better witness than one who had traveled with Jesus, lived and eaten with Him, and had even touched Him. Invariably, those who offer up heretical views of Jesus—whether they be first-century heretics or modern skeptics—can never say they met or talked with Jesus in the flesh, either before or after His resurrection.

The Testimony of the Gospel of John

The purpose behind the writing of the Gospel of John[2] seems to have been to leave the church with an authoritative eyewitness depiction of Jesus' life that not only shows He came "in the flesh" but demonstrated through signs, wonders, and healing miracles that He was "the Son of God." For that reason John did not intend to write just another biography of Jesus' life; the synoptics had done that. Instead, we find in John, among other things, ten incredible miracles that could be accomplished only through divine power. Note them as they appear in this extraordinary account of Jesus:

1. He turned the water in six large pots into delicious wine (2:1-12)

2. He healed a nobleman's son from a distance (4:46-54)

3. He healed a man who had been suffering for 38 years with a horrible affliction (5:1-15)

4. He fed 5000 men with only two loaves of bread and five fish (6:1-14)

5. He walked on water (6:15-21)

6. He healed a blind man in Jerusalem (9:1-38)

7. He raised Lazarus from the dead (11:1-45)

8. He rose bodily from the dead after three days (chapters 20–21)

9. He directed the disciples to a miraculous catch of fish requiring two boats to pull in—after they had spent a whole night catching nothing (21:1-12)

10. He appeared five times to individuals or groups after His resurrection (chapters 20–21)

Not one of the miracles listed above could have been accomplished by human power! Individually they attest to the power of God at work in Jesus; collectively they provide awesome evidence that He was more than a man, and could only be God in human flesh. Truly, no man could do all that He did—fulfill prophecy, live a sinless life, provide the world's most profound teachings, do all the miracles attributed to Him, voluntarily die sacrificially on a cross, rise from the dead, reappear many times to as many as 500 people at once and thus prove He was alive after death—and be just a man. The only explanation is, as John said, that He is "God with us"!

Jesus' Teachings Unique to John

Because John wrote his Gospel after the other three Gospels, John shied away from repeating their record of Jesus' teachings. His Gospel is a treasure trove of teachings not found in the other three Gospels. Among the most important texts are the following:

1. *Christ the Creator*

In the beginning was the Word, and the Word was with God, and the Word was God. He was in the beginning with God. All things were made through Him, and without Him nothing was made that was made. In Him was life, and the life was the light of men. And the light shines in the darkness, and the darkness did not comprehend it (John 1:1-5).

He was in the world, and the world was made through Him, and the world did not know Him. He came to His own, and His own did not receive Him. But as many as received Him, to them He gave the right to become children of God, to those who believe in His name: who were born, not of blood, nor of the will of the flesh, nor of the will of man, but of God. And the Word became flesh and dwelt among us, and we beheld His glory, the glory as of the only begotten of the Father, full of grace and truth (John 1:10-14).

John does not leave us in doubt as to what he believed in A.D. 90 about the Jesus he had walked with and talked with and followed. He doesn't call Him merely "God in human flesh," as I have several times in this book. He says Jesus was the "Word" or expression of God; He was in the beginning (before creation) with God; He created all things; He is the light of all men. Not even the best human being who ever lived comes close to measuring up to that description! Truly, as John said, He is the "only begotten of the Father."

2. *You must be born again*

Unless one is born again, he cannot see the kingdom of God....Most assuredly, I say to you, unless one is born of water and the Spirit, he cannot enter the kingdom of God....The wind blows where it wishes, and you hear the sound of it, but cannot tell where it comes from and where it goes. So is everyone who is born of the Spirit (John 3:3,5,8).

The expression "born again" is unique to John's Gospel. So far as we know, Jesus used the term only twice. Yet many Christians today use the term because it best describes that once-in-a-lifetime experience of passing from spiritual death to spiritual life through faith in Jesus. By comparing that born-again spiritual experience to physical birth, Jesus clarified the principle that, just as it is necessary to be born physically to get into this world, one must be born spiritually to qualify for inclusion in the next, eternal world.

3. *The gospel in a nutshell*

And as Moses lifted up the serpent in the wilderness, even so must the Son of Man be lifted up, that whoever believes in Him should not perish but have eternal life. For God so loved the world that He gave His only begotten Son, that whoever believes in Him should not perish but have everlasting life. For God did not send His Son into the world to condemn the world, but that the world through Him might be saved. He who believes in Him is not condemned; but he who does not believe is condemned already, because he has not believed in the name of the only begotten Son of God (John 3:14-18).

This text may be the best-known teaching on salvation in the entire Bible (and with good reason, for that is what the Bible is all about). It contains "the gospel in a nutshell." Verse 16 is unquestionably the most-loved verse in all Scripture. Uncounted numbers of individuals have professed faith in Christ and accepted salvation with only this short scripture to guide them. And they were born again and were assured of their salvation.

Why isn't the story of Nicodemus, from which this text is taken, found in the other Gospels? Perhaps the apostle John was the only disciple who accompanied Jesus to His meeting with Nicodemus, during which this exchange took place. Whatever the case, we are indebted to John for including this sublime passage from the lips of "the only begotten Son of God."

4. Valid proof that Jesus is the Christ

The best single chapter in the Bible on the deity of Jesus is John 5. It includes Jesus' witness of who He was, John the Baptist's witness, the miracles or "works" of Jesus as witnesses, the voice of the Father, and the testimony of the Scriptures (particularly fulfilled messianic prophecies). This one chapter provides awesome evidence for the deity of Jesus.

5. The last teachings of Jesus

It has long been considered that the last words of a dying man are among his most significant. That was the case with Jacob, Moses, and many others. In this long tradition, the four chapters of John 14–17 are of utmost significance, for they record the very last teachings of Jesus just before His crucifixion and resurrection.

These significant teachings discuss heaven, Jesus "the truth," prayer, clinging to Him as branches cling to the vine, the ministry of the Word and the Holy Spirit, and more. In any list of the ten most important chapters of the Bible to master, these four must be included. They lay out the essentials of the Christian life and should be read regularly as a unit.

Christ and the Resurrection

The aged apostle John left no question that, even though 50 or more years had passed since Jesus ascended to heaven and even though all the other disciples were dead, he still believed Jesus was the Christ. He confessed Jesus as the Promised One—that He had come from God, rose from the dead, and had returned to God, and will return again. John dedicated two whole chapters after the crucifixion to the fact of the empty tomb and to the postresurrection appearances of Jesus Christ.

John knew the one message that would change the face of religious teachings forever would be the fact of the resurrection of Christ from the grave. He knew that resurrection to be a fact and wanted to leave a record of it in ink so that all the world would know that the last living apostolic eyewitness regarded it to be a fact. There is no question that, to John, Jesus was God and had proven that fact by rising from the dead. John's heartbeat was that others would come to believe as he did. That's why he openly revealed his purpose in writing the Gospel of John.

> Truly Jesus did many other signs in the presence of His disciples, which are not written in this book; but these are written that you may believe that Jesus is the Christ, the Son of God, and that believing you may have life in His name (John 20:30-31).

After reading this chapter, if you still have doubts about the true identity of Jesus, I suggest you read the life of Christ by one who knew Him well. That's what John gives us in the Gospel of John. It may well change your life, as it has the lives of countless others through the ages.

Chapter Nine

The Testimony of the Apostle Paul

God also has highly exalted Him and given Him the name which is above every name, that at the name of Jesus every knee should bow, of those in heaven, and of those on earth, and of those under the earth, and that every tongue should confess that Jesus Christ is Lord, to the glory of God the Father (Philippians 2:9-11).

The dramatic conversion of the apostle Paul offers an impossible problem for the skeptic determined to destroy Christianity. How can the life transformation of this extraordinary man be explained away?

When a brilliant scholar, a member of the Sanhedrin, "a Pharisee of the Pharisees" zealous for the faith of Israel, a man who persecuted the early church and who wholeheartedly consented to the death of its first martyr, *himself* becomes converted in a miraculous way, resulting in a complete change of lifestyle and life message—there must be some potent reason. Particularly when that man becomes the outstanding spokesman for the church he once persecuted! No credible scholar, including most critics, denies the life and astonishing turnaround of the apostle Paul. Without a supernatural, resurrected Jesus, there is no adequate explanation for Paul's radically reoriented life.

A Major Turnaround

To begin, refresh yourself on the details of Paul's conversion:

> Then Saul, still breathing threats and murder against the disciples of the Lord, went to the high priest and asked letters from him to the synagogues of Damascus, so that if he found any who were of the Way, whether men or women, he might bring them bound to Jerusalem. And as he journeyed he came near Damascus, and suddenly a light shone around him from heaven. Then he fell to the ground, and heard a voice saying to him, "Saul, Saul, why are you persecuting Me?" And he said, "Who are You, Lord?" Then the Lord said, "I am Jesus, whom you are persecuting. It is hard for you to kick against the goads." So he, trembling and astonished, said, "Lord, what do You want me to do?" Then the Lord said to him, "Arise and go into the city, and you will be told what you must do." And the men who journeyed with him stood speechless, hearing a voice but seeing no one. Then Saul arose from the ground, and when his eyes were opened he saw no one. But they led him by the hand and brought him into Damascus. And he was three days without sight, and neither ate nor drank (Acts 9:1-9).

Thus began a life transformation that can only be accounted for by the supernatural. Christianity has a simple explanation for Paul's dramatic metamorphosis: he was saved, as he himself said, in a confrontation with the resurrected Christ, then indwelt by God's Holy Spirit and empowered to perform miracles, teach, preach, build churches, and write epistles. No other explanation can account for how such an antagonist to the gospel could suddenly and thoroughly change into a man who would eventually write 13 of the New Testament's 27 books.

Paul's conversion still stands as one of the greatest witnesses to the deity of Christ and the truth of Christianity. In fact, J. Gresham

Machen, one of the modern era's most able defenders of orthodoxy, counted Paul's conversion as the second greatest proof of the faith, eclipsed only by the resurrection of Christ. Something remarkable happened there on the Damascus Road almost 2000 years ago. Christianity has an explanation for it; the skeptics are still looking for one.

Paul the Credible Witness

Paul never saw Jesus during His life here on earth. He never saw Him perform a miracle, never heard Him teach, did not see Him after the resurrection until meeting Him miraculously on the Damascus Road. Yet Paul's writings show he was thoroughly familiar with the life of Jesus of Nazareth *many years before the Gospels were ever written!* The question is, where did Paul get this information?

One obvious answer is that *it was common knowledge throughout the church at the time of his conversion* (which took place from one to three years after the events recorded in the Gospels). I intend to show in this chapter that within 15 to 20 years of Jesus' resurrection, a written record from the apostle Paul was produced which referred to the basic gospel events in such a specific way that his readers must have been thoroughly familiar with the story. There simply wasn't enough time for "myth making" or embellishing the resurrection story. Such would have required at least one to two generations to develop—a time span that wasn't present in this case.

Why Was Paul Chosen?

I have long wondered why God permitted Paul, an apostle "born out of due time,"[1] to be the first to author a New Testament book. I also wondered why his Greek colleague, Dr. Luke (who also never met Jesus), became the author of one of His biographies and a complete history of the early church.

Eventually I came to see one possible reason behind God's strategy. You see, whenever these outsiders wrote on Jesus the Christ and all the supernatural elements of His life, they were reflecting the *commonly held beliefs of the church at that point in time.* Had their writings conflicted with the established views of the church, they would have been attacked and discarded immediately. But they never were.

The letters of Paul were written on papyrus and were available for checking against Mark and Matthew, once the latter works came out. Yet we are still waiting for telling instances of contradictions between Paul and the Gospel writers. That can only mean that Paul's teachings and writing were synonymous with the commonly held core beliefs of early Christianity. And while Luke may have had Mark to read before he wrote his own Gospel, it is highly likely he interviewed many individuals whose stories do not appear in Mark's Gospel.

What is important to note is the widespread acceptance by the early church of the life, person, and resurrection of Jesus—the cornerstone of our faith. What we have in Paul's writings are the essential details of what the early church believed and taught about Jesus of Nazareth.

Paul, the Earliest Witness

It isn't always possible to determine exactly when the books of the Bible were written. Most scholars agree that either James or 1 Thessalonians was written first. We believe Thessalonians was written by Paul from Corinth on his second missionary journey after his brief, three-week visit in Thessalonica, where he founded a church and then was driven out of town by hostile Jews. It is possible from these and other details to determine it was written between A.D. 49 and 51. This means it appeared from one to about four years prior to the completion of Mark's Gospel.

Paul wrote this little book because he had taught this young church a great deal about prophecy, particularly concerning the coming of the Lord. After the death of some of their new believers, they grew deeply troubled about what might happen to their departed loved ones when the Lord returned for His saints "in the air" (1 Thessalonians 4:17). Paul wrote this epistle to answer their questions.

Subsequently the Thessalonians received another letter, often called "the spurious letter." We know nothing about it, other than it caused the Thessalonians a good deal of grief. This necessitated that the apostle write a second time to correct some of the false teachings in the spurious letter. While I am tempted to show how very much Paul had taught these brand new Christians about the second coming and related events, that is not our purpose in this book. Here we need to examine what Paul said about the life, person, death, and resurrection of our Lord. It's clear those concepts were already widespread, even within such a short time of Jesus' ascension. Keep in mind that Paul was writing to Greeks who had no Old Testament background or awareness of Jesus' life and times. And what Paul said would eventually be scrutinized by the church leaders in Jerusalem. Since they never objected to the message of these letters, we know that what he wrote reflected the commonly held beliefs of the early church.

Let's now take some time to examine, right from the pen of the apostle Paul, the core doctrines he espoused to this early church.

1 Thessalonians

Note the work of the trinity:

> Paul, Silvanus, and Timothy, to the church of the Thessalonians in God the Father and the Lord Jesus Christ: Grace to you and peace from God our Father and the Lord Jesus Christ. We give thanks to God always for you all, making mention of you in our prayers (1:1-2).

Note the work of Jesus in salvation, that the gospel is called "the gospel of God" and that "God raised Jesus":

> They themselves declare…how you turned to God from idols to serve the living and true God, and to wait for His Son from heaven, whom He raised from the dead, even Jesus who delivers us from the wrath to come….We were bold in our God to speak to you the gospel of God….We were well pleased to impart to you not only the gospel of God, but also our own lives….We preached to you the gospel of God (1:9-10; 2:2,8-9).

Note the details about those who killed Jesus and how this displeased God:

> We also thank God without ceasing, because when you received the word of God which you heard from us, you welcomed it not as the word of men, but as it is in truth, the word of God, which also effectively works in you who believe. For you, brethren, became imitators of the churches of God which are in Judea in Christ Jesus. For you also suffered the same things from your own countrymen, just as they did from the Judeans, who killed both the Lord Jesus and their own prophets, and have persecuted us; and they do not please God and are contrary to all men (2:13-15).

Note that the second coming of Christ is the church's hope:

> For what is our hope, or joy, or crown of rejoicing? Is it not even you in the presence of our Lord Jesus Christ at His coming? For you are our glory and joy (2:19-20).

Note that "the gospel of God" and "the gospel of Christ" are inter-changeable, and that a preacher of that gospel is called "a minister of God":

> …and sent Timothy, our brother and minister of God, and our fellow laborer in the gospel of Christ,

to establish you and encourage you concerning your faith (3:2).

Note that both God the Father and the Lord Jesus direct the paths of Christians:

Now may our God and Father Himself, and our Lord Jesus Christ, direct our way to you (3:11).

Note that the sanctification of the church depends on the second coming:

So that He may establish your hearts blameless in holiness before our God and Father at the coming of our Lord Jesus Christ with all His saints (3:13).

Note that it is the will of God that Christians obey the commands of Jesus:

Brethren, we urge and exhort in the Lord Jesus that you should abound more and more, just as you received from us how you ought to walk and to please God; for you know what commandments we gave you through the Lord Jesus. For this is the will of God, your sanctification: that you should abstain from sexual immorality (4:1-3).

Note that participating in the rapture requires faith in the death and resurrection of Jesus:

If we believe that Jesus died and rose again, even so God will bring with Him those who sleep in Jesus. For this we say to you by the word of the Lord, that we who are alive and remain until the coming of the Lord will by no means precede those who are asleep. For the Lord Himself will descend from heaven with a shout, with the voice of an archangel, and with the trumpet of God. And the dead in Christ will rise first. Then we who are alive and remain shall be caught up together with them in the clouds to meet the Lord in the air. And thus we shall always be with the Lord (4:14-17).

Note that salvation is through our Lord Jesus Christ:

> For God did not appoint us to wrath, but to obtain salvation through our Lord Jesus Christ (5:9).

Note that the will of God is through Christ:

> In everything give thanks; for this is the will of God in Christ Jesus for you (5:18).

Note yet another reference to the second coming of Jesus:

> Now may the God of peace Himself sanctify you completely; and may your whole spirit, soul, and body be preserved blameless at the coming of our Lord Jesus Christ (5:23).

2 Thessalonians

Note that Jesus is presented equal to God the Father:

> Paul, Silvanus, and Timothy, to the church of the Thessalonians in God our Father and the Lord Jesus Christ: Grace to you and peace from God our Father and the Lord Jesus Christ (1:1-2).

Note that the early Christian churches were known as the churches of God:

> ...so that we ourselves boast of you among the churches of God for your patience and faith in all your persecutions and tribulations that you endure (1:4).

Note another reference to the second coming of Jesus, that He is called "Lord" and that Christians are called "His saints":

> These shall be punished with everlasting destruction from the presence of the Lord and from the glory of His power, when He comes, in that Day, to

be glorified in His saints and to be admired among all those who believe, because our testimony among you was believed (1:9-10).

Note that grace comes equally from God and Jesus:

We also pray always for you that our God would count you worthy of this calling, and fulfill all pleasure of His goodness and the work of faith with power, that the name of our Lord Jesus Christ may be glorified in you, and you in Him, according to the grace of our God and the Lord Jesus Christ (1:11-12).

Note that at His second coming Jesus will destroy the antichrist:

The mystery of lawlessness is already at work; only He who now restrains will do so until He is taken out of the way. And then the lawless one will be revealed, whom the Lord will consume with the breath of His mouth and destroy with the brightness of His coming (2:7-8).

Note that the penalty for refusing to believe the gospel of Christ is condemnation:

The coming of the lawless one is according to the working of Satan, with all power, signs, and lying wonders, and with all unrighteous deception among those who perish, because they did not receive the love of the truth, that they might be saved. And for this reason God will send them strong delusion, that they should believe the lie, that they all may be condemned who did not believe the truth but had pleasure in unrighteousness (2:9-12).

Note that it is equally the work of Jesus and God the Father to comfort and establish the believers:

May our Lord Jesus Christ Himself, and our God and Father, who has loved us and given us everlasting consolation and good hope by grace, comfort your hearts and establish you in every good word and work (2:16-17).

Note that Jesus is the giver of both peace and grace, and that His presence is promised to believers:

> May the Lord of peace Himself give you peace always in every way. The Lord be with you all. The salutation of Paul with my own hand, which is a sign in every epistle; so I write. The grace of our Lord Jesus Christ be with you all. Amen (3:16-18).

These texts show that within 15 to 17 years of Jesus' ascension, Paul was discussing several doctrines that were common knowledge among the early churches. Keep in mind that much of this doctrine was contrary to the strict Jewish upbringing and training of the day. For example, Paul...

- equates "God the Father" with the "Lord Jesus Christ";

- uses the "gospel of God" and the "gospel of Christ" interchangeably, for they are one gospel;

- instructs believers to await the return of Jesus;

- insists that God raised Jesus from the dead;

- says Jesus delivers us from the wrath to come; He is the source of our salvation;

- says Jesus was opposed by the Jews;

- says Jesus is alive and will take believers into His presence;

- says Timothy is a "minister of God" preaching the "gospel of Christ";

- says both "God the Father" and "Jesus the Son" direct believers' paths;

- maintains that true believers will take part in the second coming;

- says God appointed us to salvation through Jesus Christ our Lord;

- teaches that saints will be sanctified "completely" at the coming of Christ;

- says both God the Father and Jesus Christ dispense "grace."

As you consider the foregoing list of a few of Paul's early doctrinal teachings, remember that they all reflect the basic understanding of the early church. Even if some of these doctrines (such as specifics regarding the second coming) were revealed through Paul,[2] it is clear that the early church endorsed them, for these letters have been passed down to us through the centuries without a hint of censure. It appears these teachings must have been the entrenched beliefs of the early church, accepted and heard as common doctrine.

Surely Paul knew that someday the leaders of the church would visit his young churches, including that at Thessalonica, and examine his writings. He dared not as an apostle "born out of due time" teach anything that was not the common faith "once for all delivered to the saints" (Jude 3). Interestingly, he was never accused of doing so!

How much of Paul's doctrine was learned from the earliest church leaders in Jerusalem and how much he received as direct revelation from God is unclear. What we do know is his teaching was accepted, endorsed, and supported by the early church. Near the end of his life, Peter himself wrote, "Our beloved brother Paul, according to the wisdom given to him, has written to you, as also in all his epistles, speaking in them of these things, in which are some things hard to understand, which untaught and unstable people twist to their own destruction, as they do also the rest of the Scriptures."[3] Note several things:

- Peter calls Paul "our beloved brother"
- Peter says God gave to Paul a special "wisdom"
- Peter says some of Paul's teachings are "hard to understand"
- Peter says that to "twist" Paul's words leads to "destruction"
- Peter numbers Paul's epistles among "the rest of the Scriptures"

When you combine Peter's enthusiastic endorsement of Paul with the content of Paul's early letters, you must conclude that these doctrines had to be the common teaching of all the churches, starting shortly after Jesus' resurrection, ascension, and the descent of the Holy Spirit. That should not surprise us, for that is exactly what was preached on the day of Pentecost.

The Later Theology of Paul

The testimony of Paul is not confined to the books of 1 and 2 Thessalonians, but is also found in his other books. Nowhere does he contradict the writers of the Gospels. In fact, Paul endorsed in writing some of the stories and teachings found later in the Gospels. Two powerful examples are his paeans of praise to the full deity of Christ as written in the epistles to the Colossians and the Philippians:

> [God] has delivered us from the power of darkness and conveyed us into the kingdom of the Son of His love, in whom we have redemption through His blood, the forgiveness of sins. He is the image of the invisible God, the firstborn over all creation. For by Him all things were created that are in heaven and that are on earth, visible and invisible, whether thrones or dominions or principalities or powers. All things were created through Him and for Him. And He is before all things, and in Him all things consist.

And He is the head of the body, the church, who is the beginning, the firstborn from the dead, that in all things He may have the preeminence. For it pleased the Father that in Him all the fullness should dwell, and by Him to reconcile all things to Himself, by Him, whether things on earth or things in heaven, having made peace through the blood of His cross.

And you, who once were alienated and enemies in your mind by wicked works, yet now He has reconciled in the body of His flesh through death, to present you holy, and blameless, and above reproach in His sight (Colossians 1:13-22).

Let this mind be in you which was also in Christ Jesus, who, being in the form of God, did not consider it robbery to be equal with God, but made Himself of no reputation, taking the form of a servant, and coming in the likeness of men. And being found in appearance as a man, He humbled Himself and became obedient to the point of death, even the death of the cross.

Therefore God also has highly exalted Him and given Him the name which is above every name, that at the name of Jesus every knee should bow, of those in heaven, and of those on earth, and of those under the earth, and that every tongue should confess that Jesus Christ is Lord, to the glory of God the Father (Philippians 2:5-11).[4]

Paul's Unflagging Testimony

There can be no question that the apostle Paul went to his grave proclaiming the deity of Jesus Christ, including His sinless life, His sacrificial death, His bodily resurrection, His offer of redemption from sin and eternal salvation, and much more.

Paul's encounter with the living Christ on the Damascus Road that so transformed his life is indeed a powerful witness to the deity of Jesus. It also provides a powerful endorsement for his testimony of Jesus' identity, a testimony that has not been impeached for 2000 years.

Chapter Ten

The Testimony of God Himself

"This is My beloved Son, in whom I am well pleased."
And we heard this voice which came from heaven when we
were with Him on the holy mountain (2 Peter 1:17-18).

Much like an attorney who has already proven his case beyond a reasonable doubt, our God the Father adds His own audible testimonies to the awesome accumulated evidence of who Jesus really is. Three times that we know of during the life of Christ, God Himself spoke from heaven to verify the identity of His Son.

Several times in the Old Testament, God communicated from heaven to instruct or reassure the Israelites of His presence. On the most famous occasion He spoke the Ten Commandments to Moses, then wrote them in stone. Before that He had addressed Moses through the burning bush, and later spoke to Pharaoh through His servant Moses. On each of these occasions, God used His audible testimony at an enormously important time in the life of Israel.

In the same way, on three occasions during the life of our Lord, the voice of God the Father was heard audibly from heaven. We shall examine each of them, in sequence, for they too come at uniquely important times and proclaim Jesus as the Son of God.

The Voice of God at the Baptism of Jesus

When He had been baptized, Jesus came up immediately from the water; and behold, the heavens were opened to Him, and He saw the Spirit of God descending like a dove and alighting upon Him. And suddenly a voice came from heaven, saying, "This is My beloved Son, in whom I am well pleased" (Matthew 3:16-17; see also Mark 1:9-11 and Luke 3:21-22).

Earlier we examined Jesus' baptism by John the Baptist, calling special attention to the descent of the Holy Spirit like a dove to rest on Jesus, identifying Him as the Son of God. At that time we did not highlight the significant fact that all three members of the Trinity were involved in that event: Christ, who was baptized; God the Holy Spirit, who identified Jesus of Nazareth as the Messiah; and God the Father, whose voice was heard from heaven. The event was significant enough to be recorded in all four Gospels. Matthew and John were eyewitnesses, Mark may have been, and Luke renders a credible account through research and the testimony of eyewitnesses.[1]

Note too that all three of the synoptic writers recorded the same statement: "A voice came from heaven saying, 'This is My beloved Son, in whom I am well pleased.'" Jesus is identified not only by the Holy Spirit in dove form, but also by the awesome voice of God Himself recognizing Jesus of Nazareth as His unique Son, adding the distinct comment "in whom I am well pleased." This is further testimony of the holiness of Jesus from birth to the time of this event, which Luke says occurred during Jesus' thirtieth year.[2]

Who actually heard this testimony? We do not know. Certainly John the Baptist did, together with the disciples and probably other believers. Crowds of people had gathered at the Jordan River, where multitudes came to be baptized by John, most of whom were sincere believers. Yet we also know from the questions that followed that some did not believe. Evidently they either did not hear the voice, failed to understand it, or did not recognize it as from God.

Scripture makes it clear that God the Father spoke from heaven before many witnesses to identify His Son. Several of those witnesses testified to that fact in the Gospel record.

The Voice of God at the Transfiguration

After six days Jesus took Peter, James, and John his brother, led them up on a high mountain by themselves; and He was transfigured before them. His face shone like the sun, and His clothes became as white as the light. And behold, Moses and Elijah appeared to them, talking with Him. Then Peter answered and said to Jesus, "Lord, it is good for us to be here; if You wish, let us make here three tabernacles: one for You, one for Moses, and one for Elijah." While he was still speaking, behold, a bright cloud overshadowed them; and suddenly a voice came out of the cloud, saying, "This is My beloved Son, in whom I am well pleased. Hear Him!" And when the disciples heard it, they fell on their faces and were greatly afraid. But Jesus came and touched them and said, "Arise, and do not be afraid." And when they had lifted up their eyes, they saw no one but Jesus only (Matthew 17:1-8).

The transfiguration was one of the most significant events in the life of Christ and the only time He was so physically manifested before witnesses. His three closest disciples, Peter, James, and John, were given a once-in-a-lifetime opportunity to witness His essential Godlike nature shine right through His human flesh. Throughout His life Jesus was both fully man and fully God, seen and known by His fellow men. On this unique occasion He was seen in a peculiar light: God in human flesh, His divine nature within shining through His human skin.

Both Luke and Mark also include this story, emphasizing its importance. Luke adds, "the appearance of His face was altered, and his robe became white and glistening,"[3] reflecting the supernatural nature of the event. All three authors tell us that Moses and Elijah appeared with Him in that glorious place we know today as the Mount of Transfiguration. Only Luke adds that they spoke with Him "of His decease which He was about to accomplish at Jerusalem."[4] Centuries before, both Moses and Elijah had foretold that the coming Messiah would suffer for the sins of the people, fulfilling all the sacrificial requirements for the sins of the whole world.

Yet the disciples were not ready to entertain the thought that Jesus would soon be crucified in fulfillment of God's divine plan of redemption. Peter had made that clear a short time earlier when he rebuked Jesus for saying that "He must go to Jerusalem, and suffer many things from the elders and chief priests and scribes, and be killed, and be raised the third day."[5] That Peter was totally out of touch with Jesus' plan appears in the Master's curt response, "Get behind Me, Satan! You are an offense to Me, for you are not mindful of the things of God, but the things of men."[6]

Now, on that holy mountain of Transfiguration, Peter, James, and John evidently heard Jesus discussing His impending death with Moses and Elijah. It is not clear if they understood God's divine plan for His future, but somehow they did recognize Moses and Elijah, for Peter suggested, "Let us make here three tabernacles: one for You, one for Moses, and one for Elijah" (Matthew 17:4).

To understand the significance of this event, remember that Moses and Elijah were the two greatest men in the history of Israel. They were special servants of God who not only ministered in a significant way to the nation, but also were writing prophets. In those days, when an Israelite referred to "Moses and Elijah," he was alluding not only to the events in the illustrious lives of these two men, but (in the case of Moses) to the first five books of the Bible and (in the case of Elijah) to the prophets who wrote in "the spirit of Elijah." Jesus recognized this in Luke 16 when He told the rich man that He would not send Lazarus to the house of the dead man's father in order to warn his brothers to flee the future of the unsaved, because "they have Moses and the prophets; let them hear them."[7]

As great as these two men were, the next text makes it clear that they pale in the significance to the Son of God. We are told in Matthew 17:5 that a "bright cloud overshadowed them" (much like the many clouds in the Old Testament that shrouded the presence of God himself) and then "suddenly a voice came out of the cloud, saying, 'This is My beloved Son, in whom I am well pleased. Hear Him!'" No wonder that "when the disciples heard it, they fell on their faces and were greatly afraid" (verse 6). They had just heard and recognized the voice of the almighty God! And while that voice never mentioned the names Moses and Elijah, it exalted the man they knew as Jesus of Nazareth.

On the Mount of Transfiguration, just as at the Jordan River, God identified Jesus as His Son and expressed His pleasure with Him. He was saying to the disciples, and to all believers after Him, "Hear Him!" In other words, although the words of Moses and Elijah (which in that day meant the books of the Old Testament) should be revered, the people were to place Jesus' words above even them.

Peter never got over the wonder of this encounter. We noted in chapter 6 that, as on old man about to be martyred, the apostle took time to recount this wondrous event to the young believers in his charge. His words bear repeating:

> For we did not follow cunningly devised fables when we made known to you the power and coming of our Lord Jesus Christ, but were eyewitnesses of His majesty. For He received from God the Father honor and glory when such a voice came to Him from the Excellent Glory: "This is My beloved Son, in whom I am well pleased." And we heard this voice which

came from heaven when we were with Him on the holy mountain (2 Peter 1:16-18).

Could a testimony be any clearer? Peter heard the voice of God, gave testimony to its message, and thus underscored the essential deity of Jesus the Christ.

The Voice of God Four Days Before the Crucifixion

"Father, glorify Your name." Then a voice came from heaven, saying, "I have both glorified it and will glorify it again." Therefore the people who stood by and heard it said that it had thundered. Others said, "An angel has spoken to Him." Jesus answered and said, "This voice did not come because of Me, but for your sake. Now is the judgment of this world; now the ruler of this world will be cast out. And I, if I am lifted up from the earth, will draw all peoples to Myself." This He said, signifying by what death He would die (John 12:28-33).

The voice of God was heard from heaven for the third time after Jesus had presented Himself to the nation of Israel on what we call Palm Sunday. But then the nation rejected Him, and He knew that His death on the cross was close at hand.

That week some Greeks asked the disciple Philip to introduce them to Jesus. Doubtless the majority of the crowd was made up of Jews, but some Bible scholars suggest that these Greeks were present because God was preparing the Gentiles to recognize that His Son was about to die sacrificially, not only for the sins of Israel, but for the entire world.

The apostle John is the only one who records this incident.[8] While thinking of His impending death in a matter of days, Jesus admits, "My soul is troubled." That was illustrated just two days later when, in the Garden of Gethsemane, "His sweat became like great drops of blood falling down to the ground."[9] Yet although His soul was "troubled," He did not shrink from the ignominious death He was about to suffer. Instead He declared, "For this purpose I came to this hour."[10]

Then Jesus prayed, "Father, glorify Your name," and the voice of God responded, "I have both glorified it and will glorify it again"[11]—thus acknowledging that He had spoken before and that He would again glorify Him through the resurrection after His seeming defeat on the cross. The people, both believers and unbelievers alike in that crowd, recognized that the voice was supernatural. Jesus identified the source of the voice and declared that it came for their sakes. Why for their sakes?

By this time the chief priests and Pharisees were speaking out against Jesus and accusing Him of being an impostor. He knew He would be reviled and crucified and that many would turn away in disillusionment during His three days in the tomb. The voice of God "glorified Him" so that these representatives of all nations would believe in Him. Jesus stated, "And I, if I am lifted up [on the cross] from the earth, will draw all peoples to Myself,"[12] thus indicating the kind of death He would suffer.

Last, Jesus appealed to the people: "A little while longer the light is with you. Walk while you have the light, lest darkness overtake you....While you have the light, believe in the light, that you may become sons of light."[13] Since He had already introduced Himself as "the light of the world," He was calling them to become believers before the crucifixion would try the souls of both believers and unbelievers.

And the crowd's response? "But although He had done so many signs before them, they did not believe in Him."[14] This tragic comment proves that unbelievers were present on this occasion. They heard the voice of God and had viewed Jesus' miracles, yet they refused to believe. Happily, others did put their trust in Him.

That same choice to believe or to disbelieve is given to people today. The evidence is exactly the same now as it was then. People today—just as those witnesses 2000 years ago—are without excuse, for they have the testimony of the voice of God Himself, endorsing His Son.

In a Category All by Himself

God's voice resounded at His Son's baptism. The disciples heard it on a mountain at the Transfiguration. And finally that voice boomed in the ears of the public just before Jesus' crucifixion.

Not only did God three times audibly identify and validate Jesus as His Son, but later He lifted His teachings into a category all by themselves. The author of Hebrews wrote, "God, who at various times and in different ways spoke in time past to the fathers by the prophets, has in these last days spoken to us by His Son, whom He has appointed heir of all things, through whom also He made the worlds."[15]

Jesus is indeed in a category all by Himself!

Part III:
What His Works Prove About Him

Chapter Eleven

His Miracles As Witness to His Identity

If a man came onto the world scene healing lepers, restoring paraplegics, reconstructing crippled limbs, and giving sight to the blind, we would instantly acclaim him more than a man. We might even call him a god in human flesh.

If a man walked on water, calmed storms, and fed more than 5000 men at one time with a boy's lunch, we would suspect that man was more than human.

If a man stopped a funeral procession and raised the only son of a grieving widow, returning him to his mother—in front of many witnesses—we would indeed proclaim him a god. For in the history of the world, no human being has ever performed one of those miracles by his own power, much less all of them.

That must be what Jesus meant when He told the Jews who objected to His claim that He was the Son of God, "I have a greater witness than John's...the works that I do—bear witness of Me."[1] In other words, while John the Baptist was indeed a powerful witness to His deity, His miraculous works were an even greater array of witnesses.

Jesus Known for His Works

Wherever the story of Jesus has become known, news of His marvelous miracles have accompanied it, for anyone who studies His life carefully discovers that it would be impossible to separate Him from His miracles. The miraculous deeds (particularly those of bodily healing) caused thousands of people to flock to Him to hear His matchless teaching. It was His miracles that gave His teaching credibility among the people. As one who witnessed some of these miracles said, "No one can do these signs...unless God is with him."[2] It is doubtful that Jesus would have drawn much of a following had He not been able to heal the sick and raise the dead. Almost 20 centuries later, scarcely anyone would have heard of Jesus Christ had it not been for His supernatural miracles. They indeed establish His authenticity.

Throughout history some attempts have been made to eliminate His miracles from His life. A few skeptics have tried to explain them away and some rationalists have endeavored to turn them into myths (such as the agnostic David Hume, whose eighteenth-century attack on Jesus' miracles reveals feeble evidence against them), but these "explanations" usually require more faith than the miracles themselves.

Thomas Jefferson, third president of the United States, tried to rid Christianity of Christ's miracles by cutting them out of the Bible with a pair of scissors. All he succeeded in creating was literary mush. His version of the Bible never caught on because it renders the Greatest Story Ever Told into unintelligible nonsense. It strips the Son of God of the best evidence for believing He was supernatural by simply removing the evidence. Just saying, "I don't believe in the supernatural," as did Hume, Jefferson, and modern skeptics, establishes nothing. Anyone who disbelieves in God will have an inadequate view of the supernatural, making belief in miracles impossible. And of course, no one has yet offered convincing evidence that there is no God.

If a person starts by excluding the possibility that a supernatural God exists, he will reject the possibility of miracles. No proof underlies such a conviction, of course; the skeptic is merely voicing his unbelief. And that can never refute the account of Jesus' miracles. Historical evidence weighs overwhelmingly in favor of the miracles as an integral part of the Nazarene's life. Without them, Jesus would have been quickly forgotten and drifted into eternal obscurity.

Jesus' Miracles Were Important to His Work

Jesus of Nazareth ministered publicly for only three-and-a-half years, a short time to establish Himself as the Son of God for all time and to found a religion that would stand the test of the ages. Thus it was important to Him that He establish His personal credibility early in His ministry so that His work could be carried on by His followers.

The significance Jesus placed on miracles appears in His response to the disciples of John the Baptist, who asked whether He was the predicted Messiah or not. The question came some time after John had publicly identified Jesus as the Lamb of God who takes away the sins of the world. Note the Lord's answer: "Go and tell John the things you have seen and heard: that the blind see, the lame walk, the lepers are cleansed, the deaf hear, the dead are raised, the poor have the gospel preached to them."[3] Jesus knew John the Baptist was in prison, soon to be executed for confronting King Herod about his adultery. John needed something to help fortify his faith in the messiahship of Jesus, so Christ used His miracles as proof.

Jesus pointed to miracles as a "greater witness" of His deity when He said, "The works which the Father has given Me to finish—the very works that I do—bear witness of Me, that the Father has sent Me."[4] He clearly intends that His "works," a term He uses interchangeably with "miracles," identify that He is God in human flesh. He said, "The works that I do in My Father's name, they bear witness of Me."[5] Later, referring to His miracles, He registered a claim that until our day has never been refuted: "the works which no one else did."[6] As a miracle worker, Jesus is still in a category all by Himself.

The Seriousness of Rejecting Jesus' Miracles

One of the most terrifying condemnations in the Bible was reserved for the people of two cities where Jesus did many miracles. The Jews of those cities rejected Him, particularly when He made claim to deity. "Woe to you, Chorazin! Woe to you, Bethsaida!" He said. "For if the mighty works which were done in you had been done in Tyre and Sidon, they would have repented long ago in sackcloth and ashes. But I say to you, it will be more tolerable for Tyre and Sidon in the day of judgment than for you."[7]

Obviously, Jesus' miracles were meant to convince people that He was acting in the power and name of God. When the Jews rejected His claim, they were rejecting a powerful witness to His deity and thus were without excuse. To capture the significance of this, He compared their towns to the cities of Sodom and Gomorrah, which were rife with homosexuality and decadence. Those wicked cities did not, however, see Jesus perform miracles in their city or hear Him deliver His matchless teachings. Had He done so, He assures us, they would have "repented." Therefore, they will find it "more tolerable...in the day of judgment." At least they were not guilty of rejecting overwhelming evidence of His personal identity.

Miracles, then, are an overt and powerful witness to Jesus' identity. People reject them at their peril. The late Dr. Wilbur M. Smith wrote:

> We do not know any adequate reason why these early disciples should have inserted these stories concerning miracles in the Gospel records, unless they rested upon actual historical events. In fact, if the testimony of these Gospels concerning the miracles of Christ is false, then their falsehood is indeed a greater miracle than the miracles which they describe. [8]

It was not Christ's *teachings* that caused Peter and the other disciples to leave their nets and follow Him; it was the *miracle* of the net full of fish that convinced them.[9] They had fished all night and caught nothing, yet Jesus, after speaking to the crowd from Peter's boat, urged the tired fishermen (who had already cleaned their nets) to "launch out into the deep and let down your nets for a catch." When they hesitantly responded to His odd command, they caught so many fish that they had to signal to another boat for help—and both boats started to sink under the load. Such a miracle convinced Peter that this man Jesus was unlike any he had ever seen or heard about. Even the fish of the sea obeyed Him!

Five Categories of Miracles

During His brief public ministry Jesus performed hundreds of miracles, at least 39 of which are described in the Gospels. Many others were not recorded in detail but were summarized in such expressions as He "healed them all."[10] Once the fame of Jesus' miracles spread to neighboring cities, "they sent out into all that surrounding region, brought to Him all who were sick."[11] Jesus' miraculous deeds were so enormous in number that His enemies never tried to deny that He possessed supernatural power. As we will see, they erred fatally in attributing them to the devil. But even as hostile witnesses, they had to acknowledge that His miracles were real, for they transformed the lives of real people.

While an examination of all the miracles Jesus performed is beyond the scope of this book, it is possible to categorize all His miracles into five divisions: power over nature, bodily healings, casting out of demons, multiplication, and raising the dead. We will examine a few miracles from each category to demonstrate the awesome evidence they offer to the identity of Jesus of Nazareth.

1. *Miracles of power over nature*

Jesus often manipulated nature, demonstrating that He had power over the laws of nature. His first such miracle was performed at the wedding in Cana of Galilee (John 2). It is a beautiful story. Jesus, about 30 years old at the time, was attending because both He and His disciples had been invited. Shortly after the host family ran out of wine for their guests, Mary came to her son and fretted, "They have no wine." We can almost sense the desperation in her voice. Some have suggested it was a gross breach of custom not to prepare for such an eventuality and Mary, as a friend of the family, was committed to helping them serve their guests.

Jesus responded by instructing the servants to fill six huge pots (each with a 20- to 30-gallon capacity) with water. Then He changed the water into the most delicious wine the guests had tasted all through the celebration. Typical of all His miracles, this one solved a problem for someone else.

Another nature miracle occurred when Jesus calmed a vicious storm that terrified even veteran fishermen like the disciples, who had fished on the Sea of Galilee all their lives and were well aware of its treacherous history. The storm was no match for Jesus, however. The Gospel writer Mark reported, "A great windstorm arose, and the waves beat into the boat, so that it was already filling."[12] Matthew explained, "The boat was already covered with the waves."[13] Jesus, who was asleep at the time, arose, "rebuked the wind, and said to the sea, 'Peace, be still!' And the wind ceased and there was a great calm."[14] Suddenly the disciples were terrified at His power over nature, for they wondered aloud, "Who can this be, that even the wind and the sea obey Him!"[15] We can identify with their reaction, for mere human beings have no such power.

It was my privilege recently to sail on the Sea of Galilee and to retell this story aboard ship to about 100 tourists who traveled with us. Our Jewish guide verified that, to this day, violent storms can arise there suddenly and without warning. It was not hard to picture either this scene or the disciples' reaction to it. Who indeed can command even the wind and the waves? Only the Son of God!

On two occasions Christ provided His disciples a miraculous catch of fish—once in the early days of His ministry (Luke 5) and then after His resurrection (John 21). In both cases, as with all miracles, He wished to increase His disciples' faith in His divinity.

Two other miracles of nature include Peter finding the coin in a fish's mouth,[16] just as Jesus had promised, and the withering of the fig tree[17] on the same day the Lord cursed it.

My favorite nature miracle is that of Jesus walking on the water.[18] That is so humanly impossible that when people refer to an egotist, they will say in derision, "He thinks he can walk on water." Only one person has walked on water by His own power. Who else could He be but God in human flesh?

2. *Miracles of bodily healing*

Perhaps the most readily remembered miracles of Jesus are those of bodily healing. Who has not looked on a handicapped or terminally ill person and wished for the power to heal him or her? At least 17 times during His brief life, Jesus paused to heal people, most of whom were beyond all other help. Luke listed nine of these healings and noted that throngs of sick and disabled individuals came to Jesus for healing, and He "healed them all" (Luke 6:19). Possibly thousands were healed during His ministry.

In examining these miracles closely, we find that no two were replicated. Most were accomplished by the utterance of a word. He healed the centurion's servant from a distance,[19] and told the ten lepers to "go show yourself to the priest."[20] In some cases He touched the individuals, and in one case a woman placed her hand on His garment.[21]

My favorite healing miracle is the bestowing of sight to the blind man in John 9, which the Pharisees turned into a huge controversy. After speaking to the man, Jesus reached down, picked up a handful of dirt, spat on it, made it into clay, put it in the man's eyes, and told him to go wash in the pool of Bethesda.[22] The man did as he was told and the Bible says he came back "seeing." That he was truly healed of blindness is undeniable. Yet the religious leaders were upset that Jesus would perform such a deed on the Sabbath day.

It's no wonder that when Nicodemus came to Jesus by night, he said, "No one can do these signs that You do unless God is with him."[23] These miraculous events convince us that Jesus was more than a man, that in Him "dwells all the fullness of the Godhead bodily."[24] This, by the way, gives us great insight into the heart of God, for when Jesus saw the multitudes, He was "moved with compassion"[25] and healed them all, for He is tenderhearted in the face of human heartache. Isn't that what we should expect from a man who was God in human flesh?

3. *Miracles of healing those possessed with demons*

Demon possession has plagued mankind since the dawn of recorded history. And though some areas have been stricken with it more consistently than others, none have escaped. Whether in history or contemporary times, we have trouble distinguishing between insanity and demon possession. Even in this day of advanced psychiatric studies, numerous cases are hard to appraise. People diagnosed as "schizophrenic" or "mixed personalities" may act normally one moment, then suddenly scream or speak in an odd voice as though a spirit were using their body—only to awaken later and have no recollection of the event. Some will utter hurtful or blasphemous statements that oppose their basic core beliefs, then, when awakened, deny they ever said such things. Psychiatry may offer a "scientific" explanation, such as "dementia," but when some such individuals later undergo an exorcism in the name of Jesus Christ, they never again suffer another such experience. Without question, then, there is such a thing as demon possession.

During the life of Jesus, demon possession was common. That should not surprise us, in view of the purpose of His coming to this earth and of Satan's brazen temptation of Christ, mentioned in three of the four Gospels. On at least six occasions during His ministry, Jesus was confronted with demon-possessed individuals. In each case He demonstrated His power over the demons by miraculously casting them out. One of the most incredible stories that illustrates Jesus' power over demons appears in all three of the synoptic Gospels.

According to Dr. Luke's account,

> Then they sailed to the country of the Gadarenes, which is opposite Galilee. And when He stepped out on the land, there met Him a certain man from the city who had demons for a long time. And he wore no clothes, nor did he live in a house but in the tombs. When he saw Jesus, he cried out, fell down before Him, and with a loud voice said, "What have I to do with You, Jesus, Son of the Most High God? I beg You, do not torment me!" For He had commanded the unclean spirit to come out of the man. For it had often seized him, and he was kept under guard, bound with chains and shackles; and he broke the bonds and was driven by the demon into the wilderness.
>
> Jesus asked him, saying, "What is your name?" And he said, "Legion," because many demons had entered him. And they begged Him that He would not command them to go out into the abyss. Now a herd of many swine was feeding there on the mountain. So they begged Him that He would permit them to enter them. And He permitted them. Then the demons went out of the man and entered the swine, and the herd ran violently down the steep place into the lake and drowned.
>
> When those who fed them saw what had happened, they fled and told it in the city and in the country. Then they went out to see what had happened, and came to Jesus, and found the man from whom the demons had departed, sitting at the feet of Jesus, clothed and in his right mind. And they were afraid. They also who had seen it told them by what means he who had been demon-possessed was healed. Then the whole multitude of the surrounding region of the Gadarenes asked Him to depart from them, for they were

seized with great fear. And He got into the boat and returned. Now the man from whom the demons had departed begged Him that he might be with Him. But Jesus sent him away, saying, "Return to your own house, and tell what great things God has done for you" (Luke 8:26-39).

The extent of the man's possession appears in the word "Legion"—a multitude of demons that could render him so out of control that people tried to chain him up. Mark adds that during some of his spells when he went naked into the cemetery, he cut himself against the stones. Mark 5:13 also notes that "there were about two thousand" swine that ran down the precipice into the sea, showing the power of the demons that indwelt the man. No wonder he went mad!

After Jesus cast out the demons, the man was found "sitting... clothed and in his right mind." Who but Jesus could manifest such power? The demons themselves, speaking through the voice of the man, identified Jesus by saying, "What have I to do with you, Jesus, Son of the Most High God?" Such an acknowledgment was a powerful testimony, and even today missionaries share similar stories of demons cringing at the mention of Jesus' name.

4. *Miracles of multiplication*

Twice during His ministry Jesus responded to the hunger of the multitudes by feeding them miraculously. Once He multiplied the food on hand until it was sufficient to feed 5000 people; on the second occasion, 4000 were fed. The feeding of the 5000 is the only miracle (outside of the resurrection itself) mentioned by all four Gospel writers, which suggests the significance the authors attached to the event. Jesus accepted a boy's lunch consisting of five loaves and two fish, blessed it and gave it to the disciples, commanding them to feed it to the multitudes. To their amazement, the bread and fish fed all the people and the remnants filled up 12 whole baskets!

In the history of the world, no similar miracles of multiplication have been performed before so many people. These miracles elicited exactly the response such feats deserved. The disciples became even more convinced of Jesus' supernaturalness and the people flocked after Him to make Him their king. They wanted to promote Him from the carpentry shop to the palace but that is not why He came (and is probably why He repeated that miracle only once).

5. *Miracles of raising the dead*

Doubtless the most astonishing miracles of Jesus concerned His raising of the dead. Three times during His ministry Jesus did just that. First, He stopped the funeral procession of the widow of Nain's son and delivered the boy back to her, very much alive (Luke 7:11-17). Second, He raised the daughter of Jairus (Matthew 9:18-26; Mark 5:21-43; Luke 8:40-56). And most astonishing of all, Lazarus was summoned from the grave after a four-day entombment (John 11).

Jesus raised Lazarus for the express purpose of demonstrating to His disciples that He possessed absolute power over life and death. After meeting with Lazarus's sisters and identifying with the loss of their brother, He commanded that the stone be rolled from the tomb door. At first Mary and Martha protested: "Lord, by this time there is a stench, for he has been dead four days." Then, in the words of the apostle John:

> Jesus said to her, "Did I not say to you that if you would believe you would see the glory of God?" Then they took away the stone from the place where the dead man was lying. And Jesus lifted up His eyes and said, "Father, I thank You that You have heard Me. And I know that You always hear Me, but because of the people who are standing by I said this, that they may believe that You sent Me." Now when He had said these things, He cried with a loud voice, "Lazarus, come forth!" And he who had died came out bound hand and foot with graveclothes, and his face was wrapped with a cloth. Jesus said to them, "Loose him,

and let him go." Then many of the Jews who had come to Mary, and had seen the things Jesus did, believed in Him (verses 40-45).

How did the guests who witnessed the incident react to this astonishing miracle? Many "believed in Him." Christ wished to prove His identity both to those in attendance and to us today, validating His later claim that "All power is given unto Me."[26] Sadly, belief was not the only reaction. Some scurried to the religious leaders to report the event. From that time on, a plot was set in motion to kill Jesus.

We might wonder why two people viewing the same miraculous event came away with different reactions to the event, but we face the same problem today. It is always a matter of the will. As Jesus Himself said, "While you have the light, believe in the light, that you may become sons of light." John adds, "But although He had done so many signs before them, they did not believe in Him."[27] Those with closed minds rejected Him.

However—and this is crucial to keep in mind—they did not deny that Jesus raised the dead, fed the multitudes, cast out demons, healed the sick, and walked on water. It is of central importance to note that even Jesus' enemies could not deny His miraculous power! The evidence was simply too overwhelming.

Science Is Great, But Jesus Is Greater

The miracles of Jesus unquestionably attest to His deity. Even today, 2000 years later, their power and simplicity still leave us in slack-jawed wonder. We have made incredible strides in technology and science over the centuries, but His miracles still amaze us.

Although today science is able to chart the course of a hurricane and predict with some accuracy when it will strike a certain city or population center, it still cannot address a vicious, howling storm and calm it by simply saying, "Peace, be still." But Jesus did!

Although agriculturists are able to yield 30 or more bushels of wheat where formerly they could grow only ten, we do not hear of their feeding 5000 hungry people with five loaves and two fishes. But Jesus did!

Although modern science has done wonders for mental disorders, rehabilitating many to a normal life from clinical depression and worse, no doctor in a psychiatric ward ever turned to a wild man and commanded the demon spirits within him to come out and have them obey, leaving the man "clothed...sitting and in his right mind." But Jesus did!

Although modern science has performed incredible feats of healing through medicine, surgery, or other advanced forms of treatment, it has never returned sight to those born blind, healed withered limbs with the touch of a hand, or spoken a word to make a leper whole (much less ten at one time). But Jesus did!

Although doctors are able to prolong life, improve its quality, and in some cases even make death painless, eventually every doctor loses a patient to death. Never do we hear of doctors attending their patient's funeral, then four days later calling that person forth from the dead. But Jesus did!

With one loud voice, the miracles Jesus performed call to us across the ages and shout, "Jesus is the Son of God!"

Are the Miracles Still Believable?

Without question, the New Testament teaches that Jesus performed miracles. Yet can we moderns, living in the sunrise of the twenty-first century, rationally and logically believe in those miracles? If we can, they make a powerful case for the claim that Jesus was the Son of God in human flesh. He Himself challenged us to believe these miracles that confirm His identity. "Though you do not believe Me," He told the Jews, "believe the works, that you may know and believe that the Father is in Me, and I in Him."[28]

If Jesus' miracles were genuine, our decision is obvious. But we live almost 2000 years after these events occurred. How can we reasonably believe eyewitness stories that Jesus Christ performed many deeds that superseded the laws of nature?

A few skeptics have suggested that the miracle stories in the Gospels were enlarged, embellished, and increased in number as the years went on. Yet anyone familiar with Greek mythology or the religious accounts of the period after Christ will readily perceive a marked difference between them and the Gospel narratives. No winged animals or half man/half horse creatures populate the Gospels. Instead, we find Jesus dealing with real men, women, and children. Humble people who suffer the agonies of birth defects or diseases are suddenly set free. There are no fantastic details supplied, as do appear throughout the apocryphal gospels and other questionable writings of the period. Instead, we find a matter-of-fact accounting of the deeds of a remarkable individual.

Many years ago Dr. Wilbur M. Smith pointed out that, instead of the stories being embellished or increasing with the passage of time, the Gospel writers instead *decreased* the number of miracles they recounted as time went on, preferring rather to emphasize Jesus' teachings. Most scholars agree that Mark wrote his Gospel first, sometime around A.D. 60. The apostle John penned his work last, around A.D. 90; Matthew and Luke wrote sometime around A.D. 70. Dr. Smith argues:

> Though devoting only twelve chapters to the entire history of our Lord, down to the Olivet discourse on Tuesday of Passion week, Mark's Gospel contains eighteen miracles performed by Christ; whereas the Gospel of Matthew, certainly written later, in which the same period of public ministry occupies nearly seventeen chapters, contains only twenty miracles. The Gospel of Luke, written still later, gives merely twenty-one miracles; the Gospel of John, the last of all, gives only eight miracles. In other words, the first eleven chapters of the earliest Gospel, St. Mark's, records more miracles than are recorded in any other

successive eleven chapters of any of the later Gospels. Clearly then, this particular aspect of our Lord's ministry is not the product of a late mythological accretion.[29]

No, the Gospel accounts are completely trustworthy and entirely believable—even for moderns. We can be sure that the miracles attributed to Jesus in the Gospels reflect actual history, not some later literary creation. And if they are true and they did happen, they call for a personal response from each of us. What will we believe about this miracle-working Jesus of Nazareth?

His Miracles Prove He Was the Son of God

Jesus healed a woman with an issue of blood. Do you think it was difficult for her to believe that Jesus was the Son of God after 12 years of medical consultation had failed?

The wife of Jairus and the widow of Nain had a dead daughter and son returned to them alive and well. Did they struggle to believe that Jesus was God in human flesh? D. L. Moody, one of the great evangelists of the nineteenth century, reminded us, "You can't find directions in the New Testament on how to conduct a funeral because Jesus broke up every funeral He attended."

Four friends of a crippled man were forced to lower their friend through a roof to get him to Jesus because of the great crowd that blocked their way. When Jesus healed him with a word, do you think they doubted that He was the supernatural Son of God?

Multitudes that thronged after Him wherever He went saw Him heal all kinds of diseases and even raise the dead. Do you think they had a problem doubting His power came from God?

Those closest to Jesus who personally witnessed the transformations in people's lives so believed in this man that they were willing to give up their professions and normal way of life to follow Him to the end of His ministry, and were willing to travel all over the then-known world to tell His story. It is a fact of history that except for Judas, who betrayed Jesus, not one of the disciples ever recanted his commitment to Christ's cause. Even "doubting Thomas," who was convinced after meeting Jesus during a postresurrection confrontation, served Him unwaveringly until the time of his martyrdom (traditionally believed to have taken place in India) many years later.

Take Christ's miracles in their totality, and we begin to understand what Jesus meant when He said, "The works that I do, bear witness of Me." They prove His claim to be the unique Son of God. We would expect no less.

We could rest our case for the personal deity of Jesus of Nazareth on His miracles alone, but Jesus Himself did not. There is more—much more—evidence to follow.

Chapter Twelve

Jesus Received Worship

The Jewish world into which Jesus was born was intensely monotheistic. The Jews of two millennia ago considered it the worst of heresies for a human being to allow himself to be worshiped as God. Yet Jesus of Nazareth did exactly that—which is precisely why the Jews of His day took up stones to kill Him. The Old Testament prescribed death for blasphemy, and the Jews thought Jesus was more than worthy of capital punishment, since He claimed to be God, not once, but many times.

We have already seen that Jesus knew He was God, taught that He was God, and performed miracles (including His own resurrection) designed to support His claim to be God. In this chapter, we'll see that at least ten times during His life, Jesus permitted others to worship Him. That was not only criminal in the passionately monotheistic culture of the Jews, it was unforgivable—unless, of course, it was true.

Ten Instances of Unrebuked Worship

It isn't as if Jesus didn't know better. After all, it was He who rebuked Satan when the devil asked Jesus to bow down and worship him. "It is written," Jesus replied, "You shall worship the LORD your God and Him only you shall serve."[1] Jesus knew the Ten Commandments; He quoted them several times. Yet He proclaimed that He was "equal with God."[2] Several times He taught that worship belonged to God only. Yet, as incredible as it may sound, Jesus permitted Himself to be worshiped *at least* ten times—and not once did He rebuke people for worshiping Him!

1 . *At His birth*

We could excuse Jesus for the first time He permitted Himself to be worshiped. He was an infant, after all, when the wise men from the East came "to worship Him" (Matthew 2:2). The real question is, would He receive such worship during His adulthood? To do so would be criminal unless He truly was God!

2. *The blind man healed in Jerusalem*

Earlier we examined Jesus' healing of the man born blind, a miracle that enraged the religious leaders of Jerusalem because it occurred on the Sabbath. The leaders called upon the man and questioned him, encouraging him to deny that Jesus had healed him. This the man would not do: "Why, this is a marvelous thing, that you do not know where He is from," he said to them, "yet He has opened my eyes! Now we know that God does not hear sinners; but if anyone is a worshiper of God and does His will, He hears him. Since the world began it has been unheard of that anyone opened the eyes of one who was born blind. If this Man were not from God, He could do nothing."[3]

A short while after the leaders threw the man out of the temple, he met Jesus. The Lord asked him, "Do you believe in the Son of God?" The man answered, "Who is He, Lord, that I may believe in Him?" And Jesus said to him, "You have both seen Him and it is He who is talking with you." Then he replied, "Lord, I believe!" Then John adds, "And he worshiped Him."[4]

Notice Jesus did not rebuke the man or urge him to get up off his knees, as He most certainly would have if He were just an ordinary man who happened to perform miracles. It is especially significant that it is John who records this incident, for the apostle knew what it was to be rebuked for worshiping someone other than God. In the book of Revelation he records a privileged look at the events of the future as revealed by the Holy

Spirit. Twice during this remarkable experience, John was so awed by the mighty angel who showed him these visions that he fell down to worship him. And how did the angel react? "Then he said to me, 'See that you do not do that. For I am your fellow servant, and of your brethren the prophets, and of those who keep the words of this book. Worship God'" (Revelation 22:9, see also 19:10).

Everyone knows angels are mightier than men. It is natural for humans to want to worship superior beings when confronted by them, but John was forbidden to do so. The reason is simple: Only God is to be worshiped. But this same John did not hesitate to tell us of the time a man worshiped Jesus!

3. *Thomas the doubter*

John also records the response of Thomas the doubter when he came face to face with the resurrected Christ. Thomas had not been present when Jesus first showed himself to the other disciples, but a week later he was with them when Jesus made a second appearance. His famous response, "My Lord and My God,"[5] was an act of pure worship. And Jesus gave no hint of rebuke!

4. *Peter and the fish*

Luke tells of a similar event in the life of Peter. After Peter heard Jesus teach and saw Him perform the miracle of filling his nets with fish (after a fruitless night of fishing), he fell down at Jesus' knees and said, "Depart from me, for I am a sinful man, O Lord!"[6] This was another act of worship. And notice again, no rebuke from Jesus.

5. *The distraught ruler*

On another occasion, "a ruler came and worshiped Him, saying, 'My daughter has just died, but come and lay Your hand on her and she will live.'"[7] Jesus not only refused to rebuke the man; He responded to his plea and healed the man's daughter.

6. *Men in a boat*

Several miracles took place on and near the Sea of Galilee. It was there that Jesus fed the 5000. It was there that, on a stormy lake, He walked on water. It was there on another occasion that He calmed the sea with a word—after which "those who were in the boat came and worshiped Him saying, 'Truly You are the Son of God.'"[8] Nothing could be clearer: All the disciples worshiped Jesus on this occasion and still no rebuke.

7. *The Transfiguration*

When Peter, James, and John witnessed the transfiguration of Jesus, they became afraid when they heard the voice of the heavenly Father saying, "This is my Beloved Son, in whom I am well pleased. Hear Him!"[9] The scene overwhelmed them and they threw themselves on their faces at Jesus' feet. Jesus could have stopped them—but again, no rebuke.

8. *The mother of James and John*

Matthew tells of the mother of the sons of Zebedee (James and John) coming to Jesus to ask special privileges when they entered into His kingdom. She "came to him…kneeling down and asking something from Him."[10] Although the Savior did not grant her selfish request, He did not rebuke her for publicly kneeling before Him. And remember, kneeling before someone in that culture was a clear act of worship.

9. *After the resurrection*

When Jesus appeared to His disciples after His resurrection, they "came and held Him by the feet and worshiped Him."[11] No rebuke.

10. *At the ascension*

A week later in Galilee, Jesus met His disciples at the "mountain which Jesus had appointed for them. When they saw Him, they worshiped Him."[12] And once more, no rebuke.

These ten incidents prove not only that people were moved to worship Jesus, but that Jesus Himself accepted their worship. That can mean only one thing: Jesus is God in human flesh.

Confirmation from the Jehovah's Witnesses Cult

As you probably know, the Jehovah's Witnesses is a zealous cult that rejects the deity of Jesus based on some radically flawed handling of Scripture. A number of years ago while pastoring in San Diego, I received one of the group's tracts in the mail. That tract inspired me to write one in reply, pointing out the deity of Jesus as taught in the New Testament. In it I developed the argument that although Jesus was the object of worship ten times in the Gospels, on none of those occasions did He rebuke the worshipers. Then I challenged readers about the inconsistency of the Jehovah's Witnesses' own official Bible, the *New World Translation*. The publishers of that exceedingly biased work boast on page 9 that they translated each major Greek word with only one English equivalent. I pointed out that wherever they translated the Greek word *proskuneo* in relation to God, they rendered it "worship," which is correct. But wherever they translate the same word *proskuneo* when used in relation to Jesus Christ, they translate it, "do obeisance."

I find that most interesting, for there is no grammatical or exegetical reason for translating the same word two different ways—only the cult's doctrinal stance that Jesus is not God. So in my tract I asked why the Witnesses are so unwilling to "honor the Son just as [you] honor the Father,"[13] the way Jesus instructed us to. That booklet was mailed to the cult's headquarters and distributed freely to more than 250,000 people. To this day I still have not received an explanation from anyone in the Jehovah's Witnesses organization. I won't hold my breath waiting for a reply, for what could they say? *Proskuneo* means only one thing, worship, and worship is due only to God—including His Son, Jesus Christ.

Several years after writing my little booklet, I received a letter from a young construction worker thanking me for it. Neither he nor his wife were Christians when a Jehovah's Witness knocked on their door. They met with him regularly for several weeks and were almost ready to join the cult, but as the letter writer told me,

> We just did not feel right about it. We were in a state of turmoil one morning just before I went to work, so in desperation we prayed at the kitchen table for God's guidance. That afternoon, after a terrible rainstorm, I was getting out of my pickup when I spotted your little blue booklet with the large letters *Jesus: Who Is He?* [the forerunner of this book]. It was soaking wet but I picked it up and took it home, where my wife dried it out in the oven. We read it together and it convinced us we were being misled, that Jesus really was the Son of God who died for our sins and rose again the third day, just as the Bible teaches. So we prayed to receive Christ and have enjoyed wonderful "peace with God" ever since.

We should never forget that Jesus said, "If anyone wants to do His will, he shall know concerning the doctrine, whether it is from God."[14] That couple is a perfect example of this. God will bring His truth to anyone who sincerely seeks Him. In the case of this couple, God sent my booklet on a peculiar journey to accomplish His gracious purposes: It floated down a rain-filled gutter by the curb until it stopped next to his pickup truck.

Worship Is Still Due Him

Jesus not only taught He was God and demonstrated that claim by His miracles and sinless life, He also demonstrated that He was comfortable in such an exalted role by receiving the worship of one or more people on ten separate occasions. At no time did He rebuke the people for worshiping Him, an oversight that would have been considered the greatest of heresies—unless, of course, He really is God.

Michael Green, in his excellent booklet *Who Is This Jesus?* wrote,

Jesus' response was to calmly accept the worship.
They would not offer any kind of worship to any man
or statue: only to God alone. The implications of Jesus
accepting worship are obvious. He knew it was His
due! Humble though He was, full of love and service to all, He nevertheless knew who He was and
where He had come from. "He had come from God
and was going to God" as the apostle John put it in
13:3. And sometimes, just sometimes, He accepted the
worship due to God alone. It was the prelude to the
worldwide worship that would follow.[15]

Interestingly, whenever people come to believe in Jesus and
accept Him as their Lord, the first thing they want to do is to
worship Him. In a large percentage of cases, people want to get
on their knees and pray immediately. I have prayed with literally
hundreds of people in this situation; most prefer to kneel.

General Lew Wallace was not only the heroic commander of
the Union troops that successfully defended Washington, D.C.
during the Civil War, he went on to become one of the most successful writers of all time following the publication of his book *Ben
Hur, the Tale of the Christ*. Recently I had the privilege of being asked
to write a new introduction for the 2003 edition of the book for
Signet Books. In my research, I discovered that Wallace was not a
Christian during the Civil War, but had become one while research-
ing the Holy Land and the New Testament in preparation for the
writing of *Ben Hur*. In his own words he indicated that his conversion resulted in two things: "A conviction amounting to an absolute
belief in God and the divinity of Christ and the book *Ben Hur, the
Tale of the Christ*."

It is not uncommon for people such as gifted fiction writer Lew
Wallace to follow their acceptance of Jesus Christ as their Lord and
Savior with an act of worship. In his case it was using his talent for
writing to tell the story of Jesus in a way that clearly showed His
deity. *Ben Hur* became an all-time bestseller during his lifetime and

is still considered a classic. In 1959, *Life* magazine heralded it as "among the most important books ever written in America" with its solid message of the deity of Christ. That same year *Ben Hur* was made into what is considered one of the greatest motion pictures of all time, starring Charlton Heston.

In a gospel tract, my friend the late Bill Bright told the thrilling story of the late Oxford don C. S. Lewis, whose story parallels that of Wallace's.

> Similarly, the late C. S. Lewis, professor at Oxford University, was an agnostic who denied the deity of Christ for years. But he too, in intellectual honesty, submitted to Jesus as his God and Savior after studying the overwhelming evidence for His deity.

In his famous book *Mere Christianity*, Lewis makes this statement:

> A man who was merely a man and said the sort of things Jesus said would not be a great moral teacher. He would either be a lunatic—on the level with the man who says he is a poached egg—or else he would be the devil of hell. You must take your choice. Either this was, and is, the Son of God; or else a madman or something worse. You can shut Him up for a fool or you can fall at His feet and call Him Lord and God. But let us not come with any patronizing nonsense about His being a great human teacher. He has not left that open to us.[16]

Bright concluded his booklet by asking,

> Who is Jesus of Nazareth to you? Your life on this earth and for all eternity is affected by your answer to this question. Take Buddha out of Buddhism, Mohammed out of Islam and, in like manner, the founders of various other religions out of their religions

and little would change. But take Jesus Christ out of Christianity, and there would be nothing left, for Christianity is not a philosophy or ethic but a personal relationship with a living, risen Savior.

Christians do not worship statues of a dead Christ, they worship their living, resurrected Lord and enjoy a personal relationship with Him. Do you worship Him? If not, I suggest you do so today. He invites us now to choose to worship Him with joy unspeakable. Yet if we refuse that choice, He guarantees that one day we will worship Him anyway, but at that time we will do so in dread, fear, and trembling. For, as Paul reminds us, the day is soon coming when "every knee should bow...and...every tongue should confess that Jesus Christ is Lord, to the glory of God the Father."[17]

The choice is not between worshiping Jesus and refusing to worship Him. The only choice is when we begin that worship and how we conduct it. Jesus *is* Lord, and He is fully worthy of our worship. As for me and my house, we will give it gladly, freely, and often.

How about you?

Chapter Thirteen

Only God Can Forgive

One aspect of the life of Jesus of Nazareth that sets Him apart from anyone who ever lived is that He never did anything morally wrong. In 33 years of life, He never had to ask for forgiveness, from either God or man. He never had to say, "I am sorry for what I did," never had to apologize, never had to regret an action. The only people who were offended by His actions were the religious leaders of His day, who were doing the worst thing one human can do to another—deceiving people about God and His standards for gaining eternal salvation. When they took offense at Jesus or His actions, it was because He did or said something that violated their religious teachings, doctrines that ran counter to the divine teachings revealed in the Bible. It was their false teachings that were wrong, not Jesus.

Yet Jesus, who never had to be forgiven, forgave more people than anyone who ever lived. In fact, He set a pattern for personal forgiveness that has never been equaled, even though He lived at a time when the Roman philosophy of "might makes right" prevailed culturally and when the Jews championed the standard "an eye for an eye and a tooth for a tooth." In that hostile milieu He taught, "Love your enemies, do good to those who hate you....Forgive, and you will be forgiven."[1]

Not only did Jesus raise the level of loving your neighbor and forgiving your enemy to all-time highs, He demonstrated forgiveness in His personal life. He forgave the sins of others and taught His followers to do the same. When it came to forgiveness, Jesus was more than a man—He was God. And to demonstrate that fact, He not only forgave sins as a man, He forgave them as God. And that got Him into trouble.

Who Can Forgive Sins but God Alone?

Jesus never hesitated to forgive sins. That, of course, led Him into conflict with the religious leaders of His day. They knew that only Jehovah God could forgive sins and they totally rejected the possibility that He might be that Jehovah in human flesh. Yet all three of the synoptic Gospel writers include a dramatic story designed to demonstrate that Jesus, like God, had the right and authority to forgive sins. Mark narrates the story succinctly:

> He entered Capernaum after some days, and it was heard that He was in the house. Immediately many gathered together, so that there was no longer room to receive them, not even near the door. And He preached the word to them.
> Then they came to Him, bringing a paralytic who was carried by four men. And when they could not come near Him because of the crowd, they uncovered the roof where He was. So when they had broken through, they let down the bed on which the paralytic was lying. When Jesus saw their faith, He said to the paralytic, "Son, your sins are forgiven you."
> And some of the scribes were sitting there and reasoning in their hearts, "Why does this Man speak blasphemies like this? Who can forgive sins but God alone?" But immediately, when Jesus perceived in His spirit that they reasoned thus within themselves, He said to them, "Why do you reason about these things in your hearts? Which is easier, to say to the paralytic, 'Your sins are forgiven you,' or to say, 'Arise, take up your bed and walk'? But that you may know that the Son of Man has power on earth to forgive sins"— He said to the paralytic, "I say to you, arise, take up your bed, and go to your house" (Mark 2:1-11).

Jesus used this dramatic incident to teach the people of His day that He had the power to forgive sins. No witness can verify the forgiveness of sins, but he can identify the supernatural hand of God in the healing of a paralytic. In this incident Jesus connected the two. This miracle, then, is a dramatic sign of Jesus' divinity.

The people knew from the beginning that Jesus had the power to perform miracles; even His enemies knew that. What He wanted them to see was that He was most interested in their spiritual relationship to God. Having your sins forgiven is an essential part of restoring that relationship. Jesus, of course, was the key, for only through Him can anyone have their sins forgiven.

Many who heard Jesus' words believed Him and had their sins forgiven, but most of the religious leaders were hardened against Him and attributed His power to the devil. Yet even in their hostility they had to admit He had supernatural power. What they rejected was that His power included removal of sin, resulting in forgiveness.

Many people still stumble over this truth. They reject Jesus because they cannot accept that He is man's sole access to God and their only hope of having their sins forgiven. They stumble over the "stumbling stone," just as many did 2000 years ago.

Who Is This Who Even Forgives Sins?

Some time after Jesus healed the paralytic, He demonstrated His authority to forgive sins in another dramatic way. Luke tells the story:

> Then one of the Pharisees asked Him to eat with him. And He went to the Pharisee's house, and sat down to eat. And behold, a woman in the city who was a sinner, when she knew that Jesus sat at the table in the Pharisee's house, brought an alabaster flask of fragrant oil, and stood at His feet behind Him weeping; and she began to wash His feet with her tears, and wiped them with the hair of her head;

and she kissed His feet and anointed them with the fragrant oil.

Now when the Pharisee who had invited Him saw this, he spoke to himself, saying, "This Man, if He were a prophet, would know who and what manner of woman this is who is touching Him, for she is a sinner." And Jesus answered and said to him, "Simon, I have something to say to you." So he said, "Teacher, say it."

"There was a certain creditor who had two debtors. One owed five hundred denarii, and the other fifty. And when they had nothing with which to repay, he freely forgave them both. Tell Me, therefore, which of them will love him more?" Simon answered and said, "I suppose the one whom he forgave more." And He said to him, "You have rightly judged."

Then He turned to the woman and said to Simon, "Do you see this woman? I entered your house; you gave Me no water for My feet, but she has washed My feet with her tears and wiped them with the hair of her head. You gave Me no kiss, but this woman has not ceased to kiss My feet since the time I came in. You did not anoint My head with oil, but this woman has anointed My feet with fragrant oil. Therefore I say to you, her sins, which are many, are forgiven, for she loved much. But to whom little is forgiven, the same loves little."

Then He said to her, "Your sins are forgiven." And those who sat at the table with Him began to say to themselves, "Who is this who even forgives sins?" Then He said to the woman, "Your faith has saved you. Go in peace" (Luke 7:36-50).

This story is full of irony. The Pharisee who had invited Jesus to his home thought Jesus' conduct proved He was no prophet, for why would a holy person allow himself to be touched by a person he knew to be sinful? Yet Luke makes it clear Jesus acted as He did precisely *because* He knew the extent of the woman's sins as well as her heart of repentance. While the Pharisee condemned Jesus because he falsely thought the Savior was ignorant of the true character of the woman, in fact he condemned himself because it was he who was ignorant of his own wretched character.

We do not know if the Pharisee ever recognized the irony in this incident, but we do know that everyone at the dinner recognized Jesus' statement that He had forgiven the woman's sins. Not only did the Savior announce His forgiveness of the woman in verse 47, but He personally bestowed it upon her in verse 48. His action prompted the indignant question, "Who is this who even forgives sins?" Jesus heard the question, but ignored it. Instead, he continued to address the woman, granting her both salvation and peace—again, prerogatives of God alone.

Most important of all, we need to observe that while the dinner guests questioned Jesus' right and ability to forgive sins, they never doubted that He claimed to have done so.

Jesus' Classic Example of Forgiveness

While both of the preceding incidents show clearly that Jesus claimed to possess the authority to forgive sins, perhaps the most powerful evidence of this authority is found at Calvary. Twice, while hanging on His cross to purchase forgiveness for all mankind, Jesus took time to forgive specific people.

The first instance brings great comfort to those who wait until their life is almost gone before making peace with God. The conversion of the thief on the cross proves it is never too late to be forgiven, even when the torch of life is almost extinguished.

This man was a terrible sinner who admitted he deserved punishment (see Luke 23:41). At the beginning of his execution he joined his fellow thief and the hostile crowd below in mocking and taunting Jesus.[2] Yet apparently something happened in this man's heart after watching Jesus for awhile. While his fellow thief continued to "blaspheme" (in Greek, *eblasphemei,* a word that normally denotes the reviling of God) Jesus, this man rebuked the other thief and testified to Jesus' innocence. "We receive the due reward of our deeds," he said, "but this Man has done nothing wrong." Then he said to Jesus, "Lord, remember me when You come into Your kingdom" (Luke 23:41-42). And how did Jesus respond? "Assuredly, I say to you, today you will be with Me in Paradise" (verse 43).

The dual nature of Jesus is seen in this act. He was fully man in that He could die for our sins, but He was fully God in that He could forgive this dying thief of his sins.

The second instance of Jesus practicing forgiveness at Calvary is nothing short of awesome. He did what no one had ever done while dying an unjust, excruciating death. Most people think of our Lord's crucifixion in the light of some artist's painting of the event, which usually shows Jesus quite attractively. The truth is, He was beaten until He was unrecognizable. The prophet had said, "His appearance was so disfigured beyond that of any man and his form marred beyond human likeness."[3] The Roman soldiers had seen to that as they hit him with their fists, forced a crown of thorns on His head, and bruised Him.

Yet in that pathetic condition, and while being mocked by the religious leaders and the soldiers who had crucified Him, Jesus prayed, "Father, forgive them, for they do not know what they do."[4] Some time before, at the tomb of Lazarus, Jesus had prayed, "I knew that you always hear Me,"[5] and hear Him God did. Doubtless His prayer while hanging on the cross saved the lives of those who crucified Him! For instead of wiping out these rebellious people who were murdering His only begotten Son, God the Father forgave them. Jesus' prayer may well have led to the salvation of more than a few souls that day.

I am inclined to believe that many of those Jews, as well as some Romans who were clamoring for His death, were among the crowd that just 50 days later at Pentecost repented and were forgiven of all their sins—even that of crucifying Jesus!

The miracle of the salvation of some or all those who had demanded Jesus' death on the cross is the pinnacle of all miracles. That God the Father and Jesus the Son would permit the salvation of the very people who crucified Jesus is almost beyond human comprehension. I believe it, but am quick to admit that I can't understand it except in the light of Jesus' prayer, "Father, forgive them, for they do not know what they do." They knew they were crucifying a good man, but they did not know or acknowledge they were crucifying the Son of God—that is, until after the resurrection and Peter's sermon on Pentecost.

How many of the people at the foot of the cross received forgiveness of sins and salvation by faith in Christ, we will never know until we meet them someday in heaven. One thing is certain: They all could have! None of them went into a Christless eternity because they participated in the crucifixion of the Messiah—because Jesus, in essence, prayed, "Lay not this sin to their charge; they don't know what they're doing." They had no idea they were killing the King of Glory. They had no idea they were fortunate enough to live at the zenith of history when the sacrificial Lamb of God had come into the world. Jesus' prayer spared them from the consequences of their terrible sin. If they were not eternally saved on that first Pentecost day, it was because they refused to receive forgiveness for their other sins.

The worst sin of all time has to be the deliberate killing of the Lamb of God. Yet those who participated in this heinous crime are guiltless because Jesus prayed, "Father, forgive them." In doing so, He left us the greatest illustration of forgiveness in the history of the world. Only God can forgive like that! He also left us the assurance that we, too, can have our sins forgiven.

Are Your Sins Forgiven?

Jesus came into this world to provide the means of forgiveness for the sins of all mankind. Has that purpose been fulfilled for you? Have your sins been forgiven, wiped clean? That all depends on whether you have called upon Him for His forgiveness. If you have not (or are not sure you have), I urge you to do so before you close this book. He has paid the eternal debt of your sin on the cross, and only three things remain for you to do:

1. Admit it was for you and your sins that Jesus died.

2. Believe He rose from the dead.

3. Call upon Him to forgive you and save your soul.

If you will do those three things, Jesus assures you that you will be with Him in eternity, just as the thief on the cross is now with Him. And following through on these three things will do more than gain forgiveness of sins and assure you of a place in heaven. It will empower you, too, to follow Jesus' example of granting forgiveness to those who have wronged you. This is one of the greatest wonders of salvation.

A New Motivation to Forgive

It is remarkable to see the motivation to forgive on the part of those who call upon God in the name of His Son and receive the forgiveness that only He can give. Well do I remember praying with an angry, hate-filled man who had very poor relations with his entire family and anyone closely associated with Him. Over a lengthy period I was privileged to share the gospel of Christ with him, and one day he dropped to his knees and received Christ. After a few moments of experiencing the emotional "peace with God" that is quite common to those who terminate their longstanding war with Him, he suddenly stiffened and said, "God, I am going to have to forgive my father." Then he told me about the lifetime of abuse and rejection he had suffered at the hands of his father.

For years my friend had faithfully hated the man and, like most harbored hatred, the anger poisoned his emotions and ruined his relationships with those who should have been objects of love. After I assured him he did indeed have to forgive his father not because his father deserved it but because Jesus commanded it— I also pointed out that Christ, his new Master, would enable him to do so. We prayed together again; then he prayed a simple but sincere prayer in which he acknowledged that, after all these years, it would be hard to forgive a man who had so grievously sinned against him. Yet he asked God to enable him to forgive and forget the past. I then prayed that he would learn to love his father.

Afterward he was skeptical, but went home to tell his wife of his newfound faith. He called the next day to tell me, "I got the best night's sleep last night that I have had in years." He added that he had apologized to his wife for all the hurt he had brought into her life. Then he said, "I am going over to my father's house next Saturday and want to confess my anger of many years to him."

It was not easy for him, but he followed through. He later told me that during his visit his father wept and could say nothing. Within six months my friend led his father to Christ and today they are working toward building a friendship. His entire family thinks this man is a walking miracle. As one of his teens said, "My father is so different that even the dog likes him now!"

That is the power of forgiveness in action! And it is different from any other experience on earth. It is possible, however, only through Jesus of Nazareth—now the resurrected Christ. Jesus is still in the business of forgiving sins, and of enabling us to forgive others.

That's not just amazing—it's divine. Which is exactly what Jesus is.

Chapter Fourteen

The Witness of Fulfilled Prophecy, Part I

Predictions of His Ancestry, Birth, Life, and Ministry

N ow we come to the most convincing evidence of all regarding the identity of Jesus of Nazareth: the many prophecies He fulfilled during His lifetime. The Hebrew prophets had not left the Jews ignorant about how to identify their coming Messiah. As we shall see, more than 100 messianic prophecies are scattered throughout the Old Testament, some already 1500 years old by the time Christ was born.

The validity of using the Scriptures to identify the Messiah can be established by noting the activities of two elderly Bible students at the time of Jesus' birth, Simeon and Anna. Their story, found in Luke's Gospel,[1] shows them intensely anticipating the coming of the Messiah in their lifetime—so much so that they went to the temple shortly after His birth to await His appearance. They were not disappointed; they actually saw (and in Simeon's case, held) the Christ child.

Unfortunately, the Jewish leaders missed Jesus. Why? They were not looking for a suffering Messiah, but a ruling Messiah. Either consciously or subconsciously they rejected the many prophecies of a suffering Savior. Sadly, most Jews of Jesus' time didn't know their Scriptures, but were steeped in centuries-old human traditions, many of which were at variance with the Hebrew Scriptures. (A similar problem plagues many unbelievers today. They do not have a sufficient base of biblical truth from which to make valid judgments concerning Jesus' true identity.)

The truth is, a large body of evidence pointing to the identity of Jesus can be found in Old Testament prophecies, all of them written from 600 to 1500 years before He was born. Some of them are so convincing that one modern rabbi (whom we will meet later) has admitted that Jesus was indeed the Messiah—"for the Gentiles"! He expects the "Jewish Messiah" to come later. That, of course, underscores how powerful the evidence really is.

Jesus Claimed to Be the Fulfillment of Prophecy

Jesus never was confused about who He was. Early in His ministry, just after He had been tempted by Satan himself in the wilderness,

> [Jesus] came to Nazareth, where He had been brought up. And as His custom was, He went into the synagogue on the Sabbath day, and stood up to read. And He was handed the book of the prophet Isaiah. And when He had opened the book, He found the place where it was written:
>
> "The Spirit of the LORD is upon Me, because He has anointed Me to preach the gospel to the poor; He has sent Me to heal the brokenhearted, to proclaim liberty to the captives and recovery of sight to the blind, to set at liberty those who are oppressed; to proclaim the acceptable year of the LORD."
>
> Then He closed the book, and gave it back to the attendant and sat down. And the eyes of all who were in the synagogue were fixed on Him. And He began to say to them, "Today this Scripture is fulfilled in your hearing" (Luke 4:16-21).

It is almost impossible to overemphasize the importance of this event. In this text, Jesus is shown presenting Himself to His townspeople in Nazareth as the fulfillment of a prophecy from Isaiah.[2] After telling what Messiah would do when He came—activities

Jesus already was doing ("preach the gospel...heal the broken-hearted...proclaim to the captives...set at liberty those who are oppressed [even demon-possessed]...and recovery of sight to the blind...to proclaim the acceptable year of the LORD"—that is, the age of grace or the present church age), He then personalized the text and made it crystal clear that He was the object of this prophecy: "Today this Scripture is fulfilled in your hearing." That is why some tried to kill Him.

Had the Jews of Jesus' day understood this and other Old Testament prophecies, they would have recognized Jesus as the Messiah. But as He said, "You do not have His word abiding in you," thus neither in Jerusalem nor in Nazareth did they recognize Him.[3]

Further confirmation that the Old Testament prophets spoke plainly of Jesus can be seen in His encounter with Cleopas and another disciple as they returned from Jerusalem by way of the road to Emmaus shortly after His resurrection. Luke says that somehow they were kept from recognizing Him in His resurrected body. When Jesus asked about the cause of their sadness,

> Then the one whose name was Cleopas answered and said to Him, "Are You the only stranger in Jerusalem, and have You not known the things which happened there in these days?" And He said to them, "What things?"
>
> So they said to Him, "The things concerning Jesus of Nazareth, who was a Prophet mighty in deed and word before God and all the people, and how the chief priests and our rulers delivered Him to be condemned to death, and crucified Him. But we were hoping that it was He who was going to redeem Israel. Indeed, besides all this, today is the third day since these things happened. Yes, and certain women of our company, who arrived at the tomb early, astonished us. When they did not find His body, they came saying that they

had also seen a vision of angels who said He was alive. And certain of those who were with us went to the tomb and found it just as the women had said; but Him they did not see."

Then He said to them, "O foolish ones, and slow of heart to believe in all that the prophets have spoken! Ought not the Christ to have suffered these things and to enter into His glory?" And beginning at Moses and all the Prophets, He expounded to them in all the Scriptures the things concerning Himself (Luke 24:18-27).

No wonder after Jesus left them they said, "Did not our heart burn within us while He talked with us on the road, and while He opened the Scriptures to us?"[4] Now, the only Scriptures He could open at the time were the Old Testament books of Moses and the Hebrew prophets.

Using them as a base, He gave them an in-depth exposition of "the things concerning Himself." This leaves no doubt Jesus considered Himself the fulfillment of the Old Testament prophets.

At Least 109 Messianic Prophecies

Alfred Edersheim, a teacher of languages and Grinfield Lecturer on the Septuagint, wrote a classic book titled *The Life and Times of Jesus the Messiah.* In that book Edersheim claimed there were 456 messianic passages, "supported by more than 558 references to the most ancient rabbinic writings...a careful perusal of their Scripture quotations show that the main postulates of the New Testament concerning the Messiah are fully supported by rabbinic statements."[5]

Many of these 456 messianic prophecies are repetitive and some are quite obscure. But scholars agree there are at least 109 distinct prophecies the Messiah had to fulfill. For all of them to be fulfilled by one individual requires a man so unusual and a life so unique as to eliminate all pretenders and indeed all men who have ever lived—except one![6]

Answering a Possible Objection

Before addressing some of the principal prophecies Jesus fulfilled during His lifetime, I would like to address one of the problems that troubled me in my youthful questioning days. My later studies led to the discovery that I was not alone. Many honest skeptics and doubters had the same question: How do we know that these prophecies were not written *after* Jesus' life?

In ancient times, writing on papyri was difficult and most ancient documents have not survived the passage of time. Quite possibly a scheme could have been hatched to make Jesus' life *seem* prophetic by creating these "prophecies" after He had passed from the scene. Modern scholars, however, have established that such a scheme is simply not possible. The very latest the Old Testament could have been written was some 200 to 300 years *before* Jesus' birth, for that is when the Septuagint (a Greek translation of the Hebrew Scriptures) was written. Most scholars of antiquities admit that the Hebrew original must have existed at least 50 to 150 years before the Septuagint was produced. That means all 109 prophecies of Jesus' life and death had to be written at least 250 to 400 years prior to His birth. Consequently, these prophecies are more than adequate witnesses to His unique person and identity.

It gets even worse for the skeptics. A recent *Time* magazine article admitted that modern archaeological findings have "strengthened the Bible's claim to historical accuracy" and early composition. After listing several artifacts and sites of long-lost cities now found, the author referred to two tiny silver scrolls discovered inside a Jerusalem tomb:

> They were dated around 600 B.C., shortly before the destruction of Solomon's Temple and the Israelites' exile in Babylon. When scientists carefully unrolled the

scrolls at the Israel Museum, they found a benediction from the Book of Numbers etched into their surface. *The discovery made it clear that parts of the Old Testament were being copied long before some skeptics had believed they were even written.* [7]

As one person has suggested, "Only a preexisting bias against supernatural prophecy itself [such as by those holding a rationalistic worldview] or a bias against these prophecies referring to the person of Jesus can deter someone from accepting the Scriptures" as messianic prophecy written far in advance.

Consider the mathematics involved in the fulfillment of these prophecies. The probability that just 20 of those 109 prophecies could be fulfilled in one man by chance is less than one in one quadrillion, one hundred and twenty-five trillion. Most people cannot even imagine such a number. If they did, it would look something like this: 1 in 1,125,000,000,000,000.

This chapter on fulfilled messianic prophecies is written to show that the scores of prophecies Jesus fulfilled during His lifetime identify Him—and Him alone—as the predicted Messiah. Since they were all written hundreds of years before Jesus lived, we must conclude that He was more than a man, that He was in fact the Messiah and the Savior of the world. The following is some of that evidence.

Your Address as Identification

Where would we all be without an address? My ministry address, for example, is: Tim LaHaye, P.O. Box 1157, El Cajon, CA 92022, USA. I am the only person on planet earth who has that precise address; that is why, out of six billion people on earth, I am the only one who receives mail sent to that address.

Yet there are only five identification marks to my address. "USA" distinguishes my country from almost two hundred others. "El Cajon, California" separates my city from 50 other states and hundreds of other cities. The zip code narrows it down to a small quadrant of our city, and my post office box number from thousands of other boxes. My name separates me from others who have access to my box (my wife, my daughter, my son-in-law). In this way, with only five identification marks, I can be distinguished from six billion other people.

By the same token, five identification tags (in this case, prophecies written in advance) can easily identify Jesus. But His identification is not limited to five specific marks; as we said, there are over *one hundred* of them. That is why Jesus insisted the Jews of Jerusalem should have recognized Him as their Messiah. Even by that point in His life, He had fulfilled scores of prophecies required of the Messiah.

Time and space will not permit us to examine all the messianic prophecies which Jesus fulfilled in His lifetime. We shall, however, examine enough of them to make His true identity certain. How certain? Certain enough to convince even honest Jews today who are willing to examine the evidence.

One modern rabbi who rejected Jesus was honest enough to admit that when the Messiah came, he would have to be "just like Jesus of Nazareth, except for His untimely death." Another rabbi appeared in a debate on apologetics expert John Ankerberg's TV show. John identified the man as one of only three rabbis in the world who is also a scholar of the New Testament. The evidence of Jesus' messiahship was so clear to this rabbi that he concluded Jesus had indeed fulfilled the prophecies—He died and rose again from the grave—but that He was the Messiah *for the Gentiles!*

That is progress, but highlights the difficulty we have in convincing modern Jews of the identity of Jesus. This rabbi rejected Jesus as the Messiah of the Jews not because Jesus failed to fulfill any of the prophecies required of Him, but because He would have to come twice to fulfill them all. This rabbi's conclusion: "When Messiah comes, He will settle all the problems of the world. I still see wars, death, disease, poverty, etc.; therefore we are still waiting for our Messiah."

What this man didn't understand is that the Messiah had to suffer first[8] for the sins of the world. Then, in the last days, He will come again to fulfill all the prophecies concerning His second coming.

—⁓—

While we don't have space to examine all 109 messianic prophecies that Jesus fulfilled, we can examine 28 of the most specific. Many of them answered the doubts and questions I brought into adulthood. In this chapter we will consider the first 12 of these 28 prophecies, which deal with His birth, heritage, life, and ministry. In the next chapter we will consider the last 16 prophecies, which concern his death, burial, and resurrection.

Prophecies Concerning His Birth and Heritage

1 . *Messiah to come from the seed of the woman*[9]

This verse has been accepted through the ages by the rabbis and scholars of Israel as the very first qualification of the Messiah. Unlike all other men who are the result of the seed of their father, Messiah must come from the "seed of the woman." As we know today, women do not have seed. They provide the egg at conception, but it must be fertilized by the seed of the man for her to become pregnant. The New Testament makes it clear that Joseph was not the father of Jesus; no human was, as Luke said. That "holy thing" or seed was planted in Mary's womb and, for the first time in human history, a virgin conceived and bore a son. This prophecy was fulfilled by a virgin birth, which immediately put Jesus Christ in a category all by Himself.

2. *His virgin birth a telltale sign*

At least 700 years before Jesus' birth, one of the most respected of the Hebrew prophets predicted, "Therefore the Lord Himself will give you a sign: Behold, the virgin shall conceive and bear a Son, and shall call His name Immanuel."[10] This prophecy was fulfilled by the miraculous intervention of God and was confirmed by an angel,[11] both His parents, the disciple Matthew, the historian Luke, and others. Today, one of the best-known facts of Jesus' life is that He, unlike anyone else who ever lived, was born of a virgin. The fulfillment of this well-known prophecy makes Him one of a kind.

3-5. *Messiah confined to a rare bloodline*

As history progressed, God revealed an ever-shrinking list of eligible individuals who would serve as ancestors of the Messiah. Shortly after the flood, God eliminated two-thirds of the human race and predicted that it would be through the line of Shem that the Messiah would "tabernacle" with men.[12] Years later God raised up a special ethnic group known as the Hebrews and predicted in Genesis[13] that they would produce the Messiah. A short while later He confined the line to Isaac.[14] Isaac and his wife had two sons, and God eliminated half the lineage by selecting Jacob to carry on the messianic line.[15] Jacob in turn had 12 sons, and the Lord selected Judah alone to continue the lineage of Messiah: "The scepter shall not depart from Judah, nor a lawgiver from between his feet, until Shiloh comes; and to Him shall be the obedience of the people."[16]

6. *Messiah to be heir of the throne of King David*

> For unto us a Child is born, unto us a Son is given; and the government will be upon His shoulder. And His name will be called Wonderful, Counselor, Mighty God, Everlasting Father, Prince of Peace. Of the increase of His government and peace there will be no end, upon the throne of David and over His kingdom, to order it and establish it with judgment and justice from that time forward, even forever. The zeal of the LORD of hosts will perform this (Isaiah 9:6-7).

This prophecy has led many Jews to reject Jesus as their Messiah. For although He fulfilled the first part as "A child is born...a Son is given," He has yet to fulfill the rest of the prediction. He must yet reign over David's kingdom as Lord of lords.

The four Gospels say Jesus came first as a humble servant to sacrifice Himself for the sins of the people, fulfilling Isaiah 53. But the Jews of Jesus' day did not want a suffering Savior who would save them from their sins; they demanded a king who would take back control of the government and rule over the nations. They didn't realize that they (and the whole world) needed a sacrifice for sin first. Only later, when Jesus returns in power and glory, will He fulfill the rest of the prophecy.

Isaiah 9:7 confirmed that Messiah would be in the lineage of King David, reigning in his place. Therefore it is no surprise that Matthew traces the lineage of Jesus back through Abraham, Isaac, Jacob, and on through the family of Jesse and to King David himself.

That becomes especially important when one realizes that no such substantiation of bloodline could be made today. All the genealogical records of the Jews were destroyed in the Diaspora (the "dispersion" when the Jews were uprooted from their homes and scattered throughout the world), so it would be impossible to identify the Messiah by family background today. Since Jesus Christ's birth line was available in that first century, however, Jesus' credentials are clearly established.

7. Messiah to be born in Bethlehem

One of the best-known prophecies of Jesus' birth is Micah 5:2: "You, Bethlehem Ephrathah, though you are little among the thousands of Judah, yet out of you shall come forth to Me the One to be Ruler in Israel, whose goings forth are from of old, from everlasting."

Why Bethlehem? Because that was the city of David. Even today the one claim to fame of that little city is that it was the birthplace of Jesus Christ. Back then Israel had scores of cities and villages, but God selected Bethlehem because it was the city of Jesse and David.[17] And today, orthodox Jews still expect their Messiah to be born there. It is doubtful if even 1000 people lived in that town at the time Jesus was born, and today it is still small (except at that season of the year when thousands of tourists come from all over the world to celebrate the birth of its most famous citizen). Although Jesus was born in Bethlehem, He was not raised there. His expectant mother and carpenter father lived in Nazareth and went to Bethlehem only to pay their taxes, as required by law. It was during this visit that Mary gave birth to the Messiah—in the very city in which the prophets predicted He would be born. That Mary, "great with child," could have ridden on a donkey for many hard miles and still not have given birth to her Son before they reached Bethlehem is a mini-miracle itself.

8. *As a child He would be called up out of Egypt*

"When Israel was a child, I loved him, and out of Egypt I called My son."[18] One of the sad parts of the Christmas story is the decree of the pathological King Herod to kill all of Bethlehem's boys under two years of age in an attempt to eliminate any future threats to his throne. As you read Matthew's account of the event, note how Jesus had no control over being sent into Egypt:

> Now after Jesus was born in Bethlehem of Judea in the days of Herod the king, behold, wise men from the East came to Jerusalem, saying, "Where is He who has been born King of the Jews? For we have seen His star in the East and have come to worship Him." When Herod the king heard this, he was troubled, and all Jerusalem with him.
>
> And when he had gathered all the chief priests and scribes of the people together, he inquired of them where the Christ was to be born. So they said to him, "In Bethlehem of Judea, for thus it is written by the prophet: 'But you, Bethlehem, in the land of Judah, are not the least among the rulers of Judah; for out of you

shall come a Ruler who will shepherd My people Israel.'"

Then Herod, when he had secretly called the wise men, determined from them what time the star appeared. And he sent them to Bethlehem and said, "Go and search carefully for the young Child, and when you have found Him, bring back word to me, that I may come and worship Him also" (Matthew 2:1-8).

Herod's directives, of course, were meant to deceive. If God had not sent an angel to warn Joseph and Mary of the king's true plans, the young child Jesus could have been killed.

Now when they had departed, behold, an angel of the Lord appeared to Joseph in a dream, saying, "Arise, take the young Child and His mother, flee to Egypt, and stay there until I bring you word; for Herod will seek the young Child to destroy Him." When he arose, he took the young Child and His mother by night and departed for Egypt, and was there until the death of Herod, that it might be fulfilled which was spoken by the Lord through the prophet, saying, "Out of Egypt I called My Son."

Then Herod, when he saw that he was deceived by the wise men, was exceedingly angry; and he sent forth and put to death all the male children who were in Bethlehem and in all its districts, from two years old and under, according to the time which he had determined from the wise men. Then was fulfilled what was spoken by Jeremiah the prophet, saying: "A voice was heard in Ramah, lamentation, weeping, and great mourning, Rachel weeping for her children, refusing to be comforted, because they are no more" (verses 13-18).

At least three prophecies were fulfilled in this account of the birth of the Christ child. He was born in Bethlehem; He would be called out of Egypt; and there would be mourning in the land because of the loss of children. That these were fulfilled accurately cannot be merely coincidental.

Prophecies Concerning His Life and Ministry

9. *He was to be a prophet like Moses*

> The LORD your God will raise up for you a Prophet like me from your midst, from your brethren. Him you shall hear....I will raise up for them a Prophet like you from among their brethren, and will put My words in His mouth, and He shall speak to them all that I command Him (Deuteronomy 18:15,18).

Fourteen hundred years before Jesus was born, God promised Moses and Israel that He would "raise up...a prophet [singular]" like Moses. Israel had many great prophets—Elijah, Jeremiah, even Daniel—but none were as great as Moses or performed the miraculous works he did...that is, until Jesus. John Ankerberg and John Weldon point out:

> Up to the time of Christ, it can be documented that the Jews had not believed that "the Prophet" had yet arrived. Thus the leaders of Israel asked John the Baptist, "Are you the Prophet?" (John 1:21 NIV), which John denied. But when the people saw Jesus' miracles they said, "Surely this is the Prophet who is to come into the world" and "Surely this man is the Prophet" and "We have found the one Moses wrote about..."
>
> What was the evidence that persuaded the people in Jesus' own time that He was the unique prophet God said was "like unto Moses"? Could anyone but the Messiah be worthy of being considered the one who is "like Moses"? In the following material we will supply parallels between Moses and Jesus, proving that Jesus was "like Moses." But we will also prove that Jesus was much greater than Moses. Only Jesus

completely fulfilled and went beyond Moses' prophetic office and is the unique one God promised would come.

A. A great founder of religion

Moses gave God's revelation of the law and founded the religion of Israel. But Jesus gave God's complete revelation of grace and truth (John 1:17), fulfilled all the law (Matthew 5:17), and became the founder and Savior of the Christian religion (1 Timothy 2:5,6).

B. A great revealer of God

Moses revealed God in writing the Torah. Moses did not point people to himself, but faithfully wrote about God and about the one in the future whom God told him about. But Jesus claimed, "For if you believed Moses, you would believe Me; for he wrote of Me. But if you do not believe his writings, how will you believe My words?" (John 5:46,47 NASB).

Yet Jesus just didn't speak about God; Jesus claimed He was God (John 5:18; 10:30).

C. A great law-giver

Moses was the only one authorized by God to give laws to Israel. But it was Jesus who gave God's full understanding of the law and gave "new" laws to Israel. Jesus quoted the law when He said, "You have heard that it was said..." but added what no other prophet had ever dared speak: "But I say unto you" (Matthew 5:21,22). That's why "when Jesus had finished saying these things, the crowds were amazed at his teaching, because he taught as one who had authority, and not as their teachers of the law" (Matthew 7:28,29 NIV).

D. A great worker of miracles

Moses was a great worker of miracles (the ten plagues on Egypt; the parting of the Red Sea, etc.) (Exodus 7–14; Deuteronomy 34:10-12). But Jesus did even greater miracles than Moses. He said, "If I had not done among them what no one else did [his miracles], they would not be guilty of sin" (John 15:24 NIV).

In fact, no one could deny His miracles because they had been witnessed by literally thousands of people: "Men of Israel, listen to these words: Jesus the Nazarene, a man attested to you by God with miracles and wonders and signs which God performed through Him in your midst, just as you yourself know..." (Acts 2:22 NASB).

E. A great redeemer

Moses rescued Israel from the bondage and slavery of Egypt (Exodus 3–4; Acts 7:20-39), but Christ rescued the world from the bondage and slavery of sin (Matthew 20:28; Ephesians 2:1-8; Romans 3:28–4:6).

F. A great mediator

Moses was the mediator between God and Israel. But Jesus is now the Mediator between God and all humanity. First Timothy 2:5,6 says, "For there is one God and one mediator between God and men, the man Christ Jesus, who gave himself as a ransom for all men" (NIV).

G. A great intercessor

Moses was the great intercessor for Israel, preventing God from utterly destroying them when they worshiped the golden calf (Exodus 32:7-14; Numbers 14:11-20). But Jesus is a greater intercessor. He now intercedes on behalf of all mankind (John 3:16; Hebrews 7:25; note Numbers 21:4-9 and John 3:14).

H. A great prophet, judge and king

Moses was a great prophet, judge and king (Exodus 18:13; Deuteronomy 33:5). But Jesus was a greater prophet, judge and king (John 1:19-21, 29-43,45; Matthew 2:2; John 5:26-29; Hebrews 7:17).

I. Moses was like the Messiah

But Jesus was the Messiah. He told this to the common people and to those in authority, such as the Jewish high priest. "The woman said, 'I know that Messiah' (called Christ) 'is coming. When he comes, he will explain everything to us.' Then Jesus declared, 'I who speak to you am He'" (John 4:25,26, NIV). The high priest asked Jesus, "Are you the Messiah?" Jesus replied, "I am" (Mark 14:61,62).[19]

It is clear that no prophet in the history of Israel ever fulfilled God's divine promise to send a prophet "like Moses"—*except Jesus of Nazareth.* As we will see in the next chapter, Jesus did greater miracles than Moses. And He did not hesitate to raise the standards of Moses' law on the basis of His own authority: "You have heard it said [in Moses' law]...but I say to you...." Truly, this One was far greater than Moses!

10. *Messiah to be a "branch of righteousness"*

> Behold, the days are coming, says the LORD, that I will raise to David a Branch of righteousness; a King shall reign and prosper, and execute judgment and righteousness in the earth. In His days Judah will be saved, and Israel will dwell safely; now this is His name by which He will be called: THE LORD OUR RIGHTEOUSNESS (Jeremiah 23:5-6).

Many Bible scholars, both Christian and Jewish, acknowledge that the word "branch" here (and in the other three prophecies where it is also used—see Isaiah 4:2; Jeremiah 33:15; Zechariah 3:8; 6:12-13) refers to the Messiah. In verse 5 above, the Messiah or the "branch" is called a "branch of righteousness," while in verse 6 He is called "Yahweh our righteousness." In the history of the world, who could be called both "righteous" and "Yahweh"? Only Jesus of Nazareth! He alone could say—without receiving any replies—"Which of you convicts Me of sin?" (John 8:46).

Lutheran scholar Dr. Theodore Laetsch, in his commentary on the book of Jeremiah, succinctly sums up the fulfillment of this prophecy in Jesus Christ:

> It is the righteousness which the Seed of David, who is the Woman's Seed of Genesis 3:15, procures for mankind by bruising Satan's head. As the Servant of the Lord, he bore the sins of man (Isaiah 53:11), which the Lord laid on him (verse 6) who had done no wrong (verse 9) and who suffered all the penalties man had

deserved (verses 5-6). By his vicarious, substitutionary fulfillment of all the demands of the mandatory and punitive justice of God he became "our righteousness," establishing this righteousness as the norm to be followed in his kingdom. Since this righteousness was procured and established by him whom God calls "Jehovah our righteousness," it is a righteousness not only promised in the Old Testament, but as the righteousness procured by Jehovah it is as timeless as the Lord, retroactive (Hebrews 9:15).[20]

We should note that no one in history, either in the Old or New Testament eras or to this day, comes close to fulfilling this prophecy—except Jesus Christ.

11. *Jesus' ministry fulfilled the prophesied ministry of Messiah*

Arise, shine; for your light has come! And the glory of the LORD is risen upon you. For behold, the darkness shall cover the earth, and deep darkness the people; but the LORD will arise over you, and His glory will be seen upon you. The Gentiles shall come to your light, and kings to the brightness of your rising (Isaiah 60:1-3).

This is such a detailed description of what Messiah was to do when He came that it must be included here. When you examine the predictions listed below (from Isaiah 61:1-2), note their detailed fulfillment in the life of Jesus, as documented in the four Gospels.

1. "the Spirit of the Lord is upon Me…anointed me";

2. "to preach good tidings to the poor";

3. "to proclaim liberty to the captives";

4. "the opening of the prison to those who are bound";

5. "to proclaim the acceptable year of the Lord";

6. "the day of vengeance of our God" (this He did in the Olivet discourse in Matthew 24–25, repeated in Mark 13 and Luke 21);

7. "to comfort all who mourn" (this verse applies to His second coming, when He sets up His kingdom).

12. *Messiah to be preceded by a forerunner*

The voice of one crying in the wilderness: "Prepare the way of the LORD; make straight in the desert a highway for our God. Every valley shall be exalted and every mountain and hill brought low; the crooked places shall be made straight and the rough places smooth; the glory of the LORD shall be revealed, and all flesh shall see it together; for the mouth of the LORD has spoken" (Isaiah 40:3-5; see also Malachi 3:1).

We have already seen that this prophecy was fulfilled by John the Baptist, so here let us simply note the fulfillment of the prophecy:

He went into all the region around the Jordan, preaching a baptism of repentance for the remission of sins, as it is written in the book of the words of Isaiah the prophet, saying:

The voice of one crying in the wilderness: "Prepare the way of the LORD; make His paths straight. Every valley shall be filled and every mountain and hill brought low; the crooked places shall be made straight and the rough ways smooth; and all flesh shall see the salvation of God" (Luke 3:3-6).

The Evidence Mounts

These 12 fulfilled prophecies, by themselves, ought to cause even the most hardened skeptic to reconsider his skepticism. Yet we are not done! In the next chapter we will consider another 16 prophecies, this time showing how the Scriptures anticipated His death, burial, and resurrection. As you will see, they are among the most remarkable—and decisive—indicators of Jesus' identity to be found anywhere.

Chapter Fifteen

The Witness of Fulfilled Prophecy, Part II

Predictions of His Passion, Death, Burial, and Resurrection

The passion, death, burial, and resurrection of Jesus Christ was no accident, but was the fulfillment of the premeditated plan of God from before the foundation of the earth—a plan to which Jesus freely gave His consent. For He said, "No one takes it [my life] from Me, but I lay it down of Myself. I have power to lay it down, and I have power to take it again. This command I have received from My Father."[1]

At no time did the multitudes, the chief priest, the Jews, or even the Romans have power over Jesus to take His life. Instead, He became a willing sacrifice for all the sinners of the world; whoever is willing to accept that sacrifice may receive divine forgiveness. Jesus made this clear in the Garden of Gethsemane after Peter had cut off the ear of the high priest's servant:

> Jesus said to him, "Put your sword in its place, for all who take the sword will perish by the sword. Or do you think that I cannot now pray to My Father, and He will provide Me with more than twelve legions of angels? How then could the Scriptures be fulfilled, that it must happen thus?" (Matthew 26:52-54).

Centuries before Jesus' birth, Scripture provided several specific details concerning His death. Jesus knew these passages well and knew from the beginning that it was His destiny to fulfill them all.

Prophecies Concerning His Death

Jesus' death was on schedule and was the most-mentioned single event by the Hebrew prophets. The following messianic prophecies all have to do with His arrest, unjust trials, and crucifixion. None of these events could have been self-manipulated by an impostor.

13. *Messiah, "the anointed One," to be cut off "for the sins of the people" after 483 years*

Some 500 or 600 years before Jesus was born, the prophet Daniel wrote,

> Seventy weeks are determined for your people and for your holy city, to finish the transgression, to make an end of sins, to make reconciliation for iniquity, to bring in everlasting righteousness, to seal up vision and prophecy, and to anoint the Most Holy.
>
> Know therefore and understand, that from the going forth of the command to restore and build Jerusalem until Messiah the Prince, there shall be seven weeks and sixty-two weeks; the street shall be built again, and the wall, even in troublesome times. And after the sixty-two weeks Messiah shall be cut off, but not for Himself; and the people of the prince who is to come shall destroy the city and the sanctuary. The end of it shall be with a flood, and till the end of the war desolations are determined.
>
> Then he shall confirm a covenant with many for one week; but in the middle of the week he shall bring an end to sacrifice and offering. And on the wing of abominations shall be one who makes desolate, even until the consummation, which is determined, is poured out on the desolate (Daniel 9:24-27).

As incredible as it may seem, this prophecy of Daniel was fulfilled by Jesus the week before He was crucified when He formally presented Himself to the Hebrew nation as its Messiah.

It can be established that, exactly 483 years after the "going forth of the command to restore and build Jerusalem," Messiah was "cut off" and rejected by His people.

But first, some background for this passage. God sent the angel Gabriel in response to a prayer of Daniel, who was a captive like thousands of other Jews who had been taken to Babylon almost 70 years before. Daniel had been studying the prophecies of Jeremiah and realized that the time for the nation's deliverance was at hand. Jerusalem—including the temple and its walls—had lain in ruins for almost 70 years. Gabriel then prophesied the restoration of all these things and the coming of the Messiah over a period of 483 years.

Jeremiah had predicted, "This whole land will be a desolation and a horror, and these nations will serve the king of Babylon seventy years" (Jeremiah 25:11 NASB). Later, the Lord said, "When seventy years have been completed for Babylon, I will visit you and fulfill My good word to you, to bring you back to this place" (Jeremiah 29:10 NASB). Daniel was among the first deportees to Babylon in 605 B.C. when Nebuchadnezzar, the king of Babylon, had invaded Palestine. Now, in 538 B.C. (67 years later), Daniel realized from the prophecy of Jeremiah that the 70-year captivity was nearing its completion.[2]

John Ankerberg and John Weldon have carefully researched this passage and shed this light on it:

> How do we know Gabriel's message to Daniel in this prophecy is about the Messiah? Because the Hebrew word that is used is *Mashiach* and must be translated "Messiah" or "the Anointed One." As the great Princeton scholar, Professor R. D. Wilson (who was fluent in 45 languages and dialects), states, "Daniel 9:25, 26 is one of the two [Hebrew] passages where the expected Savior of Israel is called Messiah."
>
> Yet some have objected to this view, claiming that rather than speaking of the "Messiah," the "Anointed

One," Daniel is instead referring to Cyrus because, as we shall see, verses 25 and 26 declare that the "Messiah" will not arrive until some 400 years after Cyrus lived. In a similar manner, it cannot apply to the Syrian ruler Antiochus Epiphanes, since he died in 164 B.C. As we shall see, the prophecy talks about the "Messiah" coming to Jerusalem alive almost 200 years after that. Therefore, this one who is called *Mashiach Nagid*—Messiah the Prince—cannot refer to either Cyrus or to Antiochus Epiphanes. As Professor E. J. Young has said, "The non-Messianic interpretation is utterly inadequate."

Who, then, is the Messiah who will come? Whoever the Messiah is, he will appear on the scene after the rebuilding of Jerusalem (Daniel 9:25,26) and be killed before Jerusalem and the temple are again destroyed.[3]

The key to understanding the timing of this prophecy is the phrase "seventy weeks are determined for your people and for your holy city" (Daniel 9:24). The word "weeks" in Hebrew literally means "units of seven," whether of days or years.[4] In this case, the context makes it clear the term is referring to years; 70 times 7 (years) adds up to 490 years determined on Daniel's people. Ankerberg and Weldon describe in detail how that was fulfilled:

> According to this prophecy, the Messiah will appear at the end of the 69 weeks [the seven weeks (49 years) plus 62 weeks (434 years)] or a total of 483 years. After the 69 weeks (483 years) the destruction of the city and the temple will take place. [We know from history this took place in A.D. 70 under Titus and his Roman legions, who destroyed Jerusalem.]
>
> But from what year and what decree [the decree "to restore and rebuild Jerusalem"] are we to begin to count the number of years until Messiah?

The prophecy cannot refer to the decree of Cyrus [539 B.C.], Tarrenai [519-18 B.C.], or Artaxerxes [457 B.C.] because all these only refer to rebuilding the temple and not the city of Jerusalem, which the prophecy demands. Only the decree given by Artaxerxes to Nehemiah in 444 B.C. involves a decree to rebuild Jerusalem (Nehemiah 2:1-8...).

We are now ready to determine the date from the decree of Artaxerxes [444 B.C.] until after the 69th week [483 years later] when Gabriel announced the Messiah would be killed in Jerusalem. Using the accepted 360-day lunar year calendar, it turns out to be A.D. 33, the very time in which Jesus Christ lived and was crucified in Jerusalem!

The important point in this prophetic passage is this: Clearly, the Messiah had to come by the end of the 69th week—483 years after the issuing of the decree. Again, we stress that the time between the decree authorizing Jerusalem to be rebuilt [verse 25—444 B.C.] and the coming of the Messiah was to be 69 "sevens" or 483 years [7 + 62 units = 69 x 7 years]. That is the exact time that Jesus Christ was alive and ministering. And since the prophecy restricts the appearance of the Messiah to this time period, there is simply no other logical candidate for the Messiah. Again, this prophecy proves that Jesus Christ is the only possible candidate to be the Jewish Messiah.[5]

A reasonable question on this important passage is, "Did the Jewish scholars before the time of Christ accept this as a messianic prophecy?" Ankerberg and Weldon suggest they did:

> Since this text explicitly speaks of the Messiah it would be difficult for any Jewish rabbi to deny it. Still, because this prophecy predicted the Messiah was to be "cut off" [die], some have denied that it referred to the Messiah.

But to their credit, many rabbis have boldly stated this passage predicts the specific time of the Messiah's appearing so exactly that it cannot be escaped. For example, Rabbi Nehumias, who lived about 50 years before Christ, is cited by Grotius as saying that the time fixed by Daniel for the appearing of the Messiah could not go beyond the next 50 years. This leads us to conclude that if Christ was not the Messiah, then Israel had no Messiah. Again, if Messiah was to come, it had to be at the exact same time period as that in which Christ lived.

The Talmud advises, "In Daniel is delivered to us the end of the Messiah [i.e., 'the time of His appearance and death'—Rabbi Jarchi]." This prophecy was so powerful that the Talmud even records that around the time of Titus [A.D. 70] it was believed that the Messiah had already come. But the feeling was that Messiah's appearance had been concealed from the Jews until they were rendered more worthy of His appearance.[6]

Sir Robert Anderson, British statesman of the nineteenth century, wrote an excellent book titled *The Coming Prince*, in which he lays out in detail all the historical events and proves that when Jesus rode into Jerusalem on a donkey, He was presenting Himself to Israel as their Messiah. This event fulfilled Zechariah 9:9: "Rejoice greatly, O daughter of Zion! Shout, O daughter of Jerusalem! Behold, your King is coming to you; He is just and having salvation, lowly and riding on a donkey, a colt, the foal of a donkey." And when did this occur? Exactly 483 years to the day after the hands on God's prophetic clock began to move.

Although the Zechariah passage is mentioned in Mark 11:7-9 and is a bona fide fulfilled prophecy, I did not include it as such because it is one of the rare messianic prophecies that conceivably could have been staged by Jesus or His disciples. What could *not* have been staged is the timing of the event; Jesus was born and was ministering at that precise point in history and was on hand to present Himself to Israel the very year this prophecy foretold. That could not have been "staged"—that is, by anyone except God Himself! And that is the point of this whole chapter. These prophecies were all fulfilled by God Himself through His Son as a means of identifying Jesus to all the world.

14. *The messianic chapter, Isaiah 53*

More than 700 years before Jesus was born, Isaiah wrote a description of the future sufferings of the Messiah. We could add eleven more fulfilled prophecies to our list just from this chapter, but the evidence already is so weighty I will lump them all together and count them as one.

That this chapter does indeed concern messianic fulfillment can be seen in that many Hebrew synagogues, where one chapter of Isaiah is read aloud every Sabbath day, habitually skip chapter 53. Why? Because the parallels in this prophecy are so close to some of the events in the life of Jesus Christ that it is hard to explain why they rejected Him. Consequently, they think it wisest to ignore the chapter. After you examine the following 11 parallels to Jesus' life as fulfilled in the New Testament, you will understand their rationale.

Isaiah 53 Text	*New Testament Fulfillment*
1. He is despised and rejected by men (verse 3).	He came to His own, and His own did not receive Him (John 1:11 and the many times the Jews took up stones to kill Him).
2. Surely He has borne our griefs and carried our sorrows (verse 4).	He Himself took our infirmities and bore our sicknesses (Matthew 8:17).
3. He was wounded for our transgressions (verse 5).	One of the soldiers pierced His side with a spear (John 19:34).

4. He was bruised for our iniquities...and by His stripes we are healed (verse 5).

Who Himself bore our sins in His own body on the tree...by whose stripes you were healed (1 Peter 2:24).

5. All we like sheep have gone astray; we have turned, every one, to his own way; and the LORD has laid on Him the iniquity of us all (verse 6).

Christ also suffered once for sins, the just for the unjust...that He might bring us to God (1 Peter 3:18).

You were like sheep going astray (1 Peter 2:25).

6. He was taken from prison and from judgment (verse 8).

[Jesus said,] "How then could the Scriptures be fulfilled, that it must happen thus?" In that hour Jesus said to the multitudes, "Have you come out, as against a robber, with swords and clubs to take Me? I sat daily with you, teaching in the temple, and you did not seize Me. But all this was done that the Scriptures of the prophets might be fulfilled." Then all the disciples forsook Him and fled. And those who had laid hold of Jesus led Him away (Matthew 26:54-57).

7. He was cut off from the land of the living; for the transgressions of My people He was stricken (verse 8).

You denied the Holy One and the Just, and...killed the Prince of life....To you first, God, having raised up His Servant Jesus (Acts 3:14-15,26).

When we were still without strength, in due time Christ

died for the ungodly....God demonstrates His own love toward us, in that while we were still sinners, Christ died for us (Romans 5:6,8).

8. They made His grave with the wicked...[though] He had done no violence, nor was any deceit in His mouth (verse 9).	Two robbers were crucified with Him (Matthew 27:38).
9. Yet it pleased the LORD to bruise Him...You make His soul an offering for sin (verse 10).	He made Him who knew no sin to be sin for us, that we might become the righteousness of God in Him (2 Corinthians 5:21).
10. Because He poured out His soul unto death, and He was numbered with the transgressors (verse 12).	Two robbers were crucified with Him, one on the right and another on the left (Matthew 27:38).
11. And He bore the sin of many, and made intercession for the transgressors (verse 12).	Father, forgive them, for they do not know what they do (Luke 23:34). [He] was delivered up because of our offenses, and was raised because of our justification (Romans 4:25).

Probably no other chapter in all the Bible is more difficult for the Hebrew scholar who wishes to be faithful to the text and yet avoid the conclusion that Jesus is the Messiah, for Jesus fulfilled all of the aspects of Isaiah 53 (and then some). John Ankerberg and Weldon write:

Are the above parallels difficult to explain on purely rationalistic grounds? As the Scottish exegete and theologian Paton J. Gloag, once professor of biblical criticism at the University of Aberdeen, argued:

> We do not see how anyone can read this remarkable prophecy without being struck with its pointed resemblance to the character, sufferings, and death of the Lord Jesus. The portrait is complete; the resemblance is striking and unmistakable. Indeed, it seems more like a history of the past than a prediction of the future....In no portion of Scripture, even in the most evangelical parts of the New Testament, is the doctrine of the atonement, that grand characteristic of Christianity, so clearly stated. And yet nothing is more indisputable than that these words were uttered centuries before our Lord came into this world.[7]

This passage has long been acknowledged as messianic. In fact, early rabbis taught from this passage that there would be *two* Messiahs. They could not reconcile the biblical statements that clearly spoke of a suffering and dying Messiah with other passages that spoke with equal clarity of an eternally triumphant and victorious Messiah. Yet they did recognize that both pictures somehow applied to the Messiah. Rather than seeing one Messiah in two different roles, however, they saw two Messiahs—the suffering and dying Messiah, called "Messiah ben Joseph," and the victorious and conquering Messiah, called "Messiah ben David."

Dr. Raphael Patai, formerly of the University of Jerusalem, and author of 20 books on subjects relating to Jewish religious beliefs, has observed, "When the death of the Messiah became an established tenet in Talmudic times, this was felt to be irreconcilable with the belief in the Messiah as the Redeemer who would usher in the blissful millennium of the Messianic age. The dilemma was solved by splitting the person of the Messiah in two."[8] Thus, on the basis of Isaiah 53, the Babylonian Talmud boldly predicts, "Messiah ben Joseph will be slain...."[9]

The different views that orthodox rabbis have given to this passage throughout history can be found in the book *Rays of Messiah's Glory*. Famed rabbis such as the great Maimonides and Rabbi Crispin thought it was wrong to apply Isaiah 53 to the nation of Israel, as is commonly done in Jewish commentary today. Rather, they thought this passage clearly described God's Messiah:

> The weight of Jewish authority preponderates in favor of the Messianic interpretation of this chapter.... That until recent times this prophecy has been almost universally received by Jews as referring to Messiah is evident from Targum [J]onathon, who introduces Messiah by name in chapter LII.13; from the Talmud ("Sanhedrin," fol. 98,b); and from the Zohar....In fact, until Rashi [Rabbi Solomon Izaaki, A.D. 1040–1105, considered the originator of the modern school of Jewish interpretation], who applied it to the Jewish nation, the Messianic interpretation of this chapter was almost universally adopted by Jews.[10]

The "father" of modern Hebrew, Wilhelm Gesenius, has also written, "It was only the later Jews who abandoned this [messianic] interpretation [of Isaiah 53], no doubt in consequence of their controversies with the Christians."[11]

Today, many Orthodox Jews still wait for a political messiah, Messiah ben David, who will conquer and rule forever. And interestingly, there are some who accept Jesus Christ as the "other" Messiah (Messiah ben Joseph), even though they deny His deity.[12]

In a debate with Dr. Walter Kaiser on the *John Ankerberg Show*, Dr. Pinchas Lapide stated: "I fully agree with Dr. Kaiser that Isaiah 53 lends itself in many startling similarities to the life, career, and death of Jesus of Nazareth."[13]

Amazingly, Dr. Lapide even believes Jesus physically rose from the dead after being crucified because of the many compelling historical facts in favor of this belief.[14] Yet Dr. Lapide concludes that Jesus is the Messiah for the Gentiles and not for the Jews.

We have only one question: If Jesus Christ is not God's suffering Servant found in Isaiah 53, then who is?[15]

The next several prophecies concerning events of Jesus' death are so obvious they need no explanation. I will simply reproduce the Old Testament prophecy along with its New Testament fulfillment.

15. *Betrayed by a close friend*

Even my own familiar friend in whom I trusted, who ate my bread, has lifted up his heel against me (Psalm 41:9).

While He was still speaking, behold, a multitude; and he who was called Judas, one of the twelve, went before them and drew near to Jesus to kiss Him. But Jesus said to him, "Judas, are you betraying the Son of Man with a kiss?" (Luke 22:47-48).

16. *Betrayed for 30 pieces of silver*

I said to them, "If it is agreeable to you, give me my wages; and if not, refrain." So they weighed out for my wages thirty pieces of silver (Zechariah 11:12).

One of the twelve, called Judas Iscariot, went to the chief priests and said, "What are you willing to give me if I deliver Him to you?" And they counted out to him thirty pieces of silver (Matthew 26:14-15).

17. *Silent to accusations*

He was oppressed and He was afflicted, yet He opened not His mouth; He was led as a lamb to the slaughter, and as a sheep before its shearers is silent, so He opened not His mouth (Isaiah 53:7).

While He was being accused by the chief priests and elders, He answered nothing. Then Pilate said to Him, "Do You not hear how many things they testify against You?" And He answered him not one

18. *Spat on and struck*
I gave My back to those who struck Me, and My cheeks to those who plucked out the beard; I did not hide My face from shame and spitting (Isaiah 50:6).

word, so that the governor marveled greatly (Matthew 27:12-14).

They spat in His face and beat Him; and others struck Him with the palms of their hands (Matthew 26:67).

19. *Hated without reason*
Let them not rejoice over me who are wrongfully my enemies; nor let them wink with the eye who hate me without a cause (Psalm 35:19).

If I had not done among them the works which no one else did, they would have no sin; but now they have seen and also hated both Me and My Father. But this happened that the word might be fulfilled which is written in their law, "They hated Me without a cause" (John 15:24-25).

20. *Pierced through hands and feet*
I will pour on the house of David and on the inhabitants of Jerusalem the Spirit of grace and supplication; then they will look on Me whom they pierced. Yes, they will mourn for Him as one mourns for his only son, and grieve for Him as one grieves for a firstborn (Zechariah 12:10).

He said to Thomas, "Reach your finger here, and look at My hands; and reach your hand here, and put it into My side. Do not be unbelieving, but believing" (John 20:27).

21. *Scorned and mocked*
All those who see Me ridicule Me; they shoot out the lip,

The people stood looking on. But even the rulers with them

they shake the head, saying, "He trusted in the LORD, let Him rescue Him; let Him deliver Him, since He delights in Him!" (Psalm 22:7-8).

sneered, saying, "He saved others; let Him save Himself if He is the Christ, the chosen of God" (Luke 23:35).

22. Prayed for His enemies
In return for my love they are my accusers, but I give myself to prayer (Psalm 109:4).

Jesus said, "Father, forgive them, for they do not know what they do." And they divided His garments and cast lots (Luke 23:34).

23. Soldiers gambled for His clothing
I can count all My bones. They look and stare at Me. They divide My garments among them, and for My clothing they cast lots (Psalm 22:17-18).

Then they crucified Him, and divided His garments, casting lots, that it might be fulfilled which was spoken by the prophet: "They divided My garments among them, and for My clothing they cast lots." Sitting down, they kept watch over Him there (Matthew 27:35-36).

24. Forsaken by God
My God, My God, why have You forsaken Me? Why are You so far from helping Me, and from the words of My groaning? (Psalm 22:1).

About the ninth hour Jesus cried out with a loud voice, saying, "Eli, Eli, lama sabachthani?" that is, "My God, My God, why have You forsaken Me?" (Matthew 27:46).

25. No bones broken
He guards all his bones; not one of them is broken (Psalm 34:20).

The soldiers came and broke the legs of the first and of the other who was crucified with Him. But when they came to Jesus and saw that He was

The Witness of Fulfilled Prophecy, Part II

already dead, they did not break His legs....For these things were done that the Scripture should be fulfilled, "Not one of His bones shall be broken" (John 19:32-33,36).

26. His side pierced

I will pour on the house of David and on the inhabitants of Jerusalem the Spirit of grace and supplication; then they will look on Me whom they have pierced. Yes, they will mourn for Him as one mourns for his only son, and grieve for Him as one grieves for a first-born (Zechariah 12:10).

One of the soldiers pierced His side with a spear, and immediately blood and water came out (John 19:34).

27. Buried with the rich

They made His grave with the wicked—but with the rich at His death, because He had done no violence, nor was any deceit in His mouth (Isaiah 53:9).

Now when evening had come, there came a rich man from Arimathea, named Joseph, who himself had also become a disciple of Jesus. This man went to Pilate and asked for the body of Jesus. Then Pilate commanded the body to be given to him. And when Joseph had taken the body, he wrapped it in a clean linen cloth, and laid it in his new tomb which he had hewn out of the rock; and he rolled a large stone against the door of the tomb, and departed (Matthew 27:57-60).

209

A Closer Look at the Details

It is miracle enough that "God so loved the world that He sent His only begotten Son" to die for the sins of the world. But in the 13 aforementioned prophecies of Jesus' death (and others that also could be listed), we have another miracle that should compel us to accept Jesus as the Messiah of God. The literalness of their fulfillment defies human manipulation and cries out that only one man in history could have died just the way He did. Truly, though others have died by crucifixion, no one ever died like Jesus. It would serve us well to consider in a little more depth the following five specific details about His death. Taken together, it becomes impossible not to identify Him as the suffering Messiah.

He was to die a substitutionary, atoning death for others

> He was wounded for our transgressions, He was bruised for our iniquities; the chastisement for our peace was upon Him, and by His stripes we are healed. All we like sheep have gone astray; we have turned, every one, to his own way; and the LORD has laid on Him the iniquity of us all (Isaiah 53:5-6).

This prophecy, written more than 700 years before Christ was born, spoke of Jesus' sacrifice as a perfect fulfillment of the Passover lamb described in Exodus 12. Passover was first practiced by the Hebrews in Egypt when they put blood on their doorposts, which allowed them to escape the judgment of God. Later the sacrificial lamb was mandated in Exodus 12, which is why it is practiced by the orthodox Jews to this day. The scapegoat of Leviticus 16 pictured Christ carrying our sins away, while the bullock in that same chapter was like Christ, a sacrifice that pictured Him as the innocent burden-bearing Savior. And always, the shedding of innocent blood was required.

Many New Testament verses show that Christ was found innocent by all His judges, except the Jews, who could find no fault in Him except that "He made Himself equal with God" and that He performed miracles on the Sabbath day. Neither of those two charges is sin:

- if you are God (it is no sin to admit it);
- it has never been wrong to do good on the Sabbath; besides, Jesus (as God) considered Himself "Lord of the Sabbath," therefore He controlled the Sabbath, the Sabbath did not control Him. Consequently, Pilate was right: "This man [Jesus] has done nothing worthy of death."

Jesus was the innocent Lamb of God who fulfilled all the requirements of the sacrifice offering of God for the sins of mankind. The apostle Paul saw this clearly when he wrote, "Indeed Christ, our Passover, was sacrificed for us."[16] He stated this more theologically when he wrote, "He made Him who knew no sin to be sin for us, that we might become the righteousness of God in Him."[17] The apostle Peter also saw this when he wrote, "Knowing that you were not redeemed with corruptible things, like silver or gold, from your aimless conduct received by tradition from your fathers, but with the precious blood of Christ, as of a lamb without blemish and without spot."[18] In another place the apostle Paul defined the gospel in these words: "I delivered to you first of all that which I also received: that Christ died for our sins according to the Scriptures, and that He was buried, and that He rose again the third day according to the Scriptures."[19]

Subjecting an innocent man to the cruelties of death by crucifixion when He had done no wrong, but instead had healed the sick, bound up the brokenhearted, and left behind the greatest teachings ever delivered by mortal man, makes no sense—unless it was done for the specific purpose of becoming a divine sacrifice for sin. And since that death fulfilled many prophecies God had given His people hundreds of years prior to the events, human logic demands we accept the historical fact that Jesus of Nazareth was God's appointed sacrifice for man's sin. Only then do His life, ministry, and death have real purpose. As we shall see later, all that was sealed by His resurrection.

The Messiah-Savior must be hanged on a cross

Many prophecies about the death of the promised Messiah, when considered together, could be fulfilled only by crucifixion. Moses warned the children of Israel:

> If a man has committed a sin deserving of death, and he is put to death, and you hang him on a tree, his body shall not remain overnight on the tree, but you shall surely bury him that day, so that you do not defile the land which the LORD your God is giving you as an inheritance; for he who is hanged is accursed of God (Deuteronomy 21:22-23).

Death by hanging on a tree earned for the victim a special "curse." Jesus was hung on a Roman cross, a fate not possible in Israel until just a few years before Jesus' life. Historically, Jews never hanged condemned people; they stoned them to death. Yet Jesus was never stoned, even though the Jews tried several times in their anger to stone him. Why were they unable to do so? Because that did not conform to what the prophets said would happen. Instead, He was hung on a tree.

The apostle Paul addresses this matter in Galatians 3:13, where he wrote, "Christ has redeemed us from the curse of the law, having become a curse for us (for it is written, 'Cursed is everyone who hangs on a tree')."

Zechariah, another respected Hebrew prophet, added to the requirements of Messiah's death. He wrote that the Messiah would have wounds in His hands (not a customary practice for those who are hung): "One will say to him, 'What are these wounds between your arms?' Then he will answer, 'Those with which I was wounded in the house of my friends'" (Zechariah 13:6).

Again, Jesus would not die from stoning. The psalmist adds this:

> Dogs have surrounded Me; the congregation of the wicked has enclosed Me. They pierced My hands and My feet; I can count all My bones. They look and stare at Me. They divide My garments among them, and for My clothing they cast lots (Psalm 22:16-18).

If this is not a perfect description of death by crucifixion, I don't know what is. Jesus was "hanged" but not by a rope. He was nailed to a Roman cross and pierced in His hands and feet, and crucifixion *distends the victim's* bones. Was it merely coincidental that He was born during the Roman captivity of Israel, when crucifixion was "in" and stoning was "out"? A far easier explanation is that His death came about according to the precise plan and divine purpose of God.

Not a bone of the Messiah-Savior was to be broken

We have already seen that the Passover Lamb was a picture of Christ. Among the specific qualifications given for that lamb was he was to be "without blemish."[20] This concern for a perfect sacrifice was illustrated each Passover when the lamb was eaten in such a way that *none of its bones were broken.* Scripture commanded, "In one house it shall be eaten; you shall not carry any of the flesh outside the house, nor shall you break one of its bones."[21]

This was further confirmed by the psalmist when he said of God's Suffering Servant, "He guards all his bones, not one of them is broken."[22] Even though the Lamb of God (or the Passover Lamb) was to suffer terribly, none of His bones were to be broken.

When you read the apostle John's account of the death of Jesus, you see the strong hand of God Himself "guarding" the bones of the Savior against what could well have been a satanic attack:

> Because it was the Preparation Day, that the bodies should not remain on the cross on the Sabbath (for that Sabbath was a high day), the Jews asked Pilate that their legs might be broken, and that they might be taken away. Then the soldiers came and broke the legs of the first and of the other who was crucified with

Him. But when they came to Jesus and saw that He was already dead, they did not break His legs. But one of the soldiers pierced His side with a spear, and immediately blood and water came out (John 19:31-34).

The miraculous preservation of the bones of the Savior was not lost on John, an eyewitness to these events. He wrote, "He who has seen has testified, and his testimony is true; and he knows that he is telling the truth, so that you may believe. For these things were done that the Scripture should be fulfilled, 'not one of His bones shall be broken.' And again another Scripture says, 'They shall look on Him whom they pierced.'"[23]

God Himself was "guarding the bones" of the Savior and thus literally fulfilled the prophecy that "not one of His bones shall be broken"!

In addition, as Jesus hung on the cross, He called for something to quench His thirst and was given "vinegar" in fulfillment of Psalm 22:15 and 69:21 (texts that we did not include in our list of 28 fulfilled prophecies). Then Jesus said, "It is finished!"—that is, the way of salvation by the shedding of His own blood on the cross was "finished" so that now all men could be saved. Then "bowing His head, He gave up His Spirit."[24]

Notice: Jesus had such control over events that, even in death, He directed His fate. When His sacrifice of Himself was complete, He simply "gave up His Spirit."

The Messiah-Savior was to be "pierced"

After Jesus was dead, the Roman soldiers ran a spear into His side and blood and water poured out. This was not accidental; it was according to prophecy. Zechariah had said of the Messiah, "they will look on Me whom they have pierced."[25]

It is doubtful the Jews would have pierced Jesus' body with a spear, for that was totally out of their custom. Even more importantly, if they were familiar with this prophecy, that is the last thing they would have done. Consequently, the Lord had the Roman soldiers fulfill this prophecy!

Messiah to be betrayed for the price of a slave

Over 600 years before Jesus was crucified, Zechariah wrote about the price that a certain man would receive for his wages— 30 pieces of silver, which was the price of a slave. This angered the Lord and He ordered the money to be thrown on the temple floor. Note carefully the wording of Zechariah:

> Then I said to them, "If it is agreeable to you, give me my wages; and if not, refrain." So they weighed out for my wages thirty pieces of silver. And the LORD said to me, "Throw it to the potter"—that princely price they set on me. So I took the thirty pieces of silver and threw them into the house of the LORD for the potter (Zechariah 11:12-13).

The fulfillment of this prophecy is so famous even those who know nothing about the Bible know this refers to Judas Iscariot. In fact, his name is held in such contempt that no one ever names a child after him (although dogs sometimes get called Judas). At best, Judas is a tragic figure in *The Greatest Story Ever Told*. He lived at an opportune time in history and let greed cloud his thinking. After traveling as one of Jesus' trusted disciples (he served as treasurer for the group) he turned his back on the Savior and betrayed Him for "thirty pieces of silver," just as the prophet predicted. But that is not the end of the story. Read it from the eyewitness account as told by Matthew:

> When morning came, all the chief priests and elders of the people plotted against Jesus to put Him to death. And when they had bound Him, they led Him away and delivered Him to Pontius Pilate the governor.
>
> Then Judas, His betrayer, seeing that He had been condemned, was remorseful and brought back the thirty pieces of silver to the chief priests and elders, saying, "I have sinned by betraying innocent blood." And they said, "What is that to us? You see to it!" Then he threw down the

pieces of silver in the temple and departed, and went and hanged himself.

But the chief priests took the silver pieces and said, "It is not lawful to put them into the treasury, because they are the price of blood." And they consulted together and bought with them the potter's field, to bury strangers in. Therefore that field has been called the Field of Blood to this day.

Then was fulfilled what was spoken by Jeremiah the prophet, saying, "And they took the thirty pieces of silver, the value of Him who was priced, whom they of the children of Israel priced, and gave them for the potter's field, as the LORD directed me" (Matthew 27:1-10).

Think for a moment of all the prophetic details fulfilled in the tragic act committed by Judas:

- God's special Servant to be betrayed
- He would be betrayed by His own people ("a familiar friend")
- the price of betrayal is to be 30 pieces of silver
- silver, not gold, was the medium of exchange
- the 30 pieces of silver to be thrown down, not placed
- thrown in the house of the Lord
- the money to be used to buy a potter's field

It stretches all credulity to believe that these seven details, written 700 years beforehand, just "coincidentally" were fulfilled in the death of Jesus. Only God knows the future and can present it in advance so that people could identify the Messiah when He came.

Two other facts are important here. First, Jesus of Nazareth had no way of manipulating these events; they were accomplished by His enemies and a disloyal follower who plotted to kill Him.

Second, they were fulfilled in the last hours of Jesus' life, and when considered in the light of all the other prophecies we have studied in this chapter, they could have been fulfilled only in the person of one man: Jesus Christ. The evidence is overwhelmingly convincing to any objective observer.

Prophecies Concerning the Resurrection

The truth of Christianity hinges on the resurrection of Christ. Without that supernatural event—despite the fulfillment of all the aforementioned prophecies—no one would ever have heard of Jesus of Nazareth. If He had not risen from the dead, history's only mention of Him would have occurred in a long list of would-be messiahs. Yet if He did rise from the dead (proof of which will be given in chapters 16–18), everything changes. This one-of-a-kind event—a man being raised from the dead, proving that He was indeed the promised Messiah—also was predicted by the Hebrew prophets.

28. *Messiah to be resurrected*

You will not leave my soul in Sheol, nor will You allow Your Holy One to see corruption (Psalm 16:10).

David said about him: "I saw the Lord always before me. Because he is at my right hand, I will not be shaken. Therefore my heart is glad and my tongue rejoices; my body also will live in hope, because you will not abandon me to the grave, nor will you let your Holy One see decay. You have made known to me the paths of life; you will fill me with joy in your presence." Brothers, I can tell you confidently that the patriarch David died and was buried, and his tomb is here to this day. But he was a prophet and knew that God had promised him on oath that he would place one of his descendants on his throne. Seeing what was ahead, he spoke of the resurrection of the Christ, that he was not abandoned to the grave, nor did his body see decay. God has raised this Jesus to life, and we are all witnesses of the fact (Acts 2:25-32 NIV).

God will redeem my soul from the power of the grave, for He shall receive me (Psalm 49:15).

The angel answered and said to the women, "Do not be afraid, for I know that you seek Jesus who was crucified. He is not here; for He is risen, as He said. Come, see the place where the Lord lay. And go quickly and tell His disciples that He is risen from the dead, and indeed He is going before you into Galilee; there you will see Him. Behold, I have told you" (Matthew 28:5-7).

He shall see the labor of His soul, and be satisfied. By His knowledge My righteous Servant shall justify many, for He shall bear their iniquities (Isaiah 53:11).

While we were still sinners, Christ died for us. Since we have now been justified by his blood, how much more shall we be saved from God's wrath through him!...For we know that since Christ was raised from the dead, he cannot die again; death no longer has mastery over him (Romans 5:8-9; 6:9 NIV).

Long before the astonishing events unfolded, Jesus repeatedly told His disciples He would be crucified and that on the third day He would rise from the dead.[26] Yet either they did not believe Him or didn't understand Him—reactions which confounded the angels who appeared to the women at the empty tomb on Resurrection Sunday. You can almost hear the irritation in the voices of these two angelic messengers:

> Why do you look for the living among the dead? He is not here; he has risen! Remember how he told you, while he was still with you in Galilee: "The Son of Man must be delivered into the hands of sinful men, be crucified and on the third day be raised again."
> *Then they remembered his words* (Luke 24:5-8 NIV).

Without the resurrection, everything else goes for naught. But with the resurrection...ah, that's a different story! It's worth a much more in-depth look, which we'll take in the next three chapters.

The Evidence Is In

These 28 predictions were selected because they are so specific they can hardly be ignored. Even if the skeptic rules out five or six, the evidence represented in the remaining number is still staggering.

It is impossible to adequately illustrate the improbability of one person fulfilling all 28 of these prophecies. Someone has suggested that if we took only ten of these prophecies, the possibility of one person fulfilling them all would be like covering the state of Texas one foot thick with silver dollars, then flying over the state in a helicopter and, while blindfolded, reaching into that pile of loot and picking up a single marked coin.

You say, "Impossible!" I would agree. It is impossible for any one human being—other than Jesus—in the past or future to fulfill even ten of these prophecies. So if ten are that impossible, try to imagine how inconceivable it would be for anyone else to fulfill all 28, including the six about Jesus' death and those in Isaiah 53. No wonder Jesus rebuked the Jews in John chapter 5 for not recognizing that He was their Messiah—the evidence was all there in the Scriptures they claimed to believe and study, for as He said, "These are they that testify of me" (John 5:39). They were without excuse.

And so are we, if we refuse to act on this overwhelming evidence.

Part IV:
Evidence for the Resurrection

Chapter Sixteen

Jesus' Resurrection:
The Rest of the Story

A famous minister was walking the streets of Los Angeles during Easter season when he saw a young boy looking into a shop window. The lad was transfixed by a classic painting of the crucifixion of Christ. Estimating the boy to be about 12 years of age, the minister pointed to the painting and asked, "Who is that?" "That is Jesus Christ," the youth responded. "The religious leaders of His day had Him crucified—but He hadn't done anything wrong. He died for the sins of all the world." Then he proceeded excitedly to describe some of the details of Christ's life and death. After he was finished, the minister and boy walked in opposite directions.

Before the minister had walked two blocks, he heard the lad shouting to him and running in his direction. "Hey mister, I forgot to tell you the rest of the story. Three days later He rose again from the dead!"

Indeed, the bodily resurrection of Jesus, the foundational doctrine of the church, is not only "the rest of the story" but the best part of the story! The execution of Christ, considered by itself, is a tragic miscarriage of justice. Yet when you include the resurrection, the message of the cross is changed from a tragic defeat to a glorious victory. Without it, Christianity would be nothing more than a hopeless religious fairy tale, powerless to save one lost soul (much less offer salvation to the whole world).

Even Napoléon Bonaparte understood the significance of the resurrection. On board a troop ship en route to his North African campaign, he engaged one of his generals in conversation as they looked across the waters one night. "General, what are you going to do when this war is over and we return home?" The general replied, "Excellency, I think I will found a new religion." To which Napoléon responded, "That should be easy—all you have to do is die on a cross and rise again the third day!"

Napoléon was right. It is not enough to be born of a virgin, fulfill over 100 Old Testament prophecies, live a sinless and sacrificial life, and die an excruciatingly painful death, even though you are totally innocent. In order to found a religion unlike any before or since, you must rise from the dead. That is the one event that authenticates all the rest.

From Mere Martyr to Divine Savior

The life and story of Jesus is incomplete without the cross, for that is what transforms Him from being the perfect martyr to being the world's Savior. The resurrection of Jesus is what gives power to the cross and proof of the reliability of Christianity. It is also what makes it possible for individuals to have their sins forgiven, to enjoy peace with God, and to receive assurance of eternal life. Without it, Christianity is a fraud, a hoax, or at best, a delusion.

This fact was not lost on the apostle Paul, who boldly based everything he taught on the fact of the resurrection. He wrote:

> Now if Christ is preached that He has been raised from the dead, how do some among you say that there is no resurrection of the dead? But if there is no resurrection of the dead, then Christ is not risen. And if Christ is not risen, then our preaching is empty and your faith is also empty. Yes, and we are found false witnesses of God, because we have testified of God that He raised up Christ, whom He did not raise up—if in fact the dead do not rise. For if the dead do not rise, then Christ is not risen. And if Christ is not risen, your faith is futile; you are still in your sins! Then also

those who have fallen asleep in Christ have perished. If in this life only we have hope in Christ, we are of all men the most pitiable (1 Corinthians 15:12-19).

Then he adds these all-important words: "But now Christ is risen from the dead" (verse 20).

That is telling it like it is! Christianity depends entirely on the resurrection, for it confirms everything else. If the resurrection can be proven, then it follows that the Gospels that tell of the life of Jesus are accurate, that the Bible can be relied on, that there is "power in the cross," and that all believers can face death and eternity with confidence. But if the resurrection is a fraud, then there is no hope. Lost mankind is still lost.

Dr. Wilbur Smith sums up for us the importance of the resurrection to Christianity and shows how totally dependent Christianity is on that single event:

> Whatever be one's final conviction regarding the Resurrection of our Lord, it is admitted by everyone that such a supposed event is so interwoven with all the New Testament documents that to eliminate it from the Gospels, the Acts, and the Epistles, is to render the entire New Testament record hopelessly confused.
>
> It would be not only to deny certain words of our Lord in His teaching, but also to repudiate many accusations made against Him by His enemies; it would be to make the end of our Lord's life nothing but a tragedy. It would be to leave unexplained and unexplainable the formation of the Christian Church. It would be to leave us without dependable records of the early Apostolic messages. It would be to make the conversion and conviction of the Apostle Paul the greatest riddle of human history.
>
> Without the Resurrection, we do not know the ultimate end of Christ's life on earth; we do not know why

the Apostles began to preach; we do not know why the Apostle Paul became convinced of such a supernatural event; we do not know why the Sabbath day was changed; we do not know how the Christian Church came to be established.

With the Resurrection admitted as a fact, the stupendous themes of the New Testament become reasonable, and its narratives logical. Without the Resurrection we have nothing but a tissue of dermas, ethics resting in air, truth proclaimed without evidence, and we remain of all men most miserable. Whatever ultimately may be thought of the reality or unreality of this particular event, at least it must be confessed that it is inextricably woven into the fabric of the New Testament, welcoming the most careful investigation. [1]

Skeptics Understand the Importance of the Resurrection

One of the leading rationalists in the world during the first quarter of this century wrote a book on Jesus that was included in the famous *History of Civilization* series, published in English in 1935. Dr. Charles Guignebert was not only professor of the history of Christianity in the Sorbonne (which Dr. Wilbur Smith considered "the most important professorship in all France"), he was also a member of the Rationalist Press Association of Great Britain, which included John Dewey, Julian Huxley, Bertrand Russell, and H. G. Wells. No friends of Christianity there!

Guignebert utterly repudiated the idea of Christ's resurrection, as well as all the miracles of the New Testament. But at the end of his book he was forced to make the following confession:

> There would have been no Christianity if the belief in the Resurrection had not been founded and systematized the whole of the soteriology [doctrine of

salvation] and the essential teaching of Christianity rests on the belief of the Resurrection and on the first page of any account of Christian dogma might be written as a motto Paul's declaration: "and if Christ is not risen, then is our preaching and your faith is also vain." From the strictly historical point of view, the importance of the belief in the Resurrection is scarcely less. By means of that belief, faith in Jesus and in His mission became the fundamental element in a new religion which, after separating from it, became the opponent of Judaism and set out to conquer the world.[2]

David Strauss was another infamous skeptic who admitted the resurrection was "the Touchstone not of lives of Jesus only, but of Christianity itself: and is decisive for the whole view of Christianity."[3]

Any thinking person who is even generally acquainted with Christianity knows that it rises or falls on the truth of the resurrection. If skeptics, rationalists, and atheists can destroy belief in the resurrection, they can destroy Christianity. That is why so many rationalistic "scholars" have set themselves to attacking it. Yet their attacks usually prove to be a blessing to sincere seekers after truth, for they force Christian thinkers to answer their arguments and provide solid evidence that Jesus did indeed rise from the dead.

One of the skeptic's greatest dilemmas is the need to explain Christianity without the deity and resurrection of Jesus. Yet there is no way to present the argument that an unlearned Jewish carpenter came on the scene 2000 years ago and ignited a spiritual spark that has transformed the lives of billions of people... without the supernatural touch of both His life and His resurrection. So far, skeptic's attempts are so pathetic their suggestions are harder to believe than the real story.

One Bible scholar who has written a book in answer to the conclusions of the Jesus Seminar (see pages 29–31) confronts them with this dilemma:

Even the most skeptical critic must posit some mysterious X to get the movement going. But what is that X? The person, the life, the death and the bodily resurrection supply that X to not only get Christianity moving but to have sustained it for two thousand years. The resurrection of Jesus is therefore the most plausible explanation for the origin of the Christian way.[4]

I would add it is the only explanation—and we can depend on it.

The Evidence Is Overwhelming

The evidence for the resurrection of Christ is overwhelmingly powerful. We do not have to "just believe." We can look at this important doctrine through the eyes of Scripture, reason, and logic and still conclude that Jesus of Nazareth, a known figure in history, not only died by crucifixion but also rose from the dead, proving that He was indeed the Messiah and the Savior of the world.

This evidence is so compelling I am convinced that unless you just will not believe (following the example of some of the Jews of Jesus' day) or you are biased against Him (as are all rationalists, skeptics, and atheists), then you will come to accept the fact that Jesus Christ did indeed rise from the dead. My research over many years has convinced me that the evidence is so conclusive that only preconceived bias, rebellion to the truth, or lack of exposure to the truth keeps some men and women from believing.

Those who would (if they could) destroy our faith in the resurrection are faced with two insurmountable problems. First, they cannot answer the overwhelming evidence in favor of the resurrection. Second, they cannot explain the existence and great growth of Christianity without the resurrection.

The irony is that many of the classic objections (which we will examine in the next two chapters) are easily answered, while the alternatives skeptics offer are ridiculous by comparison. The burden of proof rests on the skeptics, for none of their alternatives account for the present power and strength of Christianity, still growing almost 2000 years after the foundational events occurred.

Christ's Resurrected Body of Real Flesh and Bone

At the outset let's keep in mind that when we talk about the resurrected Christ, we are talking about a real body. Some skeptics have tried to solve their dilemma of not being able to explain away the resurrection by suggesting it was "a spiritual resurrection." Or as one liberal minister told me (and he got the idea from the rationalist skeptics), "Of course I believe in the resurrection of Christ! I believe He rose in spirit." That is not only false, it is blasphemy!

Jesus rose *physically* from the dead, as He promised. A spiritual resurrection would have inspired no one. A spirit could not walk, talk, and eat with the two disciples on the road to Emmaus. Nor could a spirit Christ say to doubting Thomas, "Reach your finger here, and look at My hands; and reach your hand here, and put it into My side. Do not be unbelieving, but believing."[5] We are not told whether Thomas touched Jesus, but you can be sure a spirit Jesus would never have inspired Thomas to instantly believe; yet a physically resurrected Christ would have. And keep in mind, it was this confrontation with the physical Christ that inspired Thomas to go all the way to India, preaching the gospel of his resurrected Lord and eventually becoming a martyr. No spirit Christ would have inspired such motivation or sacrifice.

It was a physically resurrected Christ who prepared fish for the disciples and ate it with them. Only a physically resurrected Christ could have said to His doubting disciples, "Why do doubts arise in your hearts? Behold My hands and My feet, that it is I Myself. Handle Me and see, for a spirit does not have flesh and bones as you see I have."[6]

As Dr. Smith sagely wrote:

There is no such thing as the "resurrection of a spirit." Resurrection means being raised again. The spirit never has to be raised again from the grave, because it never enters the grave; a spirit can know no resurrection from the dead, because a spirit never dies! The New Testament continually insists that it was a body which was placed in the tomb, so it was a body which came forth from the tomb. It is sheer nonsense to talk about believing in a spiritual resurrection of Christ. There is no such thing. If it were a spirit that was being raised, there would be no sense in insisting on the third day. A spirit could manifest itself at any time after death.[7]

What Kind of Body Was It?

The resurrected body of Christ was indeed different from the body He died in. The latter was an ordinary human body so He could "taste death for everyone."[8] His postresurrection body was obviously different, for it had different characteristics, but still it was a physical body. Scripture does not say that before the crucifixion, Jesus walked through doors or walls to get from one place to another. After the resurrection, however, He could and did. Although His resurrected body was physical enough to handle and touch, it was supernatural enough to no longer be subject to time or space. It is similar to the body all Christians will have in the resurrection, as the apostle Paul explained:

Someone will say, "How are the dead raised up? And with what body do they come?" Foolish one, what you sow is not made alive unless it dies. And what you sow, you do not sow that body that shall be, but mere grain—perhaps wheat or some other grain. But God gives it a body as He pleases, and to each seed its own body.

All flesh is not the same flesh, but there is one kind of flesh of men, another flesh of beasts, another of fish, and another of birds. There are also celestial bodies and terrestrial bodies; but the glory of the celestial is one, and the glory of the terrestrial is another....So also is the resurrection of the dead. The body is sown in corruption, it is raised in incorruption....

Now this I say, brethren, that flesh and blood cannot inherit the kingdom of God; nor does corruption inherit incorruption. Behold, I tell you a mystery: We shall not all sleep, but we shall all be changed—in a moment, in the twinkling of an eye, at the last trumpet. For the trumpet will sound, and the dead will be raised incorruptible, and we shall be changed. For this corruptible must put on incorruption, and this mortal must put on immortality. So when this corruptible has put on incorruption, and this mortal has put on immortality, then shall be brought to pass the saying that is written: "Death is swallowed up in victory" (1 Corinthians 15:35-40,42,50-54).

Jesus' crucified body was buried in Joseph of Arimathea's new tomb, fulfilling Old Testament prophecy. Jesus then rose again the third day in an "incorruptible body" that was physical and supernatural. That's why the disciples could talk, walk, and eat with Him. And it is for that resurrected Christ that all of them laid down their lives.

The Ultimate Sign of His Deity

Throughout His lifetime, Jesus was pestered by individuals who said, "Teacher, we want to see a sign from You." Jesus had performed many signs and miracles, but after three years of such, evidently the people had become conditioned to His miracles; they expected them and tended to take them for granted. No wonder He called them "an evil and adulterous generation" (Matthew

12:39) for demanding an airtight "sign" that would forever erase all doubts of His true identity.

After rebuking their skepticism, He replied, "No sign will be given to it except the sign of the prophet Jonah. For as Jonah was three days and three nights in the belly of the great fish, so will the Son of Man be three days and three nights in the heart of the earth."[9] Jesus here mentioned one of the most incredible miracles in the Old Testament, one His audience would be quite familiar with. Everyone knew of Jonah the rebellious prophet, who was swallowed by the great sea monster and regurgitated back upon land after three days. The fact that a giant fish swallowed a man was no miracle; that has been reported several times in history. The miracle was that he lived through it. In a sense, Jonah was resurrected to fulfill the commission God had given him. Jesus used a known truth (Jonah's experience) to illustrate a future event (that He would be buried and rise again the third day), so that when it came to pass they would remember His words.

The resurrection is not only the greatest of all signs of Christ's deity; it is the ultimate sign. It alone should convince us Jesus is truly the Son of God. Without His bodily resurrection from the dead, we end up with some failed prophecies. Only the resurrection of Jesus, as all the Gospels portray it, can adequately solve that dilemma. The importance of the bodily resurrection of Jesus was never lost on the apostle Paul, for he said: "Jesus Christ our Lord...was born of the seed of David according to the flesh, and declared to be the Son of God with power according to the Spirit of holiness, by the resurrection from the dead" (Romans 1:3-4).

That event was so powerful and provable that it forms the foundation of the gospel and is essential to saving faith:

> I delivered to you first of all that which I also received: that Christ died for our sins according to the Scriptures, and that He was buried, and that He rose again the third day according to the Scriptures (1 Corinthians 15:3-4).

Clearly, the death, burial, and resurrection of Christ are essential to the gospel. Belief in the resurrection to the point of confessing it is the means of obtaining salvation: "If you confess with your mouth the Lord Jesus and believe in your heart that God has raised Him from the dead, you will be saved. For with the heart one believes unto righteousness, and with the mouth confession is made unto salvation."[10]

It could be said that the minimum faith necessary to become a true Christian is belief in the death of Christ for our sins, the burial of His body in the tomb, and the bodily resurrection. This is also confirmed by the apostle as the minimum faith necessary to be included in the coming of Christ for His church in what the Bible calls the second coming: "If we believe that Jesus died and rose again, even so God will bring with Him those who sleep [the dead in Christ] in Jesus."[11] Salvation does not require a person hear or even believe in the traditions of the church or even the miracles of Jesus (as important as they are). It does require, however, that we believe in the resurrection. It is safe to say that no person who refuses to believe in the resurrection of Christ from the dead can be saved.

The Importance of the Resurrection

It is all but impossible to exaggerate the importance of the resurrection of Jesus Christ. Here are some reasons why this is so.

It fulfills the prophecies of Jesus

The Old Testament taught that if a prophet gave a prophecy that did not come to pass, he should be stoned to death because he was a false teacher.[12] (It's a good thing for modern-day prophets that we do not practice such penalties today.) Jesus mentioned so many times during His ministry that He would rise from the dead that He would be a terrible impostor if He had not risen as He said He would, three days after He was buried. Note carefully the seven predictions Jesus made about rising again:

1. "For as Jonah was three days and three nights in the belly of the great fish, so will the Son of Man be three days and three nights in the heart of the earth."[13]

2. "Behold, we are going up to Jerusalem, and the Son of Man will be betrayed to the chief priests and to the scribes; and they will condemn Him to death, and deliver Him to the Gentiles to mock and to scourge and to crucify. And the third day He will rise again."[14]

3. "The Son of Man must suffer many things, and be rejected by the elders and chief priests and scribes, and be killed, and be raised the third day."[15]

4. "My Father loves Me, because I lay down My life that I may take it again. No one takes it from Me, but I lay it down of Myself. I have power to lay it down, and I have power to take it again. This command I have received from My Father."[16]

5. "Destroy this temple, and in three days I will raise it up." Then the Jews said, 'It has taken forty-six years to build this temple, and will You raise it up in three days?' But He was speaking of the temple of His body. Therefore, when He had risen from the dead, His disciples remembered that He had said this to them; and they believed the Scripture and the word which Jesus had said."[17]

6. "He commanded His disciples that they should tell no one that He was Jesus the Christ. From that time Jesus began to show to His disciples that He must go to Jerusalem, and suffer many things from the elders and chief priests and scribes, and be killed, and be raised again the third day."[18]

7. "After I have been raised, I will go before you to Galilee."[19]

These seven predictions make it crystal clear Jesus did not rise from the dead at the last minute as a means of salvaging a bad situation; it was His plan from the beginning. In fact, He made it the number-one proof of His divine identity. It was not the crucifixion that opened the eyes of Jesus' disciples, it was His resurrection.

Jesus' prophecies of His impending death and resurrection provide compelling proof He was an inerrant prophet. Even the angel acknowledged this when, on Resurrection Sunday, he met the women as they came to the tomb to embalm the body of Jesus: "He is not here; for He is risen, as He said" (Matthew 28:6).

The resurrection is the most-attested event in the life of Christ and the most essential event for explaining the existence of Christianity today. Not only did Jesus rise from the dead, but He did it exactly "as He said."

The Old Testament predicted Messiah would rise from the dead

Many Old Testament prophecies of the suffering Messiah-Savior also talk about His future activities (for example, Isaiah 53). These do not expressly teach the resurrection, but without it there could be no fulfillment of the future activities they predict. One of the psalms of David addresses this important event: "My flesh also will rest in hope. For You will not leave my soul in Sheol, nor will You allow Your Holy One to see corruption."[20] To whom did this prophecy pertain? In view of David's adulterous past, it is hard to believe David would refer to himself as "Your Holy One." He must have had someone far more lofty than himself in mind.

We are not left in doubt about who that personage is, for Peter, on the day of Pentecost, under the inspiration of the Holy Spirit, quoted this very passage in a sermon. He made it clear David was not speaking of himself, but of Jesus, whom "God has raised up, of which we are all witnesses."[21] Peter told his Jewish audience they had collectively as a nation crucified their Messiah, but he offered them hope when he explained that God had raised Jesus from the dead. "When they heard this, they were cut to the heart, and said to Peter and the rest of the apostles, 'Men and brethren, what shall we do?'" (Acts 2:37). The apostle explained that they could "repent, and...be baptized in the name of Jesus Christ for the remission of sins; and you shall receive the gift of the Holy

Spirit."[22] Three thousand souls accepted this offer of salvation and were added to the church that day.

The heart and core of Peter's message was that Jesus the Messiah was crucified for their sins, according to the Old Testament prophets, and God raised Him from the dead. Again we are confronted with the importance of the resurrection, for it not only fulfills Old Testament prophecy, but also forms the foundation of the gospel and the building of the church.

The resurrection of Jesus was at the core of the preaching of the gospel by the early church and remains the message of the Bible-teaching church today

The members of the early church believed their whole purpose on earth was to proclaim the resurrection of the Savior. Acts chapter 1 tells how, after the traitor Judas Iscariot had hanged himself, the disciples were led by the Spirit to select a replacement. Note what Scripture says about the requirements for Judas's replacement: "Therefore, of these men who have accompanied us all the time that the Lord Jesus went in and out among us, beginning from the baptism of John to that day when He was taken up from us, one of these must become a witness with us of His resurrection."[23] The candidates had to have a personal acquaintance with Jesus' life, teachings, ministry, and resurrection. Peter thought testifying of the resurrection was an important work of the early church.

Peter's second sermon, preached after the day of Pentecost, is as instructive as his first. On their way to the temple to pray, Peter and John healed a crippled man in the name of the resurrected Jesus Christ. Peter, seizing the opportunity to speak to the great crowd that gathered to see this miracle, reminded them that Moses had predicted God would send Israel a prophet like Moses and that Jesus had been that prophet—but they had crucified Him. He concluded by saying, "To you first, God, having raised up His Servant Jesus, sent Him to bless you, in turning away every one of you from your iniquities."[24] Again we find the resurrection at the very heart of his message.

This fact was not lost on the religious leaders. They hated the disciples for preaching the resurrection of Christ. Acts 4 tells us the high priest and other religious leaders called the disciples together and demanded, "By what power or by what name have you done this?" Peter answered, "By the name of Jesus Christ of Nazareth, whom you crucified, whom God raised from the dead." Then he identified Him as "the stone which was rejected by you builders...the chief cornerstone....Nor is there salvation in any other."[25]

So it is all through the book of Acts. Whether it concerns the first missionary journey of Paul and Barnabas or the second with Paul and Silas, it is ever the same: The resurrection of Jesus the Christ is central. Later, on the Areopagus in Athens, Greece—the citadel of man's wisdom without God—Paul preached once again the resurrection of Jesus from the dead.

It is interesting that the Athenians, the first-century forerunners of the man-centered rationalists of the eighteenth century, mocked Paul when he mentioned the resurrection. Not because it wasn't true, and not even because they had examined the evidence. They rejected the resurrection because of their preconceived bias that there is no personal God who performs miracles. And resurrection certainly is a miracle!

One thing is certain: The fact of the bodily resurrection of Jesus was at the very heart of the first-century church's message. It was also the motivating fire that ignited believers for the next two centuries, even after the death of the eyewitnesses. The result? Christianity became the prevailing religious view of the Roman empire in A.D. 312. Belief in that same resurrection has continued in both the Eastern and Western branches of the church ever since. It was the exclusive position of the Protestant reformers and is the core message of the Bible-preaching churches of today.

In fact, a rather unusual phenomenon exists today that illustrates the power of the resurrection. During the last five decades, when secular humanism as a philosophy has become the only sacred doctrine of our schools and universities, we have seen an incredible growth in both the size and number of churches. Fifty years ago a church with 1000 members was considered huge. Today many churches have 3, 10, and even 20,000 members. And they are not limited to a single denomination. Superchurches exist among several denominations. What do they all have in common? An intense belief in the bodily resurrection of Jesus Christ, just like their forebears of 2000 years ago, beginning with the eyewitnesses of the resurrected Christ.

Skeptics or disbelievers are confronted with a solid trail of both friendly and hostile witnesses to the historical fact of Jesus' resurrection, plus an unbroken trail of individuals who died for their belief in the facts as portrayed in the Gospels. If consistency of testimony means anything at all, the evidence all favors belief in the resurrection.

All major doctrines of the Christian faith depend on the bodily resurrection of Jesus

If it were possible to pull the foundation stone of the resurrection from the Christian faith, the entire church would plunge into the quicksand of oblivion, for every major doctrine is dependent on the resurrection. We do not have time or space to examine all of them, but the following six important doctrines will serve as examples.

1. *Salvation by faith is dependent on the resurrection*

In 1 Corinthians 15:3-4, the apostle Paul builds the gospel message on the fact of the resurrection. In verse 14 he says that "if Christ is not risen, then our preaching is empty." In verse 17 he says, "If Christ is not risen, your faith is futile...you *are still in your sins!*"

2. *The doctrine that we have an advocate, an intercessor before the Father day and night, is dependent on the resurrection*

There were many priests, because they were pre-
vented by death from continuing. But He, because He
continues forever, has an unchangeable priesthood.
Therefore He is also able to save to the uttermost those
who come to God through Him, since He ever lives
to make intercession for them. For such a High Priest
was fitting for us, who is holy, harmless, undefiled,
separate from sinners, and has become higher than the
heavens; who does not need daily, as those high
priests, to offer up sacrifices, first for His own sins and
then for the people's, for this He did once for all when
He offered up Himself (Hebrews 7:23-27).

My little children, these things I write to you, that
you may not sin. And if anyone sins, we have an
Advocate with the Father, Jesus Christ the righteous.
And He Himself is the propitiation for our sins, and
not for ours only but also for the whole world (1 John
2:1-2).

Christians are not perfect. Even after we are saved by faith we
occasionally sin. At such times we need an intercessor or advocate
who appears before God on our behalf. The reason we have one
working for us is because He is "the living Christ"—which is possible only through the resurrection.

3. *Our justification before God and peace with God are both dependent on the resurrection*

The apostle Paul used Abraham as an illustration of faith. In
view of Abraham's faith, the Lord imputed the righteousness of
God to Abraham, "not...for his sake alone...but also for us." This
righteousness "shall be imputed to us who believe in Him who
raised up Jesus our Lord from the dead, who was delivered up
because of our offenses, and was raised because of our justification.
Therefore, having been justified by faith, we have peace with God
through our Lord Jesus Christ."[26]

The need for justification before God to provide the righteousness of God, which produces the peace with God that every believer so desires, is based on the fact that God "raised up Jesus our Lord from the dead."[27] Paul made it very clear that justification, righteousness, and peace are dependent on Jesus' bodily resurrection.

4. *The promise of the second coming is predicated on the resurrection*

One of the best-loved passages on the second coming appears in Philippians 3:

> Our citizenship is in heaven, from which we also eagerly wait for the Savior, the Lord Jesus Christ, who will transform our lowly body that it may be conformed to His glorious body, according to the working by which He is able even to subdue all things to Himself (verses 20-21).

Note how it is the *living Christ* who will return for His church. A dead Christ, whose body lay in some hidden tomb in or near Jerusalem, could not save anyone. He would be powerless to return from glory to take us to be with Him. But a resurrected Christ? Now, that's another matter! He is more than able to come again and take us to be with Him.

5. *Individual judgment for all men is dependent on the resurrection*

In his great sermon on the Areopagus, Paul specifically tied future judgment to the resurrection. Now God "commands all men everywhere to repent, because He has appointed a day on which He will judge the world in righteousness by the Man whom He has ordained. He has given assurance of this to all by raising Him from the dead."[28]

The resurrection of Christ guarantees the fact of future judgment for all men. I believe it is this fact that causes many skeptics to try to destroy belief in the resurrection. They often seem driven more by fear than by solid evidence. Frankly, I don't blame them. The reality of facing the living Christ on judgment day—knowing that you refused to believe in His deity and resurrection—would strike cold, naked fear in the heart of any person.

6. *The "blessed hope" that Christ will resurrect us and our loved ones is dependent on the bodily resurrection of Jesus*

If Christ is not risen, not only is our faith futile but "also those who have fallen asleep in Christ have perished."[29] When evangelist Billy Graham preached at the funeral of former president Richard Nixon, with upwards of a quarter of a billion people watching on worldwide television, he quoted the "blessed hope" of the Christian faith from this passage of Scripture. Why? Why did he not quote the poets, philosophers, or mystics of the day? Because he knew they have nothing to offer about life beyond the grave. The real reason Billy Graham used this text is because it represents the only hope of the world regarding life after death.

As a pastor for 33 years, I conducted literally hundreds of funerals. In all of them I mentioned this promise and similar ones of eventual resurrection of the body. Why? Because our future resurrection is based on the resurrection of Jesus. In all other religions and literature there is nothing that comes even close.

Years ago I debated a prominent philosophy professor at UCLA who was also a board member of the American Humanist Association. The debate took place at one of that group's annual conventions. During the break, this 40-year, tenured professor told me his greatest joy was in changing the religious convictions of students in his classes. He bragged about the lad who enrolled at UCLA and planned to go on to Dallas Theological Seminary to study for the ministry. The professor had so attacked this young man's biblical beliefs that he changed his mind.

While doing my homework for the debate I read an article by this professor in *Humanist* magazine, which told about the premature death of his grandson. Very honestly, I was moved by the hopelessness of the man as he described standing at that child's crib and saying, "My son, you will live as long as I live, for you will live in my mind." Here was a brilliant scholar and author of several books, some on the myths of religion, who in the moment of death had no hope to give his grieving son and daughter-in-law beyond remembering his grandson until he died himself.

That is hope? That is tragedy! No one uses such words in the funeral parlor, where people desperately need hope. But in humanism, skepticism, and "enlightenment atheism," there is no hope beyond this life. My humanist friend who offered such tragic words could do no better. For the humanist manifesto that he had signed makes it clear that when you are dead you are dead.

I am happy to say the Christian faith still champions the principle that because Christ lives, believers too will live. The power of future resurrection does not depend on us, it is all of God. Paul made that clear when he wrote, "If the Spirit of Him who raised Jesus from the dead dwells in you, He who raised Christ from the dead will also give life to your mortal bodies through His Spirit who dwells in you."[30] The resurrection of our human bodies does not depend on us, it is totally dependent on God. And He has given us ample assurance that we will indeed be raised, for God raised His only begotten Son from the dead.

The ordinances of the Lord's Supper and baptism are based on the resurrection

Most evangelical churches have only two ordinances: baptism (which is performed once) and the Lord's Supper (which is observed periodically). Both depend on the resurrection.

Christ himself instituted the Lord's Supper, which reminds us of the price He paid for our sins. When the Spirit of God inspired the apostle Paul to instruct the Corinthian church on the purpose of communion, he wrote, "For as often as you eat this bread and drink this cup, you proclaim [testify to] the Lord's death *till He comes.*"[31] Obviously, Jesus' coming, to which we testify, depends on the resurrection. No resurrection, no communion.

The other ordinance, baptism, is expressly a testimony of our belief in the death, burial, and resurrection of our Savior. Paul wrote,

> Do you not know that as many of us as were baptized into Christ Jesus were baptized into His death? Therefore we were buried with Him through baptism into death, that just as Christ was raised from the dead by the glory of the Father, even so we also should walk in newness of life. For if we have been united together in the likeness of His death, certainly we also shall be in the likeness of His resurrection, knowing this, that our old man was crucified with Him, that the body of sin might be done away with, that we should no longer be slaves of sin....Now if we died with Christ, we believe that we shall also live with Him, knowing that Christ, having been raised from the dead, dies no more. Death no longer has dominion over Him (Romans 6:3-6,8-9).

Baptism, of course, does not save the believer, but it does identify him publicly with Christ's death, burial, and resurrection. As the apostle told the Colossian church, we are "buried with Him in baptism, in which [we] also were raised with Him through faith in the working of God, who raised Him from the dead."[32]

The resurrection that these ordinances commemorate gives Christians an assurance that enables them to sleep peacefully each night, knowing their sins are forgiven, their resurrection is secure, their advocate is Jesus Christ, and they will live with Him forever when He comes again. What could be more important to the individual believer and the church?

Half a Gospel Is No Gospel at All

D. L. Moody, the great evangelist of the nineteenth century and founder of Moody Bible Institute (one of the oldest and most faithful Christian preparation schools in America), assigned some ministerial students to conduct evangelistic tent meetings throughout the city of Chicago. The students were to preach sermons nightly as a means of winning souls for Christ and to practice their preaching. Dr. Moody personally showed up one night unannounced at one of the meeting places to hear one of his fledgling young ministers preach the gospel. The young man did quite well expounding on the death of Christ on the cross for the sins of the world, and for his hearers individually. At the close of the service, he announced that everyone should come back the next night when he would preach on the resurrection of Christ.

After the people left, Moody said, "Young man, you will not be back tomorrow night! You did not preach the gospel tonight, only half of it. Many of these people will not be back tomorrow night and consequently have heard only half the gospel!" Then he defined the gospel in the words of Paul: "Christ died for our sins according to the Scriptures, and...He was buried, and...He rose again the third day according to the Scriptures."[33]

Churches that leave the resurrection out of their message do not preach the gospel. The resurrection of our Lord is not an optional doctrine that plays front and center stage on Easter, only to be ignored the rest of the year. It should always be the message of the church, for it is the only hope for this sin-cursed world.

Chapter Seventeen

Can Jesus' Resurrection Be Proven?

Josh McDowell is one of the most able defenders of the Christian faith today, particularly when it comes to the bodily resurrection of Jesus of Nazareth. Yet Josh was not always a Christian; in fact, while in college he was a skeptic who enjoyed making fools of any Christians in the classroom who dared to ask the "wrong" questions. He was an honor student at every school he attended, including graduate school.

Josh was a born debater, and with his skeptic training and background, could not resist when challenged by some Christian students to examine the evidence for Christianity. He began by thinking all the data was in his favor. As he later said, "I didn't know there was evidence a person could evaluate with his mind" to substantiate the Christian position. "As a skeptic, I accepted their challenge to examine intellectually the claims that Jesus Christ was God's Son, that He was buried and arose three days later, and that He can change a person's life....One of the crucial areas of my research to refute Christianity centered around the resurrection. Surprisingly, I couldn't refute Christianity because I couldn't explain away one crucial event in history—the resurrection of Jesus Christ."

One day a student at the University of Uruguay said to him, "Professor McDowell, why can't you intellectually refute Christianity?" He responded, "For a very simple reason. I am not able to explain away an event in history—the resurrection of Jesus Christ."[1]

Josh has been my friend for about 35 years. We have spoken together at several conferences or conventions around the country and he spoke in my San Diego churches (his home was not far from us). On one Easter Sunday night we rented the city convention center, invited our three churches and any others that cared to participate, and listened to this former skeptic share some of his convincing evidences for believing in the resurrection. He has lectured at several hundred college and university campuses and has written several bestselling books, including such classics as *Evidence That Demands a Verdict, More Than a Carpenter,* and *The Resurrection Factor.* Today he directs an international ministry dedicated to reaching young people on college and high-school campuses with the overwhelming evidence for the deity of Christ and His resurrection. Wherever he goes he also issues a challenge to live a sexually pure life. Multiplied thousands are listening—all because he was personally convinced by the reality of Jesus' bodily resurrection.

Reasons for Believing the Resurrection

The resurrection of Jesus boasts more confirming evidence than do many other events in ancient history. I am confident you will be persuaded the evidence is both compelling and convincing. But no amount of evidence—short of Jesus' physical return to this earth to show us His nail-scarred hands—is absolute. That is according to God's plan, which requires some degree of faith. Not blind faith! We are to use our God-given brain to weigh the evidence, then make a reasoned decision to accept the biblical record as true and valid. Consider the following evidence and decide for yourself.

1. *The fact of the empty tomb*

All the famous tombs in the world—from Westminster Abbey in London to the Tomb of St. Thomas in India to the Tomb of the Unknown Soldier in Washington, D. C. or even to the many other tombs in Israel—are famous for the bodies they contain. Not so the tomb of Jesus. It is the only tomb in the world that is famous for what it does *not* contain. It was empty on that first Easter morning and it is so still. Its emptiness is a constant reminder of the angel's message to the women, "He is not here; for He is risen, as He said" (Matthew 28:6).

The significance of the empty tomb should not be underestimated. It was attested by both Jesus' friends and His enemies; it was mentioned by all four Gospel writers; it was noted by Paul and Peter and other New Testament writers. For example, Matthew wrote,

> Now when evening had come, there came a rich man from Arimathea, named Joseph, who himself had also become a disciple of Jesus. This man went to Pilate and asked for the body of Jesus. Then Pilate commanded the body to be given to him. When Joseph had taken the body, he wrapped it in a clean linen cloth, and laid it in his new tomb which he had hewn out of the rock; and he rolled a large stone against the door of the tomb, and departed. And Mary Magdalene was there, and the other Mary, sitting opposite the tomb (Matthew 27:57-61).

It would have been impossible to challenge people to worship a "resurrected" Savior if His body were still in the tomb! His disciples might have managed the deception for a time if they had moved to a city several hundred miles away from where the events in question took place. But that is not what they did. Immediately they began preaching right there in Jerusalem that He rose from the dead. And they used the empty tomb as "Exhibit A," their first piece of evidence.

You Can Believe His Friends' Report

Most of the eyewitnesses to the empty tomb were Jesus' friends. They were the principal heralds of His resurrection. And like the two Marys who came to the tomb and found the stone rolled away, they all found the tomb empty. Note the following eyewitness testimonies:

> *The Angel:* "He is not here; for He is risen, as He said. Come, see the place where the Lord lay."[2]

> *Mary Magdalene:* "Sir, if You have carried Him away, tell me where You have laid Him, and I will take Him away."[3]

> *Peter and John:* After Peter and John heard Mary Magdalene say, "They have taken away the Lord out of the tomb, and we do not know where they have laid Him," Peter "went out, and the other disciple, and were going to the tomb. So they both ran together... the other disciple outran Peter and came to the tomb first. And he, stooping down and looking in, saw the linen cloths lying there; yet he did not go in. Then Simon Peter came, following him, and went into the tomb; and he saw the linen cloths lying there, and the handkerchief that had been around His head, not lying with the linen cloths, but folded together in a place by itself."[4]

You Can Believe the Testimony of His Enemies

Everyone knows the religious leaders of the Jews were the enemies of Jesus. It was they who forced Pilate to crucify Him. After Jesus rose from the dead, some of the Roman guards at the tomb came into the city and reported to the chief priests that the tomb was empty. The leaders then "gave a large sum of money to the soldiers, saying, 'Tell them, "His disciples came at night and stole Him away while we slept." And if this comes to the governor's ears, we will appease him and make you secure.' So they took the money and did as they were instructed; and this saying is commonly reported among the Jews until this day" (Matthew 28:13-15).

I quote this account to point out how both the Roman soldiers and the Jewish leaders reacted when they were confronted with the news of the empty tomb and the missing body of Jesus. The soldiers were terrified—as well they might be, because it was Roman custom that when a guard lost a prisoner, the former had to take the place of the latter. Crucifixion and burial in Jesus' tomb was hardly appealing! When the Jewish leaders were apprised of the empty tomb and the missing body, they knew they could do nothing to replace it. You can be sure they would have displayed His body if they had it. Since they didn't, they concocted this story that the disciples took His body away. They even used bribery and promises to protect the guards to make the story stick.

These men did such a good job of spreading this rumor that, as Matthew wrote, "This saying is commonly reported among the Jews until this day" (about 30 years after the events). In other words, after 30 years, they still had not found His body! The tomb of Jesus was empty because it was empty—just as you would expect after a person rose from the dead.

If Only They Had His Body!

The Jewish leaders were eager to disprove the resurrection but couldn't because they didn't have the body. On the day of Pentecost and in the aftermath of Peter's inspired sermon in Acts 2, they saw thousands of Jews coming to believe in this resurrected Christ. Had they been able to produce Jesus' body, they would have sent most of those new converts scurrying back to their synagogues and Christianity would have died right then. Why didn't this happen? Very simply—they didn't have the body!

Gamaliel, a leader among the Jews, has been honored by Christians for almost two millennia because he was such a fair and reasonable man. In the heat of the battle for the souls of men and women after the resurrection, Peter's preaching inspired thousands to come to faith—but inflamed the hatred of Jesus' enemies. They became so furious that they discussed how to kill Peter and the other disciples:

> Then one in the council stood up, a Pharisee named Gamaliel, a teacher of the law held in respect by all the people, and commanded them to put the apostles outside for a little while. And he said to them: "Men of Israel, take heed to yourselves what you intend to do regarding these men. For some time ago Theudas rose up, claiming to be somebody. A number of men, about four hundred, joined him. He was slain, and all who obeyed him were scattered and came to nothing" (Acts 5:34-36).

Then he told about two false religious leaders whose followings had died out after them. Lastly he added,

> "Now I say to you, keep away from these men and let them alone; for if this plan or this work is of men, it will come to nothing; but if it is of God, you cannot overthrow it—lest you even be found to fight against God."[5]

We do not know if this fair-minded Pharisee ever became a Christian, but his advice under these circumstances worked out well. Immediate growth of the church does indeed support the fact of the resurrection. My point here, however, is that such reasoning— a mere five or six weeks after the crucifixion—would have been unnecessary if the body of Jesus could have been produced. That, however, was impossible, because Jesus had "risen, as He said."

Josh McDowell adds some fascinating insights on this point.

> Justin Martyr in his *Dialogue with Trypho* relates that Jerusalem authorities sent special representatives throughout the Mediterranean world to counteract the story of the empty tomb with the explanation that His followers stole the body. Why would the Jewish

authorities bribe the Roman guard and propagate the "stolen body" explanation if the tomb was occupied? Historian Ron Sider concluded that: "If the Christians and their Jewish opponents both agreed that the tomb was empty, we have little choice but to accept the empty tomb as a historical fact." John Warwick Montgomery, Dean of the Simon Greenleaf School of Law in Anaheim, California said, "It passes the bounds of credibility that the early Christians could have manufactured such a tale and then preached it among those who might easily have refuted it simply by producing the body of Jesus."[6]

And Dr. Paul Althaus, of the University of Erlangen, Germany, is quoted as saying, "The resurrection could not have been maintained in Jerusalem for a single day, for a single hour, if the emptiness of the tomb had not been established as a fact for all concerned."[7]

Tom Anderson, former president of the California Trial Lawyers Association and coauthor of the *Basic Advocacy Manual of the Association of Trial Lawyers of America,* says:

Let's assume that Christ did not rise from the dead. Let's assume that the written accounts of His appearances to hundreds of people are false. I want to pose a question. With an event so well publicized, don't you think that it's reasonable that one historian, one eyewitness, one antagonist would record for all time that he had seen Christ's body: "Listen, I saw that tomb—it was not empty! Look, I was there, Christ did not rise from the dead. As a matter of fact, I saw Christ's body." The silence of history is deafening when it comes to testimony against the resurrection.[8]

2. Who moved the stone?

Few critics (other than radical ones like Crossan and members of the Jesus Seminar) deny that a great stone was rolled in front of the tomb of Jesus, before the Roman guards were placed there to keep His friends from stealing His body. No one seems to deny that the stone was rolled away that first Easter morning.

The big question is, Who rolled away the stone? It couldn't have been Jesus' enemies, for as we have seen, they made contingency plans to cover up the fact that the stone had been rolled away and His body was missing. Outside of the explanation found in the Gospels, there are only two possibilities:

- Jesus Himself woke up from His death and rolled it away;
- The women or some other friends rolled it away.

Both of these options are a version of the "swoon theory" or the "resuscitation theory" (both of which are ridiculous and will be dealt with in the next chapter). The first imagines a Jesus so weakened that He couldn't carry His own cross (as a result of His beatings) who then, after hanging on the cross for six hours and being left for dead by Roman soldiers who were experts at crucifixion (who then thrust a spear into His side so that blood and water flowed out), miraculously woke up, found Himself tightly wrapped in grave clothes, yet got out of them without disturbing their order and proceeded to move a two-ton stone. That would take a bigger miracle than the resurrection!

The other possibility is that the women, who in three of the four Gospel accounts openly asked each other, "Who will roll away the stone for us?" nevertheless summoned the strength to open the grave. But even if they had managed such a feat, that doesn't explain how they could break the Roman seal and do all their work without disturbing the sleeping guards!

I have visited the garden tomb in Jerusalem on several occasions. Although we can't be certain it is the tomb in which Jesus was buried, it does conform to all the scriptural requirements: It is in a garden and is close to the Place of the Skull where Jesus was crucified outside the wall of Old Jerusalem. But even if it isn't the exact tomb, it is typical of those of the period. An eight- to ten-inch groove or track running downhill toward the door of the tomb was cut in the rock so that after the body was placed inside, the stone could be rolled down the groove to the block, sealing the tomb entrance. To move the stone—estimated to weigh at least one-and-a-half to two tons—back up the inclined groove would be a Herculean task for 20 women, much less a mere few! No, the women did not remove the stone. Then who did?

Josh McDowell has made an interesting discovery while studying this:

> In the Mark 16:4 portion of the Bezae manuscripts in the Cambridge Library in England, a parenthetical statement was found that adds, "And when He was laid there, he (Joseph) put against the tomb a stone which 20 men could not roll away."
>
> Later, they wrote me a letter containing all the technical terms, but on the back wrote out their conclusions in simple language.
>
> They said a stone of that size would have to have had a minimum weight of 1½ to 2 tons. No wonder Matthew and Mark said the stone was extremely large.[9]

So who moved the stone? The Bible has a simple answer: "Behold, there was a great earthquake; for an angel of the Lord descended from heaven, and came and rolled back the stone from the door, and sat on it."[10] Everyone knows that an angel would have no trouble rolling back such a stone—but that injects the supernatural! And that is just my point. Both the empty tomb and the stone rolled away require the supernatural. Without the resurrection, there is no reasonable explanation for the data.

3. *The eyewitnesses of the resurrected Christ*

As important as the moved stone and the empty tomb are in proving the resurrection, we have even greater evidence: over 500 eyewitnesses, some of whom we know by name. With all due respect to my previous two points—and as difficult as they are for skeptics to answer—the moved stone and the empty tomb transformed no one. As we shall see, it was personal confrontation with the resurrected Christ that transformed the early Christians. Thomas was so skeptical of the reports that Jesus had risen that he refused to believe even though many of his friends and all the disciples told him they had seen Him. It wasn't until he had seen Jesus for himself that he said, "My Lord and my God!" (John 20:28).

Eyewitnesses to the postresurrection appearances of Jesus provide us with powerful evidence that cannot be ignored: Jesus really did live after His crucifixion. The importance of this point was not lost on Dr. Luke, the careful first-century historian who said Jesus had shown Himself to the disciples, "to whom He also presented Himself alive after His suffering by many infallible proofs, being seen by them during forty days and speaking of the things pertaining to the kingdom of God."[11]

These "infallible proofs" are, most of all, the 500 or so witnesses of the resurrected Christ. As a group, they comprise overwhelming evidence that would stand up in any court of law in the world. Since none of the Gospel narratives include all the eyewitness accounts, we are not certain in exactly what order the appearances occurred. The following is the best list with which I am familiar:

> It is generally conceived that the New Testament records ten appearances of our Lord between the time of His Resurrection on Easter morning and His Ascension forty days later, in addition to His later appearance to the Apostle Paul on the Damascus road. It will be best for us to enumerate these appearances that the evidence may be seen in its full significance.
>
> (1) To certain women as they returned from the sepulcher, after having seen the angel who told them Christ had arisen (Matthew 28:1-10).

(2) To Mary Magdalene at the sepulcher, probably upon her second visit to it that morning (John 20:11-18; Mark 16:9-11).

(3) To the Apostle Peter, before the evening of the day of the Resurrection, but under circumstances of which we have no details (Luke 24:34; 1 Corinthians 15:5).

(4) To the two disciples, Cleopas and another, on the way to Emmaus, on the afternoon of Easter (Mark 16:12, 13; Luke 24:13-35).

(5) To the ten Apostles, Thomas being absent, together with others whose names are not given, assembled together on the evening of Easter day at their evening meal (Mark 16:14-18; Luke 24:36-40; John 20:19-23; 1 Corinthians 15:5).

(6) One week later, to all the eleven Apostles, probably in the same place as the preceding appearance (John 20:26-28).

(7) To several of the disciples at the Sea of Galilee, while they were fishing, the exact time undesignated (John 21:1-23).

(8) To the Apostles, and above five hundred brethren, at once, on an appointed mountain in Galilee (Matthew 28:16-20; 1 Corinthians 15:6).

(9) To James, under circumstances of which we have no information (1 Corinthians 15:7).

(10) To the Apostles at Jerusalem, immediately before the Ascension, on the Mt. of Olives (Mark 16:19; Luke 24:50-52; Acts 1:3-8).

A number of things should be noted about these appearances. In the first place, there is a considerable variety of circumstances attending these ten manifestations. It was not to one person, or one group of persons, that He revealed Himself at different times, nor was it to the same type of person that He revealed Himself each time. There are certain women, there are two disciples on the way to Emmaus, there are Apostles gathered together in an upper room, there are five hundred brethren meeting together at once. What a difference between such people as Mary Magdalene, Peter, James, John, and Thomas! Nor were the feelings of these different groups, at the instant when the manifestations were made to them, less various than the groups themselves: the women departing quickly from the sepulcher, with fear and great joy; Mary Magdalene standing without the sepulcher weeping; the two disciples talking in sadness of all the things which had happened; the Apostles assembled with shut doors for fear of the Jews; the brethren in Galilee gathered together in obedience to Christ's command; the seven engaged in their old occupation as fishermen; the eleven on the Mt. of Olives rejoicing in the presence of their Lord with the full assurance that it was indeed Himself.[12]

As in all the miracles of Jesus, these appearances were not staged events; they occurred in the everyday activities of life. That makes them more "infallible." No two of these appearances were exactly alike. One was in the morning; another in the evening. In some cases He ate with the disciples; one time He cooked a meal for them; another time He repeated a miracle He had performed before He was crucified (that is, the large draft of fish).

Neither were the reactions to seeing the resurrected Christ always the same. Some people were moved to "worship Him"; others wept for joy; and all were transformed by the encounter. Some skeptics, most of whom lived at least 1700 years after these events, would have us believe that all these appearances can be explained by mass hysteria or mass hallucinations. Some kind of hallucinations! Different people over a period of 40 days, never under identical circumstances, and yet they all described the object of their experiences in essentially the same way.

In fact, as we shall elaborate on in the next chapter, the apostle Paul, the first writer of New Testament Scripture, within 25 years after the resurrection, mentioned those who saw the resurrected Christ. After mentioning "Cephas" (or Peter), he wrote,

"After that He was seen by over five hundred brethren at once, *of whom the greater part remain to the present,* but some have fallen asleep [or died]."[13]

It is important to notice that most of the people who had seen Christ after the resurrection were still alive 25 years later when Paul wrote 1 Corinthians. So when the Gospel narratives began coming out, they could have offered objections to the commonly heard stories of Jesus' resurrection, if in fact they were untrue. Yet no such objections were ever raised. I find it telling that those who first denied the empty tomb, the moved stone, and the eyewitness testimonies of the resurrection did not make their appearance until almost 1700 years after the events in question.

We in the twenty-first century have a decision to make. Whose reports will we believe—500 eyewitnesses who lived in those days, or skeptical "scholars" 1700 years removed from the event? If our decision is to be made on the basis of the evidence and not merely on a distaste for the supernatural, there is only one choice: Jesus did in fact rise from the dead.

4. *The proven character of Jesus makes it easy to believe Him when He taught He would rise from the dead*

Hardly anyone in history denies that Jesus lived a holy, humble, and sacrificial life. Even those who deny His claims to deity think of Him as a great moral example, a sterling character, a model to live by. No one cast aspersions on His moral character until long after Christianity became a threat to other religions. In fact, the earliest attack on Jesus' character did not occur until the seventh century, when a handful of atheistic scholars rewrote history to make it appear He had done something immoral. This, too, would have been long forgotten had not a morally perverted Hollywood producer made it into a blasphemous movie (which, by the way, bombed at the box office, resulting in a huge financial loss).[14]

It is extraordinarily difficult for any Jesus-hater to make a case against the moral character of Jesus, so highly has His character been esteemed by many historians (even those like Thomas Jefferson, who rejected His deity but accepted His moral character as a model for modern behavior). In that sense, Jesus is in a category all by Himself. No other person in history comes close to the moral perfection exhibited by Jesus.

John R. Rice, the late evangelist and editor of the weekly *Sword of the Lord*, wrote:

> Who is there in all human history like Christ? His personality, His moral purity, His spiritual insight, His overwhelming wisdom, set Him apart as the only one of His kind. Jesus Christ is absolutely unique. When we compare with Him Socrates, or Buddha, or Mohammed, or Gandhi, or Lenin, or Shakespeare, or Napoleon, or Washington, or Lincoln, or Roosevelt, we find that there is no comparison. The sages, the intelligentsia, the learned of the world are children beside His wisdom. Their moral codes and systems are fragmentary and inadequate beside His sayings. The heroes of the world have their faults and frailties and it is taken for granted that Jesus Christ has neither fault nor frailty. He could boldly challenge His critics, "Which of you convinceth me of sin?" (John 8:46)[15]

J. Oswald Sanders wrote, "Not until Jesus came with His peerless life and matchless teaching was humility exalted as a primary virtue."[16] Jesus, by His life and teachings, rewrote the book of conduct for the whole world as it relates to character, morality, respect for others, unselfish living, and integrity. He exalted womanhood, ennobled motherhood, established the need to love and protect children, and yet did not detract from manhood. The character model and teachings of Jesus enrich all mankind.

So when Jesus spent much of His three-year ministry predicting that He would indeed rise from the dead, it is believable. Perhaps it is not sufficient in itself, but when added to the other lines of reasoning put forward in this chapter, it lays one more powerful argument on the pile of logic that maintains it was necessary for the Christ to suffer and to rise from the dead the third day.

In fact, the whole resurrection story, as it appears in the Gospels, fits well with the character of God and Christ. It does not conflict with the miracles of His life and, in fact, offers a fitting capstone for His miraculous birth, life, ministry, and death. If a man came on the world scene manifesting an impeccable character the way Jesus did, then performed all the miracles He did for other people, proclaimed the selfless teachings that put Him in a category all by Himself, then died sacrificially for sin as the lamb of God that takes away the sins of the world—why should we be surprised that He rose again the third day? Especially when that is exactly what He said He was going to do? In addition, recall that the world's greatest book predicted He would rise from the dead, and predicted this so clearly that if He wasn't the One who would fulfill these prophecies, we would have to look for someone identical to Him. No, the resurrection is the capstone of His entire life...*and it fits.*

5. Jesus' resurrection changed the day of worship

All the early followers of Jesus were Jews. Everyone knows the Jews worshiped on Saturday or the Sabbath, for so they were commanded in the Decalogue. The Sabbath was a constant reminder that in six days God created the heavens, the earth, man, and all living creatures, then on the seventh day He rested.

God even promised to bless His people for doing no work on the Sabbath, to prosper them if they kept it as a day of rest and worship. By the time Jesus came into the world, the Sabbath was one of the most entrenched customs of Israel. It was a sign the nation worshiped Yahweh God. In fact, one of the sharpest disagreements the Jews had with Jesus was over His habit of doing good works (such as healing the sick and crippled) on the Sabbath day.

So the question is, why did the early church—an exclusively Jewish institution at its inception—change the day of worship to the first day of the week, or Sunday? There is only one answer: The earliest Christians believed Jesus rose from the dead on the first day of the week. For almost 2000 years now, the pattern of Christian worship has been a physical testimony that the church has always believed Jesus rose triumphantly over death on Sunday.

I find it interesting that although Jesus gave no instruction that the early Christians were to change the day of worship, they did so anyway. They appeared to follow His own example. He not only rose the first day but appeared to His disciples on that day and on the next Sunday when Thomas was also present. The apostle John called it "the Lord's Day" (Revelation 1:10), and by the time Paul took his first missionary journey, it was customary for Christians to gather on the first day of the week for worship and Bible study. That is one reason Paul found it easy to go into the synagogues on the Sabbath day and preach to the Jews, then meet with Christians on the Lord's Day. During his life, Christian worship on Sunday was an entrenched custom!

Skeptics may not like the idea that the first Christians changed the day of worship from Saturday to Sunday to commemorate our Lord's resurrection on the first day of the week, but it is the only explanation for their behavior. There simply is no other viable alternative!

6. *The instant conversion of the apostle John*

The apostle John seems to have been very special. He was a member of the innermost circle of disciples with his brother James and Peter. These three saw Jesus transfigured and were invited to come apart to pray with Him in Gethsemane. Of the 12 disciples, they were the closest to Jesus. John was probably a young man when he was called to follow Jesus (some suggest he was only 17 years old) and outlived all the other disciples. We do know he was faithful to Christ throughout his long life and that he wrote five books of the New Testament: the Gospel that bears his name; three small letters at the end of the New Testament; and the incredible prophetic book of Revelation. John's instant conversion may make him the first true believer in Christ's resurrection, unless that honor goes to one or both Marys. Read his account of the event immediately after Mary Magdalene had been to the empty tomb and found the stone rolled away:

> Then she ran and came to Simon Peter, and to the other disciple, whom Jesus loved, and said to them, "They have taken away the Lord out of the tomb, and we do not know where they have laid Him." Peter therefore went out, and the other disciple, and were going to the tomb. So they both ran together, and the other disciple outran Peter and came to the tomb first. And he, stooping down and looking in, saw the linen cloths lying there; yet he did not go in. Then Simon Peter came, following him, and went into the tomb; and he saw the linen cloths lying there, and the handkerchief that had been around His head, not lying with the linen cloths, but folded together in a place by itself. Then the other disciple, who came to the tomb first, went in also; and he saw and believed (John 20:2-8).

The youthful John outran Peter, but stopped at the door of the tomb. Peter, the blustery disciple, ran right by him and entered. Then John stepped inside and was immediately converted by what he saw. The perfect order of the bodiless tomb sent a message to his analytical mind that something supernatural had happened. The grave clothes of Jesus were still there and in perfect order—yet no body was inside! Everything was still intact. He Himself was gone, but somehow He had left behind His grave clothes. John knew instantly that the only explanation for such a miracle was the transformation of Jesus' dead body into a new, resurrected body that was no longer subject to time and space.

If, as some late-day skeptics would have us believe, Jesus' body was stolen, why would the grave clothes still be there? If that had happened, John the eyewitness would have seen nothing that would have inspired his belief. But he did not see merely a cold slab of stone, but the perfectly wrapped but empty grave clothes. He even saw the facial handkerchief folded and set off by itself. Perfect order!

No wonder "he saw and believed" (John 20:8). I think if we had been there, we too would have believed!

7. The transformation of the eyewitnesses

Skeptics would have us believe the disciples and those who saw the resurrected Christ were highly susceptible types who could easily be duped by hallucinations. The facts suggest just the opposite. Mark, the first of the Gospel narrators, tells quite a different story:

> Now when He rose early on the first day of the week, He appeared first to Mary Magdalene, out of whom He had cast seven demons. She went and told those who had been with Him, as they mourned and wept. And when they heard that He was alive and had been seen by her, they did not believe. After that, He appeared in another form to two of them as they walked and went into the country. And they went and told it to the rest, but they did not believe them either. Afterward He appeared to the eleven as they sat at the table; and He rebuked their unbelief and hardness of heart, because they did not believe those who had seen Him after He had risen (Mark 16:9-14).

At first, Jesus' followers were slow to believe. When Mary told the disciples she had seen the Lord, they did not believe. The two men to whom Jesus appeared on the road to Emmaus had already heard reports of the resurrection, but they did not believe them. Jesus rebuked them for their unbelief and showed them from the Scriptures why everything had happened as it did. They, in turn, went to the disciples and described their whole experience, yet Mark tells us, "They did not believe them either."[17] After that, Jesus "appeared to the eleven as they sat at the table; and He rebuked their unbelief and hardness of heart." It doesn't sound like they were gullible men eager to believe!

Luke tells how Jesus said to the disciples, "Why do doubts arise in your hearts? Behold My hands and My feet, that it is I Myself. Handle Me and see, for a spirit does not have flesh and bones as you see I have."[18] You would think the disciples would have seen all the proof they needed. But no, He still had to show them His hands and His feet. And to give more proof, Jesus asked them, "Have you any food here?" (Luke 24:41). And when they gave Him some food, He ate it in their presence.

Clearly, these men were not as easily persuaded and as quick to believe as the skeptics suggest. To them, the news of His resurrection was simply too good to be true. They had seen Jesus crucified and thought it was all over. They were indeed slow to believe, but they finally came to the realization (after seeing Him *several times* after the resurrection) that Jesus had truly risen from the dead. That truth became the motivating force that transformed them into zealous and fearless witnesses of the resurrection.

It bears repeating, that as powerful as are the arguments of the empty tomb and the moved stone, these facts did not transform and motivate anyone! Had it not been for the postresurrection meetings the disciples had with the living Christ, there would have been no Christianity. Those encounters not only convinced Jesus' followers, but transformed them into dynamic witnesses of His resurrection. The book of Acts makes it clear that the resurrection became the cornerstone of the Christian faith. It was preached wherever the gospel was proclaimed and produced the most powerful motivating force in the history of the world. They went from a small group of 12 to 120 at Jesus' ascension to 3000 and then 5000 "men" on the Day of Pentecost (we can assume a similar number of women and youth). By A.D. 312, as previously mentioned, Emperor Constantine had made Christianity the state religion of the entire Roman Empire. Whether his decision was due to political or religious reasons makes no difference. The point is, in three short centuries, Christianity had become such a force that it transformed the political and religious landscape. How could this have happened unless Christians from the very beginning were energized by an unshakable belief in the resurrection of Christ?

History confirms that the early Christians were beaten, imprisoned, crucified, dismembered, drowned, thrown to lions, starved, boiled in oil, hanged, and burned. Their willing martyrdom can be explained only by their intense belief in the risen Christ.

8. *The conversion of the apostle Paul*

In chapter 8 we considered the apostle Paul's testimony on the deity of Christ. His testimony on the resurrection of Christ is so strong that we would do well to call him to the stand once more.

Recall that, before his conversion, Paul was for years a skeptic of skeptics as far as Christianity was concerned. He vehemently opposed Christ and dedicated himself to stamping out the rapid spread of Christianity. But something remarkable happened to him and instantly changed all that. He himself says his transformation occurred when he was confronted with the living Christ. Listen to his own testimony:

> My manner of life from my youth, which was spent from the beginning among my own nation at Jerusalem, all the Jews know. They knew me from the first, if they were willing to testify, that according to the strictest sect of our religion I lived a Pharisee....
>
> Indeed, I myself thought I must do many things contrary to the name of Jesus of Nazareth. This I also did in Jerusalem, and many of the saints I shut up in prison, having received authority from the chief priests; and when they were put to death, I cast my vote against them. And I punished them often in every synagogue and compelled them to blaspheme; and being exceedingly enraged against them, I persecuted them even to foreign cities.

While thus occupied, as I journeyed to Damascus with authority and commission from the chief priests, at midday...along the road I saw a light from heaven, brighter than the sun, shining around me and those who journeyed with me. And when we all had fallen to the ground, I heard a voice speaking to me and saying in the Hebrew language, "Saul, Saul, why are you persecuting Me? It is hard for you to kick against the goads." So I said, "Who are You, Lord?" And He said, "I am Jesus, whom you are persecuting. But rise and stand on your feet; for I have appeared to you for this purpose, to make you a minister and a witness both of the things which you have seen and of the things which I will yet reveal to you. I will deliver you from the Jewish people, as well as from the Gentiles, to whom I now send you, to open their eyes in order to turn them from darkness to light, and from the power of Satan to God, that they may receive forgiveness of sins and an inheritance among those who are sanctified by faith in Me."

Therefore...I was not disobedient to the heavenly vision, but declared first to those in Damascus and in Jerusalem, and throughout all the region of Judea, and then to the Gentiles, that they should repent, turn to God, and do works befitting repentance. For these reasons the Jews seized me in the temple and tried to kill me. Therefore, having obtained help from God, to this day I stand, witnessing both to small and great, saying no other things than those which the prophets and Moses said would come—that the Christ would suffer, that He would be the first to rise from the dead, and would proclaim light to the Jewish people and to the Gentiles (Acts 26:4-5, 9-23).

This angry man who dedicated himself to wiping out Christianity was so transformed by his encounter with the living Christ that he became one of the early church's most powerful evangelists and church builders. Paul's amazing transformation is a gigantic philosophical mountain that modern skeptics cannot explain away. Outside of the explanation Paul himself gave for his conversion, what could account for this astonishing, light-speed reversal? Was he driven mad by guilt? That theory is shown to be impossible by the written legacy Paul left behind in the New Testament. Yet that seems to be the only other possible explanation. And Paul himself dealt with this silly theory when he defended himself before King Festus:

> Now as he [Paul] thus made his defense, Festus said with a loud voice, "Paul, you are beside yourself! Much learning is driving you mad!" But he said, "I am not mad, most noble Festus, but speak the words of truth and reason. For the king, before whom I also speak freely, knows these things; for I am convinced that none of these things escapes his attention, since this thing was not done in a corner" (Acts 26:24-26).

No, Paul was not driven mad, either by his great learning or by terrible guilt. To the day of his martyrdom, he was one of the most lucid people who ever walked this earth. It is true he never forgot his days as a persecutor of the church, but he never doubted that he had been forgiven by the Founder of that church. That is why he so willingly gave his life to spread the news of Christ's resurrection from the dead.

Would They Die for a Lie?

History leaves no doubt that many of the earliest disciples of Jesus suffered the most horrible of persecutions and deaths. Yet among the "over five hundred brethren" who saw the resurrected Christ, there are no known defectors. We know of no one who changed his mind. Certainly there were none among the 11 disciples (not including the traitor, Judas Iscariot, who never lived to see the resurrected Christ). History never even hints that the faith of a single disciple ever flagged; none ever denied the resurrection of Jesus.

With the exception of John, every one of the 11 disciples died a martyr's death. Tradition says Peter was crucified upside down at his own request, for he thought himself "unworthy" to be crucified in the same way his Lord had been. Paul, after several long imprisonments, died a martyr's death in Rome. Thomas, who had been a "doubter" until he saw the resurrected Christ, carried his Lord's Great Commission all the way to India, where he ministered for many years and was finally martyred.

(My wife and I have stood at the tomb of St. Thomas in India, where the church for centuries has claimed his body was buried. Solid evidence for Thomas's activities is found in the Indian state of Kerala, where we ministered in many Bible churches or "brethren" assemblies. The traditional church there is known as "the MarThoma Church," named after the disciple Thomas, whom they believe first brought them the gospel. Kerala is the only Christian state in the whole of India; the rest of the nation is thoroughly Hindu. History tells us that when Portuguese missionaries sailed to India in the fifteenth century, they landed in Kerala and found Christianity so strong they went elsewhere. All this indicates that although Thomas started out his life of faith rather doubtfully, he finished extremely well.)

John, who outlived all the other disciples, pastored the great church of Ephesus for years. Tradition says he was boiled in oil yet survived, and when he was approximately 85 years old he was banished to the Isle of Patmos. From there, around A.D. 96, he wrote the last book of the New Testament, the Revelation of Jesus Christ, which thoroughly documents his continuing belief in the resurrection of Jesus and His promise to return someday to fulfill all the Old and New Testament prophecies about His future kingdom.

Now the big question: Would these disciples be so willing to suffer and die for a lie? If in fact they stole and destroyed the body of Jesus and subsequently told all the people a well-crafted lie—a lie so clever none of them was ever caught—what would cause all but one to die for their fabrication? Perhaps we could imagine one or two of them doing so—but 10 of 11? Who can believe that?

"Well," someone might say, "perhaps the disciples didn't steal the body, but nevertheless they believed a lie. They were simply mistaken that Jesus had risen from the dead. They believed He had done so, but they were wrong." Yet such a theory fares little better than the previous one. When a sword is at your throat and you are told to deny the resurrection of Christ or die, what evidence causes you to choose death over life? What prevents you from speaking the simple words, "Well, I never actually saw Him alive. You must be right…He didn't rise from the dead"? Again, we can imagine that two or even three deluded disciples might be willing to die for a mistaken belief in the resurrection of Jesus—but all 11? Isn't it reasonable to suppose that at least one of them would cave in when threatened with death? Yet none of them did so. The only explanation must be that, when confronted with death, the minds of the disciples raced back to several rock-solid, airtight reasons for maintaining their unshakable conviction that Jesus rose from the dead. Without that, what could have kept at least one or two from recanting? Yet none of them ever did so. Why not? Because they not only *believed* He had risen from the dead, they *knew* He had. They had spoken to Him. They had seen Him. They had watched Him eat. They had touched Him. They *knew*.

That is why none of them ever denied the faith, even on pain of death. There is no reason to fear death when you know your Savior has already conquered it!

My Challenge to a Skeptic

A man who formerly disbelieved in the resurrection once challenged the argument I just laid out. After granting, for argument's sake, that two or three disciples might deliberately spread such a lie convincingly, I asked, "But would they die for it?"

"Possibly," he said, "if they were really courageous men."

"But would 11 out of 12 (including Paul) die for a lie they spread, knowing it was not true? For history shows they all became martyrs, except for John."

His face brightened, as though he had thought of an idea that would drive a spike into my argument. "I can explain it: esprit de corps. They all gathered in a group, drew strength from each other, and died together!" He was clearly elated with his idea.

"The problem with that," I replied, "is that no two disciples died together!" Every one of them sealed his testimony that he had seen the resurrected Christ with his own blood—each of them separate from the others. Some perished in Israel, some in Syria, some in Rome, others in Italy and India. Some think Peter died in Babylon.

The man immediately saw the error of his theory and eventually committed his own life to the resurrected, living Christ.

Friend, we can believe those first eyewitnesses who claimed to see Jesus' glorified body three days after His crucifixion, for they not only lived out their faith by their testimony and their effective works, but they sealed it with their blood. No other religion in the world comes close to having so much confirmed evidence for the truth of its central claims.

Jesus really did rise again from the dead. There simply is no other viable explanation for what happened 2000 years ago.

Chapter Eighteen

The Best of the False Theories of Jesus' Resurrection

Skeptics have had a lot of time to develop their arguments against the resurrection of Christ—almost 2000 years by now. They have had centuries to formulate, process, and refine their own explanations of what happened to the body of Christ after He was crucified. So what have they come up with?

The flawed theories we are about to look at are the best the skeptics have to offer after almost two millennia of thought. But before we get to them, I would like to quote my mentor, Dr. Wilbur Smith, who makes a unique observation in this regard:

> In considering the varied, and often fantastic, theories that have been proposed from time to time to rationalistically explain away what the New Testament sets forth as a stupendous miracle, the Resurrection of our Lord, the author would like to make a statement that he has not seen emphasized in any book on the Resurrection that has come to his hand, namely, that from the very beginning of Christ's work on earth, and throughout the New Testament, the Resurrection of Christ was bitterly and continually opposed.
>
> When the chief priests and Pharisees said to Pilate on Saturday of Passion Week, "Sir, we remember that the deceiver said, while He was yet alive, 'After three days I will rise again.' Command therefore that the sepulchre be made sure until the third day, lest His disciples come by night, and steal Him away, and say unto the people, He is

risen from the dead: so the last error shall be worse than the first" (Matthew 27:63-64), they were, even before Christ rose from the dead, determined that such an event must not occur. *They did not want Him to rise from the dead, and they made every possible provision that He shouldn't rise from the dead. This is not the way men act who are seeking for the truth.*

On Sunday...when the Sanhedrin gave money to the soldiers, and told them to lie about what had happened, they gave added testimony that, though they were the religious leaders of the Jewish people, they were not seeking the truth. They did not want the truth. One thing only they did want, to keep people from believing that Jesus had risen from the dead.

The church has always had to contend with people like that, some of them in their own ranks, who do everything they can to keep people from knowing the truth. Shortly after the church began its glorious career, we read that the priests, the rulers of the temple, and the Sadducees were "grieved that they (the disciples) taught the people, and preached through Jesus the Resurrection from the dead," manifesting their hatred of the truth by throwing the Apostles into prison (Acts 4:1-22).[1]

Dr. Smith then pointed out that, years later, when the apostle Paul was in Athens, he preached the cornerstone of the gospel: the resurrection of Jesus. And the reaction of those Greek humanist philosophers? Skepticism.[2] Some mocked and some said they would give him another hearing.[3] Still later, while defending himself in Jerusalem before the Sanhedrin (of which he had been a member before his dramatic conversion and life transformation), he said, "Concerning the hope of the resurrection of the dead am I being judged."[4] The Pharisees were willing to concede that Christ might have risen from the dead, for they believed in life after death. But the Sadducees went ballistic, for they were militantly opposed to the resurrection—and not just Jesus' resurrection, but anyone's. That is why they exhibited such great hostility against the early church and refused to be persuaded. They were worse than doubting Thomas; they wouldn't believe even if they saw someone who had been raised from the dead.

Is it not true that, in the Gospels and in the book of Acts, those who are seen to take a deliberate stand against the resurrection of Christ make no effort to investigate the evidence for themselves? The more one looks into the New Testament opposition to the truth of Christ's resurrection, the more one sees how it is but a prophecy of the antagonism against the same truth in our modern day.[5]

The False Theories

Once again, remember that the theories we are about to consider are the best the skeptics have to offer. Keep in mind, too, that most of these theories were developed not by men who were honestly seeking the truth, but by people determined not to believe in the resurrection of Christ. Judge for yourself the strength of their arguments.

The Swoon Theory

The old idea that Jesus fainted or swooned temporarily was invented long before medical science had developed an understanding of how devastating shock is to the human body. Today any medical person would admit that if the crucifixion hadn't killed Jesus, the tightly wrapped grave clothes, the cold, damp, sealed tomb, and three days without treatment certainly would have. Then there was the huge stone that the weakened victim would be required to move. Yet that isn't the worst of it. How does a weakened and emaciated Christ, a man who would have taken weeks to recover, inspire His disciples to go out and proclaim His resurrection in power? The swoon theory is so ridiculous that even the famous nineteenth-century skeptic David Strauss wrote,

> It is impossible that one who had just come forth
> from the grave half dead, who crept about weak and

ill, who stood in need of medical treatment, of bandaging, strengthening, and tender care, and who at last succumbed to suffering, could ever have given to the disciples that impression that He was a conqueror over death and the grave—that He was the Prince of Life—which lay at the bottom of their future ministry. Such a resuscitation could orally have weakened the impression which He had made upon them in life and in death—or at the most could have given it an elegiac voice—but could by no possibility have changed their sorrow into enthusiasm, or elevated their reverence into worship.[6]

It would be hard for an evangelical Christian like myself to improve on the dismissal of the swoon theory by the above-quoted skeptic. I would add, however, a dilemma that would arise if such an impossibility had occurred. If Jesus had just revived and crawled out of the tomb, why, when the Jews of the day were confronted by reports of His resurrection, didn't they scour land and sea to arrest and present Him as "Exhibit A" and thus totally destroy the reports? The answer is simple. He was not there; He was "risen, as He said"!

People Looked for Jesus in the Wrong Tomb

The idea that Jesus' body was placed in the wrong tomb or that the women came to the wrong tomb is preposterous. The people of the day were not such idiots as to be so easily convinced of a resurrection if one never took place. To make such a claim makes a gross liar out of Joseph of Arimathea, who would have to be part of any such conspiracy (although John Dominic Crossan of the Jesus Seminar says that even *Joseph* was a literary fiction. According to Crossan, just a few scant decades after the events in question, the church simply invented a major figure connected with the Sanhedrin…akin to someone today inventing a Supreme Court justice from the 1970s *without anyone catching the deception!*). You can be sure Joseph would have raised a howl of protest if the story got out that he had allowed his new family tomb to be used to bury the body of the crucified Jesus, if in reality he had not!

Besides, you can be sure the world's greatest tomb search would have opened every grave until the Lord's body had been found, even if it meant rolling away the stone from every tomb in the garden. Yet there is not the slightest hint in recorded history that anyone ever looked in any other tomb. Remember, the religious leaders *never* denied that Jesus' body was missing. Why bribe Roman soldiers to say that His disciples came and stole His body if in fact the body was obtainable? Even the Jews knew His body was missing, which is why they did not look for it.

And in any event, how could the women have gotten confused about the location of Jesus' body? Matthew reports that when Joseph of Arimathea took Jesus' body down from the cross, he put it in his "new tomb" (some would have us believe he didn't know where his new tomb was!) while Mary Magdalene was present, with the other Mary sitting opposite the tomb. These are the women who came to the tomb early the following Sunday—and we are supposed to believe they looked in the wrong place? Incredible! Mark tells us these two women watched Joseph take Jesus' body down from the cross, anoint it temporarily, wrap it in grave clothes, then lay Him in the tomb and roll a stone against the door. Then Mark adds, "And Mary Magdalene and Mary the mother of Jesus observed where He was laid."[7] And no one could find that tomb three days later? Highly unlikely.

When my father died I was overwhelmed with grief. He was buried in a cemetery that had over 500 other graves. Do you think I would have a hard time remembering which one was his just three days after the funeral? Hardly. His entombment was sealed in my mind forever—and I was only nine years old! I can find that grave yet today, after 60-plus years.

There is no way the women could have been confused about the tomb. (Nor is it likely the angels were confused about which stone to roll away.) No, they had the right tomb, all right—and it was empty!

Wild Dogs Ate His Body

Modern skeptics, such as John Dominic Crossan, have suggested that wild dogs ate the body of Jesus. Crossan dismisses the Gospel accounts that Jesus was buried in a tomb and thinks it more likely that He was buried in a shallow grave that wild dogs immediately dug up in order to consume the body.

There are a couple of major problems with this theory: First, this possibility was never suggested by anyone until almost 2000 years after the event in question! Had this been a real possibility, is it likely Jesus' enemies would have missed it? Second, why would the Jews have claimed Jesus' disciples stole His body from a "tomb" if they suspected it had been buried in a shallow grave? Why give this new faith a boost? The story they paid the Roman soldiers to tell makes no sense—unless, of course, His body really had been buried in a tomb, it was now missing, and a desperate explanation immediately had to be concocted. The "wild dog" theory is nothing but a wild exercise in desperation.

It is hard for me to understand how brilliant "scholars" can offer suggestions as ridiculous as this. Many years ago the skeptic professor C. H. Guignebert laid the groundwork for Crossan's theory when he wrote, "The truth is, that we do not know, and in all probability the disciples knew no better, where the body of Jesus had been thrown after it had been removed from the cross, probably by the executioners. It is more likely to have been cast into the pit for the executed than laid in a new tomb."[8] Dr. Wilbur Smith responded,

> Here is the kind of historical writing that ought to be designated as "my theological." No matter how great Professor Guignebert's learning may be... when he makes a statement like this, which cannot be supported by the slightest particle of evidence from the New Testament documents (nor from any other documents which anyone knows about) he only

reveals his own determination to strip the career of Christ of all of its supernatural elements, even if it necessitates manufacturing conclusions which are utterly, absolutely unsupported by any testimony.... A theory that has no evidence for its support need not be given any further consideration.[9]

We should observe, too, that such "explanations" for the missing body could only be made centuries after the events. We find no such explanations prior to the modem era because those who lived closer to the event in question would have laughed any such suggestion out of existence. It would be like trying to suggest that America's first president was Benedict Arnold, not George Washington; that the nation broke away from the French, not the English; and that Valley Forge was a lowland iron smelter, not the encampment grounds of the Continental Army.

Unknown Persons Stole the Body of Jesus

This spurious suggestion, like the others, has zero supporting evidence. For good reason it was not raised for two millennia. If it were true, why didn't those unspecified individuals who stole the body come forward to receive the generous reward the authorities no doubt would have offered for the body? You can be sure that in a small community like the one where Jesus was buried, rumors of His corpse floating around would have surfaced—but the Jews never bothered looking for the body because they knew it was gone. Any rumors that existed had to do with His resurrection!

Dr. Joseph Klausner, a modern-day Hebrew University professor in Jerusalem, has offered a slight variation on this theory. He suggests that Joseph of Arimathea thought it unfitting that a crucified one should be buried in his new ancestral tomb, so he secretly removed the body close to the Sabbath and buried it in an unknown grave. In his book *The Resurrection of Jesus*, Dr. James Orr somewhat sarcastically answered this suggestion:

This interesting little deception of Joseph, so likely in a good man, and first brought to enlighten these last years, successfully took in the whole Christian church and combined with imaginary appearances, created its faith in the resurrection![10]

Remember, Joseph is presented as a "good man" who must have had a good working relationship with the highest Jewish council, from whom he secured permission to take Jesus' body down from the cross. Some believe he was a member of the council itself. In any case, he took the body down by permission. Had he put it in another tomb, you can be sure he would have been the first person the authorities would have contacted in their efforts to locate the body. If he burned it or disposed of it in another way, they would have had him on every street corner in Jerusalem, proclaiming the story. *Nothing like that ever happened.* In fact, no record exists that anyone even tried to contact him. That makes perfect sense if the Gospels are right in claiming that the Roman soldiers themselves told these leaders about their confrontation with the angel at the tomb. The leaders knew the body was gone, so there was no point in looking for it. The only option they had was to spread false rumors about why the body was gone. And this they did.

A related theory is that the enemies of Jesus stole the body. This suggestion can easily be dealt with, for if His enemies had stolen the body, you can be sure they would have produced it immediately to quell the spread of this new faith based entirely on His bodily resurrection. Yet they never did.

The Disciples Stole the Body

The only false theory with any semblance of plausibility is the one the Jewish leaders in Jerusalem advanced. As Matthew explained:

> Some of the guard came into the city and reported to the chief priests all the things that had happened

[the stone was rolled away, His body was gone, and several of his followers had come to the tomb and were told by two men in shining white, "He is not here; He is risen, as He said"]. When they had assembled with the elders and consulted together, they gave a large sum of money to the soldiers, saying, "Tell them, 'His disciples came at night and stole Him away while we slept' [how did they know the disciples did the deed if they were asleep?]. And if this comes to the governor's ears, we will appease him and make you secure." So they took the money and did as they were instructed; and this saying is commonly reported among the Jews until this day (Matthew 28:11-15).

Unfortunately for those who propound conspiratorial theories that would explain away the resurrection, this story picked the wrong grave robbers. Anyone but the disciples! Remember, ten out of eleven of them died for such an enormous "lie." This theory made no sense then, and still makes no sense today.

Is it likely the disciples could have "turned the world upside down"[11] with their false stories about being eyewitnesses to the resurrected Christ's activities, if in fact it was all a big lie? Hardly. That would require a much bigger miracle than the resurrection itself. The truth is, the theory that Jesus' friends stole His body introduces more problems than it solves.

The Vision Theory

The vision theory is perhaps the most widely believed false explanation for the resurrection. It seeks to avoid impugning the integrity of the disciples by instead making them honest and sincere fellows who were emotionally distraught by the death of their leader. This theory claims it was only natural that, since Jesus had predicted His resurrection, His followers had visions that He kept His word. Therefore they saw Him and conversed with Him and even thought they ate with Him.

One nineteenth-century critic, French skeptic Joseph Renan, is typical of those who hold to this theory. His conjectures have been summarized as follows:

> The so-called appearances of the Risen Christ were due to the excited state of mind in which the disciples were after the death of their Master. Overwrought and mentally distraught by the shock of His death, and yearning for His presence, they saw apparitions or visions of Him. But these were purely subjective— phantasms or mental hallucinations. They longed to see Him; they expected to see Him; and they thought they did see Him. Their thought was perfectly honest, but it was nevertheless a hallucination.
>
> For persons in a state of unusual mental excitement and expectancy, especially when they are also of a highly strung nervous temperament, such visions are, it is represented, common phenomena of religious history, and are often contagious. So it was in the case of the appearances of Jesus. They began with the women, probably with Mary Magdalene, an excitable and nervous person. Her story that she had seen the Lord was eagerly embraced; it spread with lightning rapidity, and with the force of an epidemic. What she believed she had seen others believed they too must see, and they saw. The visions were the product of their dwelling in fond and affectionate memory on the personality of their Master, which, after the first shock of despair was over, they came to feel was such that He must have survived death.[12]

Renan would have us believe that the early Christians' faith in the resurrection resulted from mass hallucinations shared by 13 people (whose names we know), plus the 500 eyewitnesses to the resurrected Christ. Yet all the disciples died as martyrs rather than recant of their faith in that resurrection. At best, it's a stretch to imagine that 11 men and several women all had the same visions, and that a few years later, Saul of Tarsus—formerly a vicious enemy of the new church—had the same visions. (Oh yes, and in the case of the original disciples, after 40 days all the dreams stopped.)

I'm not an authority on dreams, but I've never heard of mass, identical dreams in which all the persons (and no others) who *appear* in the dream also *have* the dream (while no one else does). That does tax my credulity. I myself can never dream the same thing twice, and my dreams even come out backward. Even my wife and I, when going through a time of mutual emotional pressures, can dream of the same subject—but our dreams are never close to being similar.

Beyond that, healthy people never have the least difficulty in distinguishing between a dream or vision and reality. A vision may get a missionary like Paul to "come over to Macedonia and help us,"[13] but it will never lead a large group of individuals to lay down their lives for the bodily resurrection of a man they never saw outside of their vision. Visions may supplement God's leading in a person's life, but mass visions will never account for 20 centuries of Christianity!

The Telegram Theory

This has to be one of the strangest theories ever devised. Of this odd idea one scholar wrote,

> This really assumes that the ascended Lord, ascended in His Spirit, not in His body, telegraphed back pictures of Himself to the minds of the Apostles in such a vivid way that they actually were led to believe they had seen the risen Lord in their midst. Just how any true scholar can ever consider such a fantastic theory as this, we do not quite know.[14]

Since this theory was conceived about 100 years ago, we can give its inventor an A for technological foresight, because we can now send pictures to each other from cell phones. But he receives an F-minus in theology. (Incidentally, the creator of this theory was a liberal leader of a church that did not believe in the bodily resurrection of Jesus. He was evidently trying desperately to preserve his liberalism and his church's traditions.)

Should this theory require evaluation, may I suggest you read Luke's account of the conversation between the resurrected Christ and the two men on the road to Emmaus (Luke 24:1-35). Then ask yourself if such an encounter could possibly be transmitted by mental "telegraph." Is a bodily resurrection really harder to believe than *that*?

Besides, such a theory destroys the integrity of Jesus Christ. He promised His disciples He would rise again. To fail to keep that promise—yet command His disciples to go into all the world and preach a gospel based on a physical (not telegraphed) resurrection—would be outrageously dishonest. That would be impossible for the holy Son of God and certainly out of character with everything else He did.

The Opinion of a Brilliant Scholar

Dr. J. Gresham Machen was one of the greatest thinkers ever to graduate from Princeton. He was an ardent defender of the resurrection and penned the following comment, which helps us realize Jesus was in a category all by Himself even before He rose from the dead:

> You and I have never seen a man who rose from the dead; but you and I have never seen a man like Jesus. Do you not see, what we are trying to establish is not the resurrection of an ordinary man about whom we know nothing, but the Resurrection of Jesus. There is a tremendous presumption against the resurrection of an ordinary man, but when you come to really know Jesus as He is pictured to us in the Gospels,

you will say that whereas it is unlikely that any ordinary man should rise from the dead, in His case the presumption is exactly reversed. It is unlikely that any ordinary man should rise, but it is unlikely that this man should not rise; it may be said of this man that it was impossible that He should be holden of death.[15]

Dr. Machen is right. The resurrection, though supernatural, so fits the life and character of Jesus that it is natural—for Him. That it was a supernatural event should not surprise us; His whole life was supernatural. But there is one great question His resurrection solves: It explains how the church came into existence.

No one, particularly a skeptic, has ever managed to provide a tenable suggestion about how the church could ever have exploded onto the world scene as it did had it been built on a hoax, a vision, a deception, or even a mental telegraph. There is an easy answer: Jesus, the world's most unusual man, really did rise from the dead.

Over against the feeble objections to the resurrection as represented in the aforementioned theories stands one of the greatest miracles of all. As one of the recent defenders of the faith against the well-advertised skeptics of the Jesus Seminar wrote in *Jesus Under Fire,*

> The birth and rapid rise of the Christian church… remain an unsolved enigma for any historian who refuses to take seriously the only explanation offered by the Church itself. The resurrection of Jesus is therefore the most plausible explanation of the origin of the Christian way of life.[16]

The Good That Comes from the False Theories

The Bible tells us, "Surely the wrath of man shall praise [God]."[17] That is what these false theories do: They make it easier to believe that the greatest Man who ever lived would have the greatest death on record and be one-of-a-kind in resurrection. The theories we just examined are the best the skeptics have to offer—but they all have the same, fatal problem. They are harder to believe than the real story! Dr. Wilbur Smith wrote,

> Not one of these theories has ever met with general acceptance, even among radical critics and rationalists. Those who deny the reality of Christ's Resurrection differ among themselves as to what theory most plausibly can be used to escape the significance of the evidence presented by the New Testament. When one puts them all together, and realizes how unreasonable they are, without foundation in fact, divorced from all the evidence that we have, involving, some one and some another, falsehood, corruption, deception, theft, fraud, ecstasies of visionary experiences, etc., it is inevitable that we should be convinced that if Christ did not rise from the dead, nobody knows anything about the conclusion of His life, and the New Testament documents are proved worthless. But we have seen that the New Testament documents are not worthless. They are of the greatest historical value.
>
> Furthermore, if the Resurrection did not take place, we do not know how the church was founded. If Christ did not rise from the dead on the third day, we do not know how He ended His life. And to think that One, the greatest man who ever walked this earth, between the awful experience on the cross and the end of His life whenever that was, should have been buried in the obscurity of some unknown village in Palestine, where His name once had been on the lips of every living person, is simply beyond all reason.
>
> My own frank opinion is that the Holy Spirit so guided the writers of these four Gospels, recording the events relating to Christ's Resurrection, that they were enabled to write a story which, though it relates to a stupendous miracle, is so rational, so reasonable, so logical, so close to facts which

could never be imagined, that their testimony simply cannot be broken. If, after these last one hundred years of the sharpest, bitterest, most unmerciful criticism of these records, a criticism more terrifically severe than any other documents have ever endured, the Resurrection narrative still stands unshaken, unmutilated, unharmed, men ought to be persuaded that the things here spoken of are according to the truth as it is in Christ.[18]

Don't Let Your Presuppositions Get in the Way

The evidence for the resurrection of Jesus from the tomb is so overwhelming that anyone who examines it should be convinced, provided his presuppositions do not stand in the way. Basically there are two:

The first is skepticism or atheism. Although some atheists do become Christians, many reject resurrection facts out of hand because they just do not believe in God or the supernatural. And obviously, the resurrection is a supernatural event. Most atheists simply refuse to examine the evidence objectively.

The second is more subtle. Paul warned that some would reject the truth because they "had pleasure in unrighteousness."[19] Everyone knows, or should know, that Christianity lays out a righteous way of life. "Go and sin no more" was not only a command of Jesus to a fallen woman, it is His will for all His followers. Some people, when confronted with the truth of the resurrection, reject it along with the Christian way of life that the resurrection demands.

If a seeker is unencumbered by either of these two deadly presuppositions, however, the overwhelming evidence for the resurrection makes it easy to accept as historical fact. Consider how easy it is to believe…

IF you believe in God, THEN it is easy to believe God could raise Jesus from the dead.

IF you believe Jesus is the Son of God come in the flesh, THEN it is easy to accept His resurrection.

IF you believe He was miraculously conceived of a virgin, THEN it is not hard to accept His resurrection by that same divine power.

IF you can accept that, as God in human flesh, Jesus lived a sinless life so He could die a sacrificial death, THEN you will have no trouble accepting the resurrection.

IF you read and accept His prophecies that He would rise from the dead, THEN it is easy to see how the resurrection narrative fits all those requirements.

IF you believe Jesus "is the truth," THEN it is not hard to believe He "showed Himself alive" after the resurrection.

IF you believe the miracles were evidences of His deity, THEN accepting the resurrection as a divine miracle is automatic.

IF, however, you do not believe any of the above, THEN you will find it difficult to believe the resurrection, no matter how much evidence confronts you.

No matter what you believe, you cannot deny the abundance of evidence that indicates Jesus did rise that first Easter morning. A mountain of evidence points to His resurrection, and nothing in 2000 years has come close to disproving it.

The Power of the Resurrection

The apostle Paul wrote of his desire to "know Him and the power of His resurrection."[20] Transformed lives provide the ultimate test of that power. Those who have believed the resurrection and received Christ as their Lord and Savior experience "the power of His resurrection," enabling them to live the Christian life. For most, that means a drastic change. Why? Because everyone who becomes a Christian is a sinner. Some are worse than others (like Paul, who persecuted the church). Others are blasphemers; still others are more "run of the mill" kind of sinners. Yet all of them, after conversion, are given the power to live as new creatures in

Christ. Once an individual bows his or her knee to the Savior and experiences the resurrected Christ, he or she has the power to overcome every obsessive sin that has dominated his or her life. From addictions to drugs, alcohol, prostitution, depression, anger, you name it—Jesus has cured it and continues to cure it today.

In all the years I have seen men and women come to faith in the resurrected Christ, I have yet to find one person who regretted the experience. By contrast, scores still testify that "Jesus changed my life!" You can be sure they were speaking not of a dead Jesus still in Joseph's tomb, but of the resurrected Christ alive in the world today.

The challenge now, as always, is to "taste and see that the LORD is good" (Psalm 34:8). In other words, accept Him as your Lord and Savior and experience for yourself "the power of His resurrection."

Part V:
Who Do You Say He Is?

Chapter Nineteen

Evidence That Demands a Verdict

If a brilliant man came into your community and began attracting huge crowds of people who would stand for hours on end to hear Him lecture, amazing them with teachings that seemed far wiser than those of the best-educated men of the day—even though He had no formal education beyond His training in a carpenter's shop—would you be impressed enough to go and hear Him for yourself?

And if that man began to heal all kinds of diseased, crippled, and even demon-possessed people who came to Him, and then if that man began performing miracles that had outstripped anything that had ever been done—miracles that defied human logic, such as walking on water, feeding multitudes with nothing but a boy's lunch, and turning water into the most delicious wine you have ever tasted—would you be inclined to think that man had supernatural powers?

And if that same man raised at least three people from the dead, in plain view of many credible people, and if the holiest prophet in your generation called this man the Lamb of God and the Son of God and further witnessed that He was the promised Messiah, would you believe it? Would you at least be inspired to investigate His claims more fully for yourself?

And if your research into the Hebrew prophets unearthed more than 30 specific prophecies relating to the time and location of His birth, to details concerning His amazing life, and even to specific events about His death that matched perfectly with prophecies given hundreds of years before His birth, would you conclude this man, who was unlike anyone else, before or since, came from God?

And if you also heard this man say, "I am equal with God," "I have power to raise the dead," "I and the Father are one," "I am the Judge all men will stand before in eternity," and "I am the only begotten Son of God who has come to seek and to save the lost," would you believe Him?

These are the questions the people of Jesus' day faced, head-on. Many, like the disciples, believed in Him. One spoke for them all when he said to Jesus, "You have the words of eternal life."[1] They accepted Him as God in human flesh, come into the world to do what no one else could ever do: die for the sins of the whole world. The disciples and thousands of others like them went to an early grave as martyrs because they refused to give up their belief in the deity of Jesus of Nazareth. They had joyfully committed their lives to serving Him and would willingly give up their lives to serve Him to the end. They found the evidence of His deity and His status as the Messiah-Savior so compelling that they prayed, "My Lord and my God!"

Why the Jewish Leaders Rejected Him

Of course, not everyone accepted Jesus, even though they admitted that no man could do such miracles or give such marvelous teachings "unless God is with him."[2] Some, when confronted with His miraculous power to heal all kinds of diseases, said He did these things by the power of Satan. In this they blasphemed.

Why did they reject Him? Jesus gave the answer in John 5:40. After Jesus confronted His opponents with the Scriptures that He said "testify of Me" (verse 39), He told them, "You are not willing to come to Me that You may have life." In the original Greek text, the word "willing" is in the past tense. That is, they "willed not" to come to Him. They did not reject Jesus as the Christ on the basis of evidence or logic. They could not use the Scriptures to prove He was not the Messiah come in the flesh. They could not point to some moral flaw that precluded Him from being the sinless Son of God. They rejected Him, as He said, because of their *will*. Their problem was not mind, reason, evidence, or facts; it was will. They flat-out refused to consider the evidence directly in front of them.

In the final analysis, the decision to accept or reject Jesus always comes down to a matter of the will. If people stubbornly refuse to believe, regardless of the strength of the evidence, they will live and die in unbelief. If people are open, however, God will send them ample evidence to support their belief. Jesus said, "My doctrine is not Mine, but His who sent Me. If anyone wants to do His will, he shall know concerning the doctrine, whether it is from God or whether I speak on My own authority."[3] Jesus promises God will send all the information and evidence an honest seeker needs in order to believe.

My friend Dr. John Hunter of England is a good example. He has served His Lord faithfully for over 50 years. John was not always a Christian, however. As a fighter pilot in the Royal Air Force during World War II, he had many harrowing experiences. One day, knowing that he could die at any given hour, he prayed this simple prayer: "God—if there is a God—I hope you will hear my prayer and reveal yourself to me. If you do, I will accept you and serve you." In His grace, God heard that sincere prayer and brought into John's life some individuals who knew and shared the gospel with him. Finally he learned enough about Jesus to become a believer. He invited Him into his life and was wonderfully converted.

He is not alone! Many people have prayed that kind of simple but sincere prayer and have seen God respond. The Ethiopian eunuch in Acts 8 is another example of a sincere individual seeking God (he had gone to the temple in Jerusalem to find peace with God, but left Israel empty). The Lord led the evangelist Philip into the desert to meet him and lead him to Christ. Like millions of others, after receiving Christ, "he went on his way rejoicing."[4]

That was not the story, of course, for the Jewish leaders of Jesus' day, who "willed not" to come to Him. Jesus' teachings conflicted with their preconceived biases, which were based on man-made traditions that had accumulated through the centuries rather than on Scripture. Their minds were made up and their wills set; consequently, they rejected the truth Jesus taught.

The Importance of the Human Will

Two things are said to be certain in life: death and taxes. A third should be added to that list: choice. Every man or woman must sometime in their lifetime make a choice to either accept God or reject Him. That choice goes back to the Garden of Eden, it is operational today, and will even operate during the millennium to come when Christ returns to set up His kingdom of peace and righteousness on earth.

Even before God had created Eve, Scripture tells us He planted a garden called Eden.[5] In it he put Adam, the first man, and all kinds of trees. God let Adam have access to all of them, with the exception of the tree of the knowledge of good and evil. Of this tree, Adam and his wife Eve were forbidden to eat. You know the story: They disobeyed and ate from that tree...and the universal choice of whether to obey or disobey God was presented to the entire human race. All through the ages men and women have faced the problem of whether to obey God or reject His will. God gave to Adam and Eve a free will, which was passed on to their children and has been passed on to every human being since.

Cain and Abel are two more examples of individuals with a free will. Cain chose to disobey God, and Abel chose to obey Him. Likewise, every person who has ever lived has been faced with that choice.

God's way is the way of righteousness or right living. Man's way is the way of doing his own thing. Some who choose their own way choose evil living; others choose to do what is right in their own eyes.[6] And in every age, people have been free to choose their own way.

That was true in the days of Noah, when the world became so corrupt that God had to destroy all but eight people and start the human race over again. Later God set apart the Hebrew race through Abraham and Sarah. Then He began to reveal prophecies about the future ages so people would have a more detailed record of His will.

To prepare the world for His Messiah-Savior, who would offer a permanent sacrifice for mankind's sin, God provided prophecies about His coming Son so that those who were alive at the time of Messiah's life would pick Him out from among the multitude of other people who had lived and were alive. Those who willed to do God's will had no difficulty recognizing and accepting their Messiah. Those who "willed not" to come to Him rejected Him, despite the evidence.

This scenario is still the same today!

In fact, the most important decision a person can ever make relates to how he or she exercises his or her own free will. The eternal destiny of everyone on the planet is determined by that decision. For as Jesus Himself said, "Most assuredly, I say to you, he who hears My word and believes in Him who sent Me has everlasting life, and shall not come into judgment, but has passed from death into life."[7] This is not just one of the many claims of Christ that prove He is the divine Son of God; it is His offer of eternal salvation to all who will believe. And now that you have been confronted with the evidence for Christ's deity and the many reasons for believing in Him, you, too, if you are not a Christian, are forced to make a decision about Him.

The Most Important Question in the World: What Do You Think of Jesus?

One day near the end of His three-year ministry, Jesus was walking along the road with His disciples and asked them this question: "Who do men say that I, the Son of Man, am?" They answered, "Some say John the Baptist, some Elijah, and others Jeremiah or one of the prophets."[8] All those answers are respectful, for they include some of the greatest names in the Bible. Most of us would feel complimented if someone mistook us for any of them. Not so Jesus! He then turned to the disciples and asked pointedly, "But who do *you* say that I am?" (Matthew 16:15).

That is the most important question in the world. Who do you say Jesus is?

Note very carefully Peter's classic answer: "You are the Christ, the Son of the living God" (verse 16). Jesus approved of Peter's answer, for He said, "Blessed are you, Simon Bar-Jonah, for flesh and blood has not revealed this to you, but My Father who is in heaven. And I also say to you that you are Peter, and on this rock I will build My church, and the gates of Hades shall not prevail against it. And I will give you the keys of the kingdom of heaven, and whatever you bind on earth will be bound in heaven, and whatever you loose on earth will be loosed in heaven."[9]

It is important to notice that Peter's human intelligence did not reveal the answer to him, even though he had witnessed the many events in the life of Christ mentioned in this book. His experience had convinced him that Jesus was indeed the Messiah-Savior of Israel. To that open heart God the Father revealed the classic truth, "You are the Christ, the Son of the living God." This statement, a message from God through the apostle Peter, was so important that Jesus said He would build His church on that testimony. And He did! Now, two millennia later, we can number in the billions those souls who have embraced Jesus Christ as "the Son of the living God."

Notice also that because of his testimony, Peter was given "the keys of the kingdom of heaven"—that is, he was the first person to preach the gospel and offer forgiveness of sin and salvation in Jesus' name both to the Jews (Acts 2) and to the Gentiles (Acts 10).

It was Peter who unlocked the door of the kingdom of heaven (or the door to salvation by faith) to a waiting world.

Peter gave the right answer to Jesus' soul-searching question, "Who do you say that I am?" That same question is now asked of you: Who do you say that He is? Your eternal destiny is determined by your answer.

Jesus: The World's Only Sinless Savior

The first time I went on the mission field, I visited the Chamula Indians in Mexico. In the largest village of that tribe, we visited a large, formerly Catholic church. After the revolution some 70 years before, the Indians had driven the Catholic workers out of their territory and set up their own form of worship. When I walked to the altar at the front of their church, I was amazed to find a large cross in it—but on the cross, instead of a replica of Christ, there was a fellow Chamula Indian.

Our missionary guide (who was having a vital ministry with these Indians) explained that when they originally set up their own native religion, the leaders "found the best man in their tribe and crucified him" in an attempt to provide "a Chamula savior."

Obviously they were sincere. But with due respect to the man they considered "the best in their tribe," he had two fatal flaws: He was not divine, consequently he was not perfect. For to be an adequate sacrifice for the sins of mankind, a savior must be more than a man—He must be God in human flesh, and He must be a spotless lamb without flaw or blemish.

Only Jesus of Nazareth qualifies!

In 1994 a large symposium on the religions of the world met in Chicago. It was attended by over 7000 representatives from every major religion in the world. My friend Erwin Lutzer, the pastor of Chicago's Moody Memorial Church, attended that symposium in person and described his experience:

I walked through the display area in search of a sinless prophet/teacher/Savior. I asked a Hindu Swami whether any of their teachers claimed sinlessness. "No," he said, appearing irritated with my question, "if anyone claims he is sinless, he is not a Hindu!"

What about Buddha? No, I was told, he didn't claim sinlessness. He found a group of ascetics and preached sermons to them. He taught that all outward things are only distractions and encouraged a life of discipline and contemplation. He sought enlightenment and urged his followers to do the same. He died seeking enlightenment. No sinlessness here.

What about Baha'ullah? He claimed he had a revelation from God that was more complete, more enlightened than those before him. Though he was convinced of the truth of his teachings, he made few personal claims. He thought his writings were "more perfect" than others, but he never claimed perfection or sinlessness for himself.

When I came to the representatives of the Muslim faith, I already knew that in the Koran the prophet Mohammed admitted he was in need of forgiveness. They agreed. "There is one God, Allah and Mohammed is His prophet" is the basic Muslim creed. But Mohammed was not perfect. Again, no sinlessness there.

Why was I searching for a sinless Savior? Because I don't want to have to trust a Savior who is in the same predicament as I am. I can't trust my eternal soul to someone who is still working through his own imperfections. Since I'm a sinner, I need someone who is standing on higher ground.

Understandably, none of the religious leaders I spoke with even claimed to *have* a Savior. Their prophets, they said, showed the way but made no pretense to be able to personally forgive sins or transform so much as a single human being. Like a street sign, they gave directions but were not able to take us where we need to go; if we need any saving, we will have to do it ourselves. The reason is obvious: No matter how wise, no matter how gifted, no matter how influential other prophets, gurus, and teachers might be, they had the presence of mind to know that they were imperfect just like the rest of us. They never even presumed to be able to reach down into the murky water of human depravity and bring sinners into the presence of God.

How different was Christ!

"Which of you convicts Me of sin? If I speak truth, why do you not believe Me?" (John 8:46). He pointed out hypocrisy in the lives of His critics, but none of them returned the compliment.[10]

Only Jesus was perfect enough to meet the requirements for dying for the sins of the world. And that is the reason Jesus came into the world. Dr. Lutzer adds other testimonies about Jesus' sinless life:

Judas, an apparent friend turned enemy, said, "I have sinned by betraying innocent blood" (Matthew 27:4).

Pilate, who longed to find fault with Christ, confessed, "I find no guilt in this man" (Luke 23:4).

Peter, who lived with Him for three years, said He "committed no sin, nor was any deceit found in His mouth" (1 Peter 2:22).

The apostle Paul said that God the Father "made Him who knew no sin to be sin on our behalf, that we might become the righteousness of God in Him" (2 Corinthians 5:21).

Jesus was either sinless or the greatest of sinners for deceiving so many people about His sinlessness. As C.E. Jefferson puts it, "The best reason we have for believing in the sinlessness of Jesus is the fact that He allowed His dearest friends to think that He was."

Why was Christ exempt from the sin with which we are so well acquainted? If He, like us, would have had a human father, He would have had a sin nature that is passed on from father to son. If He had been the son of Adam in a natural way, He would have been a sinner.

The virgin conception preserved His sinlessness. Mary experienced a special miracle that ensured the perfection of her son. He was like us but with an important difference.[11]

Sin: The Universal Problem

From the days of Adam and Eve on, all individuals have been plagued by the same problem in relation to God: sin! As the Bible says, "All we like sheep have gone astray; we have turned, every one, to his own way."[12] It also says, "There is none righteous, no, not one...." "All have sinned and fall short of the glory of God."[13] Only Jesus of Nazareth could ask His contemporaries, "Which of you convicts Me of sin?"[14] and get no response. All the rest of us would be ashamed to ask that question, for we know all too well we are flawed and sinful.

That is why God could say through His prophet Isaiah, "'Come now, and let us reason together,' says the LORD, 'though your sins are like scarlet, they shall be as white as snow.'"[15] God sent His Son to be our sacrifice for sin, that through Him we might have forgiveness and everlasting life. Such salvation can be obtained only by faith in Jesus Christ, who said of Himself, "I am the way, the truth, and the life. No one comes to the Father except through Me."[16]

Jesus: The Solution to Sin

Over 100 years ago (the first time the World's Fair came to Chicago), another large symposium on religion was held. Seven hundred people crowded the pavilion to hear one of the most brilliant Hindu speakers in the world, Swami Vivekananda. He did not disappoint them, for he was magnificent as he laid out the philosophical facets of Hinduism, the religion of his homeland, finishing to thunderous applause. He was followed by a famous

Christian clergyman who, for some reason, chose not to present the philosophy of Christianity. Possibly he feared the simple story of the Son of God dying for the sins of a rebellious human race would pale by contrast to the beautiful ideals of Hinduism.

When the chairman announced that the next speaker chose not to speak, a thick silence hung over the pavilion. In desperation, the chairman asked if anyone would care to speak on behalf of Christianity. Suddenly, someone sitting in the back, a Chicago Sunday-school teacher named Joseph Cook, walked forward and said, "I would like to tell a story." Then he told Shakespeare's tale of Macbeth and how Lady Macbeth and her husband had connived to kill the king, after which her guilt drove her to the edge of madness. Finally, when she could no longer rid her hands of the bloodguiltiness of her sin, she cried that famous line, "Out! Out, damned spot!"

Turning to Swami Vivekananda, Joseph Cook asked, "Sir, what relief does Hinduism have to offer Lady Macbeth to cleanse her sin?" The flustered swami admitted that Hinduism had no means of forgiving sin.

Joseph Cook then reached into his pocket for his New Testament and said, "I would like to show you Christianity's remedy for her sin." He read: "If we walk in the light as He is in the light, we have fellowship with one another, and the blood of Jesus Christ His Son cleanses us from all sin. If we say that we have no sin, we deceive ourselves, and the truth is not in us. If we confess our sins, He is faithful and just to forgive us our sins and to cleanse us from all unrighteousness."[17] Then Cook explained how Christ died on the cross for the sins of the whole world and invited those who had never done so to receive the Savior.

Years later, when I visited one of the greatest Hindu temples in India, I saw a sincere young man kneel before a marble motif carved on the floor of the temple. Suddenly he began bowing low and banging his forehead against that raised marble motif until blood flowed down his face. When I asked why he did so, I was told, "He is trying to atone for his sins." The scene reminded me of that Chicago story and the fact that Hinduism still has no remedy for sin. And neither does Confucianism, Islam, Taoism, or any other religion in the world. Only Christianity can offer forgiveness of sins through the shed blood of Jesus Christ and eternal salvation through faith in Him.

How could one man die for the sins of the whole world? The answer is found in who He was. That was not a mere man who was nailed to that cross; that was God in human flesh. Only the death of the Son of God could save billions of people. And Jesus Christ is that Son of God.

Bringing It All Together

For a short time in my early years I wanted to be a courtroom attorney. No other area of law appealed to me; what I thought attractive was the opportunity to present factual evidence before a jury in order to convince the jurors my client was innocent. This book is the closest I have come to that long-abandoned dream.

In this book, we started with the fact that Jesus of Nazareth was more than a 33-year-old carpenter. No other person in history has exerted such a remarkable influence on humanity in such a short time. That alone has lifted Him to a level of esteem shared by no other person. Who else's birth has been used to divide human history into two periods—before His birth and after it? Every time we write the date on a check or document we do so in reference to the birth of our Lord.

His prominence alone demands that we ask, "Who is this man?" To find the answer we must turn to the most reliable documents of the ancient world, the four Gospels. They tell us Jesus claimed to be the Messiah, the Son of God, that He died for the sins of mankind, and that He rose again for people's justification. To this evidence we added the testimonies of many personal eyewitnesses whose reputations are still so revered their names remain among the most popular even today (John, Peter, James, Paul, Mark, Luke, and so on).

We then examined who Jesus said He was and the miracles He performed to prove His claims—miracles that have not been duplicated in 2000 years since His death and resurrection. We summoned John the Baptist, the holiest man in Israel since Daniel (who lived 500 years earlier). John knew Jesus from childhood and testified to His absolute holiness; he even identified Him as the Lamb of God. We then examined the three times God Himself called Jesus "My Son," elevating Him above Moses and Elijah.

Then we looked at 28 of the more than 109 prophecies Jesus fulfilled during His lifetime, all of them clearly identifying Him as the promised Messiah. He is, indeed, one of a kind—so much so that one rabbi was forced to admit that He was "the Messiah—to the Gentiles!" True enough; but He's also the Messiah to the Jews. That will become clear when He appears the second time (perhaps any day now!).

Next we examined Jesus' death. He did not die like an ordinary man, but as even the skeptic Renan said, "He died like a god." He didn't have to die; He had done nothing wrong, as even His judge, Pilate, said: "I find no fault in Him" (John 19:6). No one took Jesus' life from Him; rather, He laid it down of His own accord. As He said in the Garden of Gethsemane as the mob arrived to take Him away, "Do you think that I cannot now pray to My Father and He will provide Me with more than twelve legions of angels?"[18] Jesus freely gave His life a ransom for others. As He said, "No one takes it from Me, but I lay it down of Myself."[19] In a real sense, Jesus was the only person who ever lived who did not have to die. That alone puts Him in a category by Himself.

By that point in the book, the evidence we had presented for the deity of Christ had grown to such overwhelming proportions that I was tempted to rest my case. Yet if I had stopped there, I would have omitted the most convincing evidence of all: His bodily resurrection from the grave three days after His crucifixion. Not four days or two days or a week later, but on the third day—just as He and the Hebrew prophets had predicted!

The evidence for Jesus' resurrection is simply awesome. Not only did 10 men (11, if we include Paul) who knew Him well suffer martyrdom rather than repudiate their testimony that they saw Him and touched Him during His 40 days of postresurrection appearances, but their testimony was affirmed by 500 other witnesses as well.

Last, we examined the six most popular false theories of Jesus' resurrection and confronted doubters and skeptics with their biggest dilemma: How do you explain the existence and magnitude of Christianity today without a risen Savior? A crucified Christ would have motivated no one. Without His resurrection, Jesus would have been an unknown character in history. It was the resurrected Christ who challenged His unlearned disciples to "go therefore and make disciples of all the nations...and lo, I am with you always, even to the end of the age."[20] They so believed Him they went out and turned the world upside down—from paganism to Christianity in just 300 years. Today, billions of people have embraced the Christian faith, all because of His resurrection. Without it, Christianity would not exist.

I Rest My Case

A trial lawyer eventually comes to the place where he must finally rest his case—not because he has presented all the evidence available, but because more proof is unnecessary. We have reached that point. Now it is time for you to evaluate the evidence presented and, like a good juror, make your decision. You now have to decide: Is Jesus the Christ, the Son of God, as He and His followers claimed? Or is He an impostor or a demented fool? Those are your options.

Just remember, your decision will last for eternity. Make it carefully!

The Roman centurion who watched Jesus die on the cross didn't wait until the resurrection to make his decision. He was so convinced by what he saw that day that he declared, "Truly this Man was the Son of God!"[21]

What is *your* decision? Now that you have been exposed to the evidence, you are faced with the same decision that confronted the Jews of Jesus' day: Who do you think Jesus is? If you are convinced by the evidence outlined in this book, will you personally receive Him? Will you say, as some of them did, "Yes, I believe Jesus is the Son of God, that He lived a sinless life, that He died a sacrificial death, and that He rose from the dead as He promised. Therefore I invite Him into my life"? Or will you follow the example of those who chose not to believe despite all the evidence? The choice is yours.

If you would like to accept Him as your Lord and Savior, simply pray a prayer like this:

> Dear heavenly Father, thank You for sending Your Son Jesus into the world to die for my sins. I admit I am a sinner and I ask Him to come into my life, cleanse my sin, and save my soul. I hereby give myself to You. Thank You, in the name of Your Son, Jesus, for saving me. Amen.

If you prayed this prayer, know that the Bible assures you that "whoever calls on the name of the LORD shall be saved."[22] Congratulations! You are now a full-fledged member of the family of God. And yet you should realize the adventure isn't over; it's just begun. You have just embarked on an exciting journey of faith. Based on the truth and logic you found in this book, you found reason enough to pray to receive Christ. That makes you a newborn babe in Christ. Spiritually, you are an infant who needs to grow in order to realize your full potential in Christ. The best way to nurture your new faith is to follow the example of the early believers in the first century, who continued in the apostles' word and doctrine. Today, that means several things.

First, begin to read the Word of God daily. Get yourself a modern translation of the Bible and start reading from the Gospel of John. When you're done with that, start at the beginning of the New Testament and read it through. Think of the Bible as your spiritual food. Whenever you read it, hear it taught, study or memorize it, you are building up your new spiritual life. You will benefit in the early days of your newfound faith by reading another book I wrote titled *How to Study the Bible for Yourself* (Eugene, OR: Harvest House Publishers).

Second, find a Bible-teaching church where you can learn more about God's Word. Look for a godly place where you can find fellowship with others who share your faith. The person who guided you to *Why Believe in Jesus?* is probably a good resource to help you find a strong church in your city that will help you grow spiritually.

Third, it's important you pray regularly. By receiving Christ you have become a child of God; therefore, you have access to God through prayer. That is how you seek His guidance in all you do. Jesus is alive and in heaven (where the Bible tells us He makes intercession for us before the Father),[23] so you can talk to Him on a regular basis.

And finally, the Bible teaches we should confess Christ before others. I suggest you review the many truths you have learned about who Jesus really is and share some of them with your friends. Most people who have not accepted Christ have never heard the logic and reason found in the Word of God,which produces faith. Not only that, many people will never hear those truths unless a friend like you shares what you have learned. Don't be discouraged if some of your friends are not interested right away. They may become interested later as they see the changes Christ brings about in your life.

You will find, in the course of your witnessing, that the identity of Jesus of Nazareth is always the key to Christian faith. If a person does not have faith, it is usually because he has never been convinced that Jesus is the Son of God who came in the flesh, died a sacrificial death on the cross, and rose again. Books like this one are written to help address this challenge. As the Bible says, "Faith comes by hearing, and hearing by the word of God."[24]

Remember, God does not expect us to "just believe." He wants us to take what we see in His Word, examine it with our mind in the light of historical evidence, and come to a reasonable conclusion. It is my conviction that the evidence presented in this book is so overwhelming that any unbiased person should be convinced that Jesus Christ truly is the Son of God, just as He claimed. And so we say, along with the apostle John:

> Truly Jesus did many other signs in the presence of His disciples which are not written in this book; but these are written that you may believe that Jesus is the Christ, the Son of God, and that believing you may have life in His name.[25]

Notes

Almost a Skeptic
1. Isaiah 1:18.
2. Luke 19:10.
3. 2 Peter 1:16.
4. Philippians 2:9.
5. 1 Peter 3:15.

Chapter 1: The Most Extraordinary Person Who Ever Lived
1. Matthew 5:44.
2. Luke 6:28.
3. Luke 6:38.
4. Matthew 8:20.
5. John 1:46.
6. Dr. Carl F. H. Henry, *The Identity of Jesus of Nazareth* (Nashville: Broadman Press, 1992), 20.
7. Henry, *The Identity of Jesus of Nazareth,* 20.

Chapter 2: What About the Skeptics?
1. John 3:2.
2. Matthew 5:21-22.
3. Robert Funk, Roy Hoover, and the Jesus Seminar, *The Five Gospels: The Search for the Authentic Jesus* (New York: Macmillan Publishing Co., 1993), 37.
4. Douglas Groothuis, *Jesus in an Age of Controversy* (Eugene: Harvest House, 1996), 21.
5. Groothuis, *Jesus in an Age of Controversy,* 20.
6. 2 Peter 1:16.
7. For further study on the Jesus Seminar, read the following books. All these authors are well qualified to attend a Jesus Seminar meeting but have not been invited: Michael J. Wilkins and F. P. Moreland, *Jesus Under Fire* (Grand Rapids: Zondervan Publishing House, 1995); Gregory A. Boyd, *Cynic, Sage or Son of God* (Wheaton, IL: Victor Books, 1995); Ben Witherington III, *The*

309

Jesus Quest (Downers Grove: InterVarsity Press, 1995); Douglas Groothuis, *Jesus in an Age of Controversy*.

8. Romans 10:9-10.

9. Amy Nickell and Tony Stanciu, *Rutherford*, a publication of the Rutherford Institute, Vol. 5, No. 12, December 1996.

Chapter 3: The Credibility of the Gospel Accounts

1. Henry H. Halley, *Halley's Bible Handbook* (Grand Rapids: Zondervan Publishing House, 1927), 414.

2. John 20:31.

3. Halley, *Halley's Bible Handbook*, 752.

4. Merrill F. Unger, *Unger's Bible Dictionary* (Chicago: Moody Press, 1957), 598.

5. I. Howard Marshall, "John, Gospel of" in the *New Bible Dictionary*, 2nd ed. (Wheaton, IL: Tyndale House Publishers, 1982), 610.

6. Henry M. Morris, *The Defenders Study Bible* (Grand Rapids: World Publishing, 1995), 1130.

7. Mark 3:13-19; Luke 6:12-16.

8. Dr. Carsten Peter Thiede and Matthew D'Ancona, *Eyewitness to Jesus* (New York: Doubleday, 1996), 163.

9. Thiede and D'Ancona, *Eyewitness to Jesus*, 163.

10. Gregory A. Boyd, *Cynic, Sage or Son of God* (Wheaton: Victor Books, 1995), 239.

11. Boyd, *Cynic, Sage or Son of God*, 239-40.

12. Halley, *Halley's Bible Handbook*, 458.

13. Colossians 4:14.

14. Sir William M. Ramsay, *St. Paul: The Traveler and the Roman Citizen* (Grand Rapids: Baker Book House, 1962), 69.

15. Sir William M. Ramsay, *The Bearing of Recent Discovery on the Trustworthiness of the New Testament* (London: Hodder & Stoughton, 1935), 222.

16. Dr. Wilbur M. Smith, *The Supernaturalness of Christ* (Boston: W. A. Wilde Co., 1940), 55.

17. Smith, *The Supernaturalness*, 36.

18. Smith, *The Supernaturalness*, 42.

19. Smith, *The Supernaturalness*, 61.

20. Josh McDowell, *The Resurrection Factor* (Nashville: Thomas Nelson Publishers, 1981), 25-26.

21. Eduard Meyer, *Origin and Beginning of Christianity* (Berlin, 1909), 178.

22. Thiede and D'Ancona, *Eyewitness to Jesus*, 169.

23. Smith, *The Supernaturalness*, 148.

24. John 14:26.

Chapter 4: Various Opinions of Jesus of Nazareth

1. J. Oswald Sanders, *Christ Incomparable* (Ft. Washington, PA: Christian Literature Crusade, 1952), 89-90.

2. John Cunningham Geikie, *The Life and Words of Christ* (New York: D. Appleton & Co., 1893), 13-14.

3. Exodus 20:7.

4. J. B. Lightfoot, "Epistle of Polycarp to the Church at Philippi," *The Apostolic Fathers*, Part II, Vol. 2, No. 3 (New York: MacMillan and Co., 1889), 476.

5. Edgar J. Goodspeed, *The Apostolic Fathers: An American Translation* (New York: Harper & Row, 1950), 85.

6. Lightfoot, *The Apostolic Fathers*, 572.

7. Lightfoot, *The Apostolic Fathers*, 569.

8. Kirsopp Lake, trans., *The Apostolic Fathers*, Vol. 1 (Cambridge, MA: Harvard University Press, 1965), 173ff.

9. Alexander Roberts and James Donaldson, trans., *Irenaeus*, Vol. 1, Book 4, Ante-Nicene Christian Library: Translations of the Writings of the Fathers (Edinburgh, Scotland: T. & T. Clark, 1869), 278.

10. Justin Martyr, *First Apology*, I:xii; I:xiii.

11. Matthew 16:16.

12. Sanders, *Christ Incomparable*, 90-91.

13. Sanders, *Christ Incomparable*, 90.

14. Adapted by an unknown source from James A. Francis, *The Real Jesus and Other Sermons* (Philadelphia: The Judson Press, 1926), p. 123.

Chapter 5: Who Jesus Said He Was

1. John 8:59; 10:31.

2. John 7:46.

3. Matthew 12:41; 12:42; Luke 20:17; John 8:58.

4. Dr. Henry Morris II, *Many Infallible Proofs* (El Cajon, CA: Master Books, 1974), 75-76.

5. See Numbers 28:9-10; 1 Samuel 21:1-6; Matthew 12:11-12.

6. John 11:24.

7. Daniel 12:2.

8. Revelation 20:11.

9. John 14:6; Acts 4:12.

10. 1 John 2:23; 4:15; 5:10-12.

11. John 5:24.

12. Exodus 3:13-14.

13. See John 4:26; 8:12; 10:7,11,36; 14:6.

14. Matthew 28:18.

Chapter 6: The Testimony of John the Baptist

1. Matthew 11:11.
2. Luke 7:26.
3. Malachi 3:1.
4. Arthur W. Pink, *Exposition of the Gospel of John* (Grand Rapids, MI: Zondervan Publishing House, 1945), 50.
5. Luke 1:41.
6. Luke 1:66-67,76-77,79-80.
7. John 3:30.
8. John 1:26-27.
9. John 1:6-9.
10. John 1:15.
11. Luke 1:35 KJV.
12. John 1:1.
13. Matthew 3:13-14.
14. John 1:29.
15. 1 Peter 1:19.

Chapter 7: The Testimony of the Apostle Peter

1. 2 Peter 1:16-17.

Chapter 8: The Testimony of the Apostle John

1. See John 13:23; 19:26; 20:2; 21:7,20.
2. That is, beyond its explicitly evangelistic mission; see John 20:31.

Chapter 9: The Testimony of the Apostle Paul

1. 1 Corinthians 15:8.
2. See Galatians 1:11-12,15-22; 2:1-2; Ephesians 3:2-5.
3. 2 Peter 3:15-16.
4. Compare the latter part of this passage with Isaiah 45:23, in which God says, "I have sworn by Myself...to Me every knee shall bow, every tongue shall take an oath." Paul clearly has this text in mind as he writes, thus once more equating Jesus with God.

Chapter 10: The Testimony of God Himself

1. Luke 3:21-22.
2. Luke 3:23.
3. Luke 9:29.
4. Luke 9:31.
5. Matthew 16:21.
6. Matthew 16:23.
7. Luke 16:29.

8. John 12:20-33.

9. Luke 22:44.

10. John 12:27.

11. John 12:28.

12. John 12:32.

13. John 12:35-36.

14. John 12:37.

15. Hebrews 1:1-2.

Chapter 11: His Miracles As Witness to His Identity

1. John 5:36. Note: Jesus referred to Himself as the "Son of Man" in Matthew, the "Son of God" in John and elsewhere. He did this because the noun "God" was so holy to the Jews they would not even utter it. Therefore, Matthew, who wrote his Gospel primarily to the Jews, did not want to offend them by using the forbidden noun. There is no contradiction, for they are used interchangeably; besides, He was both God and man in human form, so both titles rightly apply to Him. For further insight into the significance of the title "Son of Man," see Daniel 7:13-14.

2. John 3:2.

3. Luke 7:22.

4. John 5:36.

5. John 10:25.

6. John 15:24.

7. Matthew 11:21-22.

8. Dr. Wilbur M. Smith, *The Supernaturalness of Christ* (Boston: W A. Wilde Co., 1940), 148.

9. Luke 5:1-11.

10. Luke 6:19.

11. Matthew 14:35.

12. Mark 4:37.

13. Matthew 8:24.

14. Mark 4:39.

15. Mark 4:41.

16. Matthew 17:27.

17. Matthew 21:18-22.

18. Matthew 14:22-32.

19. Matthew 8:5-13.

20. Luke 17:11-19.

21. Luke 8:43-48.

22. No one knows why Jesus mixed dirt into clay and "anointed" the man's eyes—but I have a theory. Is it possible the man lacked eyeballs, so the Creator fashioned the organ required for sight? I can almost hear your complaint: clay made out of dirt and spittle, compatible with the human body? No problem. He is the one who made man in the first place (John 1:3; Colossians 1:16-17), so fashioning a set of eyeballs would be a minor project. And if we ask about compatibility, Genesis 1 declares that man was created from "the dust of the earth," so dust or clay would be perfectly compatible with human tissue.

23. John 3:2.

24. Colossians 2:9.

25. See Matthew 9:36; 14:14; 15:32; 20:34; Mark 1:41; 6:34; 8:2; Matthew 9:36.

26. Matthew 28:18 KJV.

27. John 12:36-37.

28. John 10:38.

29. Smith, *The Supernaturalness of Christ*, 118.

Chapter 12: Jesus Received Worship

1. Matthew 4:10.

2. John 5:18.

3. John 9:30-33.

4. John 9:35-38.

5. John 20:28.

6. Luke 5:8.

7. Matthew 9:18.

8. Matthew 14:33.

9. Matthew 17:5.

10. Matthew 20:20.

11. Matthew 28:9.

12. Matthew 28:17.

13. John 5:23.

14. John 7:17.

15. Michael Green, *Who Is This Jesus?* (Nashville: Thomas Nelson Publishers, 1990), 53.

16. C. S. Lewis, *Mere Christianity* (New York: Macmillan, 1960), 56.

17. Philippians 2:10-11.

Chapter 13: Only God Can Forgive

1. Luke 6:27,37.

2. Matthew 27:44; Mark 15:32.

3. Isaiah 52:14 NIV.

4. Luke 23:34.

5. John 11:41 NIV.

Chapter 14: The Witness of Fulfilled Prophecy, Part I: Predictions of His Ancestry, Birth, Life, and Ministry

1. Luke 2:25-38.

2. Isaiah 61:1-3.

3. John 5:38.

4. Luke 24:32.

5. Alfred Edersheim, *The Life and Times of Jesus the Messiah,* Vol. 1, rev. ed. (Peabody, MA: Hendrickson Publishers, 1993), 163-64.

6. Dennis Pollock, "Messiah Has Come," *Lamplighter Journal* (December 1994), 8.

7. Michael D. Lemonick, "Are the Bible's Stories True?" *Time* (December 18, 1995), 67 (emphasis added).

8. Isaiah 53.

9. Genesis 3:15.

10. Isaiah 7:14.

11. Matthew 1:20-25.

12. Genesis 11:10-32.

13. Genesis 12:3.

14. Genesis 17:19.

15. Genesis 28:13-14.

16. Genesis 49:10. Note how carefully this prophecy was fulfilled. The Jews enjoyed a time of self-rule even after the captivity of Babylon, until this freedom was terminated just before the ministry of Christ began around A.D. 30. As you know from history, the Romans were their captors then and removed from them the ability to put to death those guilty of religious sins. That is seen in the account of Jesus' crucifixion, for the Sanhedrin did not have the authority to put Jesus to death; that is why they took Him to Pilate. Only when Pilate gave the word could they crucify Him.

17. Isaiah 11:1.

18. Hosea 11:1.

19. John Ankerberg and John Weldon, *The Facts on Jesus the Messiah* (Eugene, OR: Harvest House Publishers, 1993), 17-19.

20. Dr. Theodore Laetsch, *Jeremiah* (St. Louis, MO: Concordia, 1965), 191-92.

Chapter 15: The Witness of Fulfilled Prophecy, Part II: Predictions of His Passion, Death, Burial, and Resurrection

1. John 10:18.

2. John Ankerberg and John Weldon, *The Facts on Jesus the Messiah* (Eugene, OR: Harvest House Publishers, 1993), 36.

3. Ankerberg and Weldon, *The Facts on Jesus*, 37.

4. We have terms like that in English. Suppose I said that "seventy dozen years are determined on America." I would mean, 70 times 12, or 840 years. Or I could say "seventy gross are determined," and that would mean 70 times 144, or 10,080. The context makes it clear Gabriel meant "sevens" (or weeks) of years; therefore it is seven times 70, or 490 years.

5. Ankerberg and Weldon, *The Facts on Jesus*, 38.

6. Ankerberg and Weldon, *The Facts on Jesus*, 39.

7. As cited in Ankerberg and Weldon, *The Facts on Jesus*, 32. Delitzsch and Gloag, *The Messiahship of Christ*, Book 2 (Minneapolis: Klock & Klock, 1983), 286-87.

8. As cited in Ankerberg and Weldon, *The Facts on Jesus*, 32; Dr. Raphael Patai, *The Messiah Texts* (New York: Avin, 1979), 166.

9. As cited in Ankerberg and Weldon *The Facts on Jesus*; Patai, *The Messiah Texts*, 167.

10. As cited in Ankerberg and Weldon, *The Facts on Jesus*, 33; David Baron, *Rays of Messiah's Glory: Christ in the Old Testament* (Grand Rapids, MI: Zondervan, n.d.), 225-29.

11. As cited in Ankerberg and Weldon, *The Facts on Jesus*, 33; Delitzsch and Gloag, *The Messiahship*, 295.

12. As cited in Ankerberg and Weldon, *The Facts on Jesus*, 32; Ben Blisheim, "Messianic Judaism—An Alternative" (privately published manuscript), 6.

13. As cited in Ankerberg and Weldon, *The Facts on Jesus*, 33; transcript of television program, *Do the Messianic Prophecies of the Old Testament Point to Jesus or Someone Else?* Dr. Walter Kaiser, Jr. and Pinchas Lapide (Chattanooga, TN: The Ankerberg Theological Institute, 1985), 22.

14. As cited in Ankerberg and Weldon, *The Facts on Jesus*, 33; Dr. Pinchas Lapide, *The Resurrection of Jesus: A Jewish Perspective* (Minneapolis: Augsburg, 1983), 7, 126-31, 137-50.

15. Ankerberg and Weldon, *The Facts on Jesus*, 32-33.

16. 1 Corinthians 5:7.

17. 2 Corinthians 5:21.

18. 1 Peter 1:18-19.

19. 1 Corinthians 15:3-4.

20. Exodus 12:5.

21. Exodus 12:46.

22. Psalm 34:20.

23. John 19:35-37.

24. John 19:30.

25. Zechariah 12:10.

26. See Matthew 16:21; 17:22-23; 20:18-19; Luke 9:22; 18:31-33.

Chapter 16: Jesus' Resurrection: The Rest of the Story

1. Dr. Wilbur M. Smith, *The Supernaturalness of Christ* (Boston: W. A. Wilde Co., 1940), 193-194.
2. Smith, *The Supernaturalness*, 189-90.
3. Smith, *The Supernaturalness*, 190.
4. William Lane Craig, *Jesus Under Fire* (Grand Rapids: Zondervan Publishing House, 1995), 160.
5. John 20:27.
6. Luke 24:38-39.
7. Smith, *The Supernaturalness*, 194-95.
8. Hebrews 2:9.
9. Matthew 12:39.
10. Romans 10:9-10.
11. 1 Thessalonians 4:14.
12. See Deuteronomy 18:20-22.
13. Matthew 12:40.
14. Matthew 20:18-19.
15. Luke 9:22.
16. John 10:17-18.
17. John 2:19-22.
18. Matthew 16:20-21.
19. Matthew 26:32.
20. Psalm 16:9-10.
21. Acts 2:32.
22. Acts 2:38.
23. Acts 1:21-22.
24. Acts 3:26.
25. Acts 4:7,10-12.
26. Romans 4:23–5:1.
27. Romans 4:24.
28. Acts 17:30-31.
29. 1 Corinthians 15:18.
30. Romans 8:11.
31. 1 Corinthians 11:26.
32. Colossians 2:12.
33. 1 Corinthians 15:3-4.

Chapter 17: Can Jesus' Resurrection Be Proven?

1. Josh McDowell, *The Resurrection Factor* (Nashville: Thomas Nelson Publishers, 1981), 6,8.

2. Matthew 28:6.
3. John 20:15.
4. John 20:2-8.
5. Acts 5:38-39.
6. McDowell, *The Resurrection Factor*, 66.
7. McDowell, *The Resurrection Factor*, 91.
8. McDowell, *The Resurrection Factor*, 66.
9. McDowell, *The Resurrection Factor*, 53-4.
10. Matthew 28:2.
11. Acts 1:3.
12. Dr. Wilbur M. Smith, *The Supernaturalness of Christ* (Boston: W.A. Wilde Co., 1940), 197-99.
13. 1 Corinthians 15:6.
14. The movie was *The Last Temptation of Christ*.
15. John R. Rice, *Is Jesus God?* (Wheaton, IL: Sword of the Lord Publishers, 1948), 140.
16. J. Oswald Sanders, *Christ Incomparable* (Ft. Washington, PA: Christian Literature Crusade, 1952), 203.
17. Mark 16:13.
18. Luke 24:38-39.

Chapter 18: The Best of the False Theories of Jesus' Resurrection

1. Dr. Wilbur M. Smith, *The Supernaturalness of Christ* (Boston: WA. Wilde Co., 1940), 206-07.
2. Acts 17:18.
3. Acts 17:32.
4. Acts 23:6.
5. Smith, *The Supernaturalness*, 207-08.
6. David Strauss, *The Life of Jesus for the People*, 2nd ed. (London: Williams and Norgate, 1879), 412.
7. Mark 15:47.
8. Charles Guignebert, *Jesus* (New York: Alfred A. Knopf, 1935), 536.
9. Smith, *The Supernatural*, 210.
10. James Orr, *The Resurrection of Jesus* (New York: Hodder & Stoughton, 1908), 129.
11. Acts 17:6.
12. Murray J. Harris, *Three Crucial Questions About Jesus* (Grand Rapids: Baker Books, 1994), 42.
13. Acts 16:9.
14. Smith, *The Supernaturalness*, 219.

15. J. Gresham Machen, *The Christian Faith in the Modern* Hodder & Stoughton, 1936), 214-15.

16. William Lane Craig, *Jesus Under Fire* (Grand Rapi Publishing House, 1994), 160.

17. Psalm 76:10.

18. Smith, *The Supernaturalness*, 220.

19. 2 Thessalonians 2:12.

20. Philippians 3:10.

Chapter 19: Evidence That Demands a Verdict

1. John 6:68.

2. John 3:2.

3. John 7:16-17.

4. Acts 8:39.

5. See Genesis 2.

6. See Judges 21:25.

7. John 5:24.

8. Matthew 16:13-14.

9. Matthew 16:16-19.

10. Erwin Lutzer, *Christ Among Other Gods* (Chicago: Moody Press, 1994), 62-64.

11. Lutzer, *Christ Among Other Gods*, 64.

12. Isaiah 53:6.

13. Romans 3:10,23.

14. John 8:46.

15. Isaiah 1:18.

16. John 14:6.

17. 1 John 1:7-9.

18. Matthew 26:53.

19. John 10:18.

20. Mark 16:15; Matthew 28:20.

21. Mark 15:39.

22. Acts 2:21.

23. Romans 8:34; Hebrews 7:25.

24. Romans 10:17.

25. John 20:30-31.

World (New York:

s: Zondervan

ouse Books

ye

phecy Library™

/hat You Need to Know

ting the End Times

End Times Prophecy Study Guide

The End Times Controversy

The Rapture

Understanding Bible Prophecy for Yourself

—ɯ—

God Always Keeps His Promises

How to Study the Bible for Yourself

I Love You, But Why Are We So Different?

The Promise of Heaven